WITCHDOCTORS and PSYCHIATRISTS

WITCHDOCTORS and PSYCHIATRISTS

The Common Roots of Psychotherapy and Its Future

E. FULLER TORREY, M.D.

*Revised edition of THE MIND GAME
by E. Fuller Torrey, M.D.*

Jason Aronson Inc.

*Northvale, New Jersey
London*

To my wife, Barbara
The most important of my sources:
the source of my best ideas and confidence

About the Author

E. Fuller Torrey, M.D., is a clinical and research psychiatrist in Washington, D.C. The original edition of this book was published in 1972, shortly after he completed his training in psychiatry and obtained a master's degree in anthropology from Stanford University. Dr. Torrey is the author or editor of nine books and over one hundred lay and professional papers. His most recent books are *The Roots of Treason: Ezra Pound and the Secret of St. Elizabeths,* which was nominated by the National Book Critics Circle as one of the five best biographies of 1984, and *Surviving Schizophrenia: A Family Manual,* for which he received a Special Award from the National Alliance for the Mentally Ill in 1984.

Contents

PART III   *Toward the Future of Psychotherapy*

Preface

Twenty years ago, Fritz Perls and Gestalt therapy were regarded by the establishment as the lunatic psychotherapy fringe, California creations of the San Andreas fault. Now Gestalt is mainstream, and seekers of the psyche migrate from Arica and the Anubhave School of Enlightenment to Zaraleya Psychoenergetic Technique, traveling by way of either Sector Therapy or Vector Therapy, depending on their maps.

In 1980, *The Psychotherapy Handbook* listed over 250 brands of this activity.[1] For the traditionalist there is Art Therapy, Poetry Therapy, Dance Therapy, Drama Therapy, and Music Therapy. Those more practical may want to try Money Therapy, Reality Therapy, or Breathing Therapy. Stay-at-homes can try Videotherapy, Soap Opera Therapy, or Therapy via Telephone, while those with a sense of humor may want to sample Shadow Therapy or Mirror-Image Therapy. Trouble keeping appointments? Try Past Lives Therapy or Future-Oriented Psychotherapy. The athletically inclined may want to sign up for Bio Scream Therapy, Primal Therapy, or Creative Aggression Therapy, while intellectual types will feel more comfortable with Paradigmatic Psychotherapy, Paraverbal Therapy, Logotherapy, Eidetic Therapy, Hypnosymbolic Psychotherapy, or Phenomeno-Structural Psychotherapy.

You can have your therapy alone (e.g., Self Therapy), in crowds (e.g., Office Network Therapy), or even on the streets (Street Therapy—to improve the survival skills of the client). And when you have tired of all of the above, you still have the avant-garde awaiting you: Ajase Complex, Lomi Body Work, Senoi Dream Group Therapy, Vita-Erg Therapy, Tibetan Psychic Healing, or the Samadhi isolation tank (a soundproof tank of warm water in which you can reexperience being in a womb).

Who qualifies as a "therapist" has become equally confusing. Once upon a time psychiatrists, psychologists, and (with supervision) psychiatric social workers were exclusive caterers to the banquet of ego and id. In the last two decades, however, the psychotherapy field has been invaded by mail order ministers, encyclopedia salesmen, assorted misfits and odd opportunists who have claimed equal standing. Navaho medicine men have organized and claimed eligibility for third-party reimbursement, and the United States Senate discussed a bill "to assure that professional mental health services . . . are efficacious, safe, and appropriate to the patient's needs."[2] Overseas a Mganga Association of indigenous therapists in Tanzania claimed thirty thousand members, and the World Health Organization officially recommended the use of "all the possible resources at its command to promote and develop traditional medicine."[3]

What are we to make of this chaotic mélange of psychotherapies and psychotherapists? The following chapters will attempt to provide a framework for an understanding. Part I shows that four basic components underlie all types of psychotherapy: a shared worldview, the personal qualities of the therapist, the expectations of the client, and an emerging sense of mastery. Therapists all over the world use these basic components and enhance them by specific techniques of therapy. Part II examines psychotherapists in action in various cultures and shows that psychiatrists and shamans, ministers and *mgangas*, do remarkably similar things. Part III then follows the consequences of this analysis into the practical realm of who should do psychotherapy, how they should be paid, and how clients can be protected.

Since the original edition of this book, great strides have been made in understanding the human brain and human behavior. We now have a much better understanding of psychotherapy, both how it works and why it works. The numbers of individuals who are unhappy with their lives are legion, and many will seek amelioration through one or more types of psychotherapy. It is the obligation of all of us in the "mental health" field to educate potential clients so they can better differentiate the helpers from the hucksters.

The revisions to the book incorporate changes in the field since 1970. The literature has mushroomed; a bibliography on *Themes in Cultural Psychiatry* for 1975–80 alone lists 1,643 books and articles.[4] I have attempted to select the significant advances and changes, therefore, rather than create an encyclopedia. Chapters 1, 5, 9, 10, and 12 are virtually new, while Chapters 11, 13, and 14 are radically revised. The remaining chapters have been revised and updated as was necessary.

I am indebted for help with this edition to the staff of the medical library at St. Elizabeths Hospital for their kind assistance, and to Ms. Karen Thomas and Ms. Judy Miller for typing the manuscript.

Preface to the Original Edition

This book is an attempt to provide a framework for understanding the activities of psychotherapists around the world. As such it is an ambitious—some would say arrogant—undertaking. To attempt it as a psychiatrist just out of the nest leaves me open to attack. "Wait until you are more experienced, wait until you are older and wiser, then you will understand," call the voices.

But I am not certain that experience brings truth or that age brings wisdom. Too often added years seem only to bring the encrustations of time, obtunding self-criticism and impelling self-justification. Perhaps it is only from the vantage point of the nest's edge that the relationship of witchdoctors and psychiatrists can be clearly seen.

A framework for a general understanding of psychotherapists can be approached by asking questions. What does a psychotherapist do? Is he effective? What does his effectiveness come from? How can he be made more effective? What is the effect of his personality? How should he be selected? What kind of training should he have? What should be his role in society? In what ways is he a product of his culture?

These questions are important and they are not asked often enough. Formal psychotherapy is an institution in our culture, enshrined in psychiatry, psychology, and social work. We tend to accept our inherited institutions without criticism and pass them on mechanically to posterity. This transfer guarantees obsolescence. Insofar as this book focuses attention on these questions, it will accomplish its purpose. The answers proposed are intended only to invite innovation and experimentation.

I realize that many readers may not agree with my general thesis. From preliminary readings it appears that the strongest opposition is likely to come from those who want to pretend that witchdoctors do not exist (e.g., highly educated members of Western subcultures and cultures from developing countries) and also from those who want to believe that psychiatrists are special and different (e.g., people who have had long-term therapy). If the book only forces these people to clarify and codify the nature of their opposition it will have accomplished much.

In the process of writing this book I have had to contend with the ethnocentrism and bias that always lurk at the periphery of my own vision. Many times I thought myself free, only to turn and find it behind me. The more introspective I became, the more I found that it had invaded the very depths of my thought. As long as our culture nurtures it in so many subtle ways, its complete eradication seems a task for Sisyphus.

The anthropological literature on therapists in other cultures is vast. A bibliography published in 1923 listed 650 studies of Siberian shamans alone—even at that time. I have selected from this array in anthropology and related fields what seemed to be the most promising items to study in greater detail. Undoubtedly I have missed many of merit. Especially conspicuous by their absence are studies of therapists in Latin America (which are mostly in Spanish) and the Middle East (which are few in number and mostly in Arabic).

This book will focus on the healer, the therapist. It will attempt to show how much of his effectiveness comes through his sharing of a common worldview with the patient, through certain personality characteristics, and through expectations that the patient has of him. It will then show how another source of his effectiveness, the techniques of therapy, are basically the same whether they are used by a witchdoctor or a psychiatrist. The book will then examine the varieties of therapists found in the United States and in other countries. Finally it will look at the implications of the foregoing for mental health services both here and elsewhere and examine some of the problems and resistances to putting the changes into operation.

Brief portions of the book are borrowed from articles I have published elsewhere. Excerpts from Chapters 2, 3, and 4 are found in my article in *The Archives of General Psychiatry*, volume 20. Some of the material for Chapter 6 was used for a chapter in *Current Psychiatric Therapies*, volume 10. Part of Chapter 10 was included in the *Community Mental Health Journal*, volume 6. And portions of Chapter 8 were published by the *Stanford M.D.*, volume 9.

I owe much gratitude to Paul Beavitt, Rosa Miller, and Robert Campos, who helped with different parts of my field work. Linda Hess, Norman Reynolds, and Halsey and Jane Beemer provided invaluable criticism of the manuscript. Sue Heller added wise counsel, and Joan Wolfe provided not only excellent typing but contributed many helpful suggestions as well.

The human brain is not an organ of thinking but an organ of survival, like claw and fangs. It is made in such a way as to make us accept as truth that which is only advantage.

ALBERT SZENT-GYÖRGI

Chapter 1

Introduction: Problems of Living and Psychiatric Imperialism

Psychotherapy, the world's second oldest profession, is remarkably similar to the first. Both involve a contract (implicit or explicit) between a specialist and a client for a service, and for this service a fee is paid. The expectations of the client and the personality characteristics of the specialist are important in determining the success of the transaction. Both professions claim that their specific techniques are crucial, though evidence suggests that underlying nonspecific factors may really be the important determinants of a successful outcome. One makes the mind feel better, the other makes the body feel better. Both, furthermore, are difficult to study, for they are essentially human transactions. When they are taken apart on the dissecting table, a part of the interaction ceases to exist.

In this age of Masters and Johnson, psychotherapy deserves equally as rigorous a scrutiny as sexuality. It is after all big business, with an estimated 150,000 psychotherapists in the United States, utilizing over 250 brands of psychotherapy.[1] Office-based psychiatrists and psychologists collected $1.7 billion in fees in 1980.[2] Almost two thirds of the psychiatrists' fees came from government and medical insurance plans, while over one third of the psychologists' fees came from the same sources.[3] Analyzing what is done in the name of psychotherapy, then, is no longer an idle luxury; rather it is an obligation for those concerned about the allocation of public resources.

Problems of Living

Psychotherapists everywhere are effective in helping people with certain kinds of problems and ineffective with other kinds. The problems with which they are most successful are those arising from a person's relationships with other people (e.g., family, friends, superiors, etc.) and those arising from a person's feelings about himself or herself. The first are often referred to as interpersonal problems and the second as intrapersonal problems, and both can be subsumed under the shorthand "problems of living." They are part of the human condition, inevitable concomitants of growing up and interacting with other people. They occur in all of us to a greater or a lesser degree "because people are complicated, not because they are disordered, and because life is hard and painful."[4] When problems of living become so troublesome or disabling that they impair the person's ability "to love and to work" (as Freud phrased it), then the person may seek help from a culturally designated healer. In Western cultures this healer is called a psychotherapist, or simply a therapist.

There are kinds of problems and conditions for which psychotherapists have comparatively little to offer. These include brain diseases, and in such conditions the contribution of psychotherapists is to simply help the person learn to live with the condition. It has long been known that multiple sclerosis and Alzheimer's disease are brain diseases, and in the last decade the evidence has become very strong that schizophrenia and manic depressive disease (now officially called bipolar disorder) are also brain diseases.[5] In these illnesses neurophysiological and neurochemical abnormalities arise from the disease process, though in none of them have the precise causes been identified. Since these are diseases, they belong within the medical model and individuals who are afflicted by them should appropriately be referred to as patients. By contrast, people with problems of living, since they do not have diseases, do not belong within the medical model and should be referred to by a nonmedical term such as clients. Patients with brain diseases should be treated by physicians (e.g., neurologists, internists, or psychiatrists specially trained in brain diseases). Psychotherapists are only useful as ancillary personnel to help such patients learn to live with their disabilities. Those who use psychotherapy to try and cure such brain diseases are wasting time and the patients' money, as Freud himself discovered when he tried to use psychoanalytic therapy on a patient with schizophrenia. Psychotherapists in Western culture as well as those in other cultures have generally learned through trial and error that patients with schizophrenia and manic-depressive disease are not good candidates for their skills.

The other conditions for which psychotherapists are ineffective are inborn personality disorders, the product of either genetic endowment or chemical in-utero alterations which change the brain irrevocably. Examples include such things as antisocial personality disorder and homosexuality, both of which have been subjected to psychotherapy with remarkably ineffective results. In fact, the use of psychotherapy to change homosexuals to heterosexuals was such a failure over the years that the American Psychiatric Association ultimately dropped homosexuality from its list of official "diseases." As with brain diseases, psychotherapy is effective with members of this group only in helping them to come to terms with their condition—learning to live with what cannot be changed.

Psychotherapists everywhere in the world spend the vast majority of their time working with clients who have problems of living. This is not surprising, since these are the people who are helped by the psychotherapeutic process. Recent analyses of problems seen by psychologists in private practice showed that the most common complaints of their clients were marital and family problems, job-related problems, and physical complaints caused by stress and anxiety (psychosomatic problems).[6] Similarly, psychiatric social workers spent most of their office time with clients complaining of marital and family problems, problems with their children, and psychosomatic problems.[7] Psychiatrists in private practice, when compared with psychologists, are said to be "more similar than dissimilar when compared with each other."[8] In a recent study, only 6 percent of clients seen by private psychiatrists had been hospitalized for psychiatric reasons (an indication of how few of them had brain diseases such as schizophrenia), and only one quarter of them were said to have any impairment in function or activity.[9]

It is not just psychotherapists in Western cultures who spend most of their professional time on problems of living. Exactly the same situation exists for psychotherapists everywhere in the world. A *mganga* in Tanzania, a *marabout* in Iraq, and a *balian* in Indonesia see the same panoply of clients who have problems with their husband or wife, their children, in-laws, co-workers, or neighbors, who have a fear of failure or a sense of inadequacy. Often the presenting complaint is masked as anxiety, depression, or physical ailments due to the stress, but the underlying problems of living are the bread and butter of psychotherapists everywhere.

A recent development of psychotherapy in the United States has been the evolution of its use from problems of living to enhancement of living. No longer do clients have to have a problem to go into therapy; they may simply decide that they want more out of life. Clients may say that their relationships are not meaningful, that they are unable to express themselves or to express emotions as they would like to, that they want to find meaning in life, or that they are simply bored with life. The use of psychotherapy for enhancement of living has become fashionable in some social circles, with no more stigma attached than to other educational endeavors, such as taking a great books seminar or learning a new language.

As psychotherapy has become fashionable, however, it has spawned an extraordinary variety of activities taking place under that heading. Most of them are legitimate, and clients engaging in them achieve the self-education and sense of well-being that they are seeking. A few of the newer types of psychotherapy appear to be less legitimate, to have been organized principally for the well-being and economic success of the therapist. Psychotherapy researcher Dr. Morris Parloff may have had some of these latter types in mind when he wrote:

> It is recognized that participants in each of these disciplines report having been helped and improved, and a goodly proportion claim

to have experienced peak states and enlightenments. It now appears that the achievement of enlightenment in our culture has attained such frequency and commonality as to raise questions about the criteria used to identify these rather extraordinary states. I strongly suspect that some are merely experiencing the vapors, while others may mistake for peak experiences and enlightenment the happy sensations that follow clearing one's sinuses.[10]

It is the intent of this book to provide a better understanding of what psychotherapy is and how it works; in this way clients may become more sophisticated consumers of psychotherapy services and better able to separate the valuable from the frivolous and even destructive.

The Spectrum of Witchdoctors

Psychotherapy both for problems of living and for enhancement of living has been found to be most effective for individuals who are already functioning well. The criterion for the best therapy candidate is well known as the YAVIS individual—young, attractive, verbal, intelligent, and successful. A brochure advertising primal therapy advises that the best candidate is the person "who is an adult, who has lived a little bit, has developed some strong functioning somewhere, either in a profession or some talent, who is not extremely dependent, [and] who is not so fragile that they can't function."[11] And when 421 psychotherapists were asked to check adjectives describing their "preferred patient," the adjectives checked most frequently were "intelligent," "alert," "frank," "cooperative," "sincere," "sensitive," and "curious." "In fact," the authors concluded, "if 'anxious' were removed from the list of the 25 most descriptive adjectives, the preferred patient would appear to be an unusually productive and creative person."[12]

It is not necessarily that psychotherapists have only such clients in their practice; many persons seeking psychotherapy are in fact very unhappy, uncomfortable with themselves, and impaired in their functioning. Rather what such studies demonstrate is that psychotherapists themselves recognize that the best candidates for psychotherapy are those individuals who are already functioning well. As Dr. Parloff summarized it:

> All forms of psychotherapy tend to be reasonably useful for patients who are highly motivated, experience acute discomfort, show a high degree of personality organization, are reasonably well educated, have had some history of social success and recognition, are reflective and can experience and express emotion.[13]

It is relatively easy for us to accept the fact that psychotherapists in our culture help people with problems of living. Even when the traditional forms of these psychotherapists—psychiatrists, psychologists, and psychiatric social workers—have been broadened to include nurses, marriage counselors, family counselors, clerics, and paraprofessionals, we can still encompass the expanded psychotherapist roles. We are also aware that bartenders, hairdressers, taxi drivers, waitresses, and friends who are good listeners may offer useful advice on problems of living, but such interactions are usually not called psychotherapy. Psychotherapy involves a series of contacts between a socially sanctioned healer and a client who seeks relief, and usually involves the payment of a fee or donation in remuneration for the services.

It is much more difficult for us to accept the fact that other cultures have psychotherapist equivalents, and that these individuals use the same techniques and get about the same results as psychotherapists in our own culture. A *curandero,* an *espiritista,* or a medicine man from a subculture within the United States seems far removed from a psychiatrist, psychologist, or psychiatric social worker and yet, as will be shown, they perform a remarkably similar function. When we venture to third world countries to look for their psychotherapists and are confronted by witchdoctors, then our credulity becomes strained beyond accustomed limits.

"Witchdoctor" is a generic term applied by Western cultures to therapists in other cultures, especially those in Africa. The Africans themselves of course do not use the term; each tribe or area has its own term for the therapist in its own language. Examples are *izinyanga* in parts of South Africa, *ganga* among the Zulu, *mganga* among Swahili speakers in East Africa, *chimbuki* among the Ndembu in northern Rhodesia, *mulogo* in parts of Uganda, *bulomba* among the Temne in Sierra Leone, *babalawo* among the Yoruba in Nigeria, and *baroom xam-xam* among the Lebou in Senegal. The last certainly sounds more impressive than "witchdoctor"; it translates as "master of knowledge."

There are other generic terms for therapists in other parts of the world. "Medicine man" is the one used most often for North American Indian tribes, though each tribe has its own word for the healer. "Shaman" is a word that originated in Siberia for the therapist in the Tungusian tribes; it became widespread as the generic term throughout Alaska and parts of Asia. More recently it has been used to designate therapists everywhere who become possessed. As with witchdoctors and medicine men, each group has its own word; if you approach a group asking for their shaman you will as likely be shown to their outhouse or hotel as to their therapist. Examples of such names are *llubu* in Tibet, *angakok* among Alaskan Eskimos, *dehar* in Afghanistan, and *miko* in Japan.

Other terms for therapists are more regional. There is the *curandero* throughout Latin America, the *medium* throughout the Caribbean, and the *marabout* in many Muslim countries. Some terms are used to indicate a specific function of the therapist. For instance, "soothsayer," "seer," and "diviner" refer to his or her ability to foretell events or find lost objects; "sorcerer" or "devil doctor" refer to the ability to cast spells.

It is inaccurate to assume that therapists from different cultures are the same, even when the same generic term is used. For instance, a psychiatrist who has studied Japanese shamans noted the wide variety among their selection, training, and function, even in different parts of Japan.[14]

In this book, the term "witchdoctor" will be used generically to cover all therapists in other cultures. Similarly, the term "psychiatrist" will be used as shorthand for all formally trained therapists in our Western cultures, including psychoanalysts, psychologists, psychiatric social workers, and trained counselors. "Witchdoctor" is a curious word. Unlike "horse doctor" or "baby doctor," which indicate who or what is treated, it implies a therapist who is simultaneously a witch.

The term apparently arose out of the eighteenth- and nineteenth-century European exploration of Africa. The world was simpler then, and the new cultures were rapidly assigned their proper status in the Order of Things. We were white; they were black. We were civilized; they were primitive. We were Christian; they were pagan. We used science; they used magic. We had doctors; they had witchdoctors. This simplistic reductionism is still remarkably prevalent in our thinking about other cultures, though it is being reevaluated. It afforded an easy way to inflate the self-esteem of the white races, though of course at the expense of others.

The witchdoctors, being semireligious in function, were especially anathematized by the colonizing whites, who often were there to spread the Christian faith. Witchdoctors quickly became equated with the devil. Thus it was, and still is, difficult for us to see them as they really are. It was partly to dispel this negative stereotype that I chose the term "witchdoctors" to juxtapose "psychiatrists." Terms with fewer negative connotations, such as "shamans" or "medicine men," could have been chosen. The end result, however, might then be agreement by the reader that there *are* a few real psychotherapists among shamans or medicine men, but "what about those others—all those evil and primitive witchdoctors." I have chosen instead to deal directly with the term "witchdoctors" so that psychotherapists in other cultures, performing the same function as psychiatrists in Western cultures, cannot be dismissed with a single pejorative epithet.

The Functions of Witchdoctors

Therapists in other cultures may include many diverse functions under their job description. Paviotso Indian shamans, for instance, were supposed to control the weather, charm the antelopes before the hunt, and make the warriors invulnerable to bullets.[15] This was in addition to their more traditional healing duties. Some traditional therapists act as the tribe historian by passing on the lore, and others overlap the political leadership of the tribe. But for the therapist to be the *most* important political personage is unusual; more often he is a close adviser to the political chief.

Therapists in almost all cultures are closely allied with religious functions. Some of the most successful of the modern African witchdoctors are associated with the Christian sects.[16] In Latin America, the *curanderos* utilize Catholicism and in Bali the *balians* utilize Hinduism in their therapeutic techniques. Often the therapists and the religious leaders are one and the same person, as are the Buddhist monks in Thailand and the *hodjas* in Turkey. It is only recently in our own culture, as a matter of fact, that therapists have become completely secularized.

The main function of therapists in all cultures is to treat illness. In our culture we distinguish rather sharply between physical illness and mental illness, and we have separate therapists for each. A psychiatrist, for instance, is not expected to treat a case of pneumonia. Most other cultures do not make such a sharp distinction, with the result that therapists in these cultures treat a wide variety of physical as well as mental and social problems.

The specialization of therapists exists in all cultures. The degree of specialization is roughly proportional to the technological complexity of the society, although this is not always the case. The Wolof and Lebou tribes in Senegal, for instance, have six distinct types of healers.[17]

Within the realm of what we call mental illness, the most common division of personnel in other cultures is into herbalist, diviner, and healer. The herbalist prepares and dispenses medicines. The diviner makes diagnoses (as well as often finding lost objects and predicting the future), and the healer treats people. The healer always has the most training and the most prestige. Often people will begin with the herbalist and work up, depending on how difficult a case it is.

Another common division of the therapist's functions in many cultures is that between public and private. The public functions include such things as presiding over ceremonies, exorcising evil spirits at the building of a new house, and giving charms to departing warriors. In our culture these functions are performed by politicians, priests, and the Department of Defense. The private functions of seeing clients individually and in groups coincides with our use of the term "therapist."

It can be seen, then, that different cultures divide up the world differently. This will be dealt with at length in Chapter 2. There is no exact equivalent of a "psychiatrist" in other cultures and we should not expect other cultures necessarily to follow our division of functions. The functions we assign to a psychiatrist are found in other cultures, and these are the subject of this book. But the reader should not be surprised to find, for instance, that the Iroquois medicine man who is doing psychoanalytic dream interpretation is also in charge of the weather, and acts as judge and philosopher in the tribe.

The functions of therapists constantly evolve. This can be seen quite clearly in our own culture. Over the past twenty years the psychiatrist has begun to move out of his private office and involve himself in community action and social planning. This extension of his purview is the cause of much debate. So in other cultures: The functions of an Eskimo shaman today may be quite different than they were one hundred years ago. Therapists, like clothing styles and dating patterns, are part of the culture and change with it.

But what about the evil functions of witchdoctors? Everybody knows that one of the most important things that witchdoctors do is to put a hex on people. Actually this is a relatively unimportant and infrequent function of most witchdoctors. It is another stereotype that arose out of the writings of the missionaries. *Belief* in witchcraft and hexing *is* very common, but it is rare to find a therapist who will admit to doing it. It is always the other therapist who is believed to be guilty of it, never the one you are talking to.

This is not to deny that therapists perform these evil functions. It is just a comparatively rare phenomenon. When therapists who are believed to do these things exist in a culture, they are usually given a separate name. For example, in Latin America, a *bruja*, translated as "witch," is believed to cast hexes. He or she is quite distinct from the *curandero*, or healer, in the minds of the people.

In some cultures the occurrence of witchcraft and its occasional use by the therapist is part of the cultural judicial system. Among the Tenino Indians, for instance, the shaman occasionally would cast a hex on an unknown criminal who had not been caught. When word of it spread, the criminal often found himself becoming sick and quickly confessing.[18]

Magic or Science?

In contrast to the abundant anthropological literature, there are remarkably few psychiatric studies of therapists in other cultures.[19] This paucity is difficult to explain in view of the more numerous studies in every other area of cross-cultural psychiatry.[20] One reason non-Western therapists and their techniques have been ignored is that they are automatically relegated to the realm of "mere magic and superstition." Only occasionally are they even dignified with the rubric "prescientific psychiatry."[21] This is to distinguish them from therapists in our culture, who are thought to employ techniques based on modern science.

The truth is not even close; it is a quantum jump away. The techniques used by Western psychiatrists are, with few exceptions, on exactly the same scientific plane as the techniques used by witchdoctors. If one is magic, then so is the other. If one is prescientific, then so is the other. The only exceptions are some of the physical therapies, in particular drug and shock therapy, which have been shown in controlled studies to be effective in producing psychiatric change.

It is difficult to comprehend this. We are used to thinking of psychiatrists as men of science and witchdoctors as men of magic. Even when we do note it we quickly forget. A good example is found in Redlich and Freedman's textbook of psychiatry. On one page they observe that if we used psychiatric therapies based only on scientific evidence, then "not much would remain, because there are very few truly scientific therapies in our field.[22] One page later, however, they have already forgotten their own admonition and lapse back into the stereotype: "The technique must be based on some scientific rationale to deserve the designation of psychotherapy; it cannot be a mystical or magical procedure."[23] They then proceed to make the inevitable but fallacious assumption that Western psychiatric therapies are based on science.

In order to be scientific, a phenomenon must be explainable by underlying laws. These laws are arrived at by observation, measurement, experimentation, induction, hypothesis formulation, and testing. The rationale for most therapies used by witchdoctors and psychiatrists is not arrived at in this way—rather the techniques are used on sick clients, the clients get well, and therefore the techniques are thought to work. This is logical, empirical psychiatry and is found among witchdoctors and psychiatrists.[24] And both witchdoctors and psychiatrists make the assumption that their clients get well because of the techniques. As we shall see, other elements are probably involved.

The dilemma arises because we confuse the general level of technology in the culture with the psychiatric techniques. We implicitly and automatically assume that therapy that goes on in an office in a modern skyscraper or in a complex medical center must be scientific, whereas therapy that goes on in a grass hut must be magical. We also confuse the educational level of the practitioner with the therapy; M.D.'s and Ph.D.'s automatically are thought to do scientific things, whereas "uneducated" persons automatically are thought to do magical things. And finally, we confuse the theories of causation with the therapies; if a person believes a mental disorder is caused by hormonal imbalance or a missing gene, then the therapy is automatically thought to be scientific, whereas if the theory of causation involves evil spirits, then the therapy must be magical. In fact, psychiatric therapies are very similar all over the world and are relatively independent of the level of technology, the education of the therapists, or the theories of causation. Psychotherapy is just as scientific—or pre-scientific—in rural Nigeria or the mountains of Mexico as it is in New York or San Francisco. Or, as phrased by Dr. Kenneth Calestro, "psychotherapy is the bastard progeny of a long tradition of neo-religious and magical practices that have risen up in every unit of human culture."[25]

It is important to challenge this stereotype of witchdoctors using magic and psychiatrists using science if we hope to see them as they really are. It may be, however, that there is still too much magic in our lives to permit us to give up the stereotype easily. We divine the future with our horoscopes. We have our superstitions about the number 13 and our lucky charms to wear around our neck to ward off evil. We buy ten million rabbit-foot charms each year.[26] We knock on wood and walk around ladders. We consult Jeane Dixon and other mediums who communicate with spirits. We are able to transform bread and wine into body and blood, at least in our minds. And at the end of the day we are advised to pray:

> From ghoulies and ghosties and long-leggety beasties
> And things that go bump in the night,
> Good Lord, deliver us!

It may be that we don't want to see this magic in our lives, so we just see it in witchdoctors and call what we do "science."

If we hope to learn about witchdoctors and psychiatrists, we will have to get outside ourselves. We will have to dispose of our condescension when we approach other cultures and begin to understand that they have something to teach us. Too much of the cross-cultural literature is tinged with psychiatric imperialism.[27] The original sin was probably ethnocentrism, which may be defined as revolving around one's own navel. We must learn to look out on the world not through the cord but with a broader view.

PART I

THE COMPONENTS OF PSYCHOTHERAPY

Chapter 2

A Shared Worldview: The Principle of Rumpelstiltskin

A doctor can give penicillin to any patients who have certain kinds of infections and the patients will get well. The penicillin does not depend upon a common language or a shared worldview. Communication is not even necessary.

This is not true for psychotherapy. Communication is its essence. And real communication presupposes not only a shared language but a shared worldview as well. When this exists, the principle of Rumpelstiltskin, the first of the four components of all psychotherapy, becomes possible. Let me illustrate.

The psychiatrist looked thoughtfully at his client. "You looked angry when you were just talking about your father. You often look angry when you talk about him. I wonder if something happened to you once that made you very angry at him." At this point the client broke down sobbing, blurting out a forgotten history of neglect and deceit by a thoughtless father toward a little girl. Afterward the client felt better. After several more sessions in which she was able to explore her feelings of anger, she began to get better.

The witchdoctor stared solemnly at the small shells. They had landed in a pattern resembling the shape of a large animal. He picked up one shell and examined it minutely. "You have broken a taboo of your family. It has offended the sacred bear that protects your ancestors. That is why you are sick." The client and her family breathed a sigh of relief. It was as they had suspected. Now that they knew for certain what was wrong, they could proceed with the necessary sacrifices. After these had been made, the client began to get better.

Both therapists are able to name what is wrong with their client. The very act of naming it has a therapeutic effect. The client's anxiety is decreased by the knowledge that a respected and trusted therapist understands what is wrong. The identification of the offending agent (childhood experience, violation of a taboo) may also activate a series of associated ideas in the client's mind, producing confession, abreaction, and general catharsis.

This is the principle of Rumpelstiltskin. Based upon personality studies by the Brothers Grimm in the early nineteenth century, the principle illustrates the magic of the right word. In the Grimm Brothers' version, the word is the name of an evil man who wants to take the queen's baby. The only way the baby can be saved is by the queen naming him correctly. At the last moment, she finds the right name—Rumpelstiltskin—whereupon the baby is saved and the queen lives happily ever after.

The naming process is one of the most important components of all forms of psychotherapy. It is also one of the most commonly overlooked components. Every healer who has ever had the experience of observing a patient's relief after solemnly telling him that he was suffering from idiopathic dermatitis or pediculosis knows how important the name is. It says to the patient that someone understands, that he is not alone with his sickness, and implicitly that there is a way to get well. It is used by all therapists everywhere, by witchdoctors and psychiatrists equally effectively.

Very little research has been done on the naming process as it is used by therapists. One of the few analyses of it is that by anthropologist Claude Lévi-Strauss. In a comparison of shamans and psychoanalysts, he says that the goal of both is to bring to a conscious level conflicts and resistances that have remained unconscious in the patient. The naming process, the use of words as symbols for what is wrong, is effective not because of the knowledge per se that the words convey, "but because this knowledge makes possible a specific experience, in the course of which conflicts materialize in an order and on a level permitting their free development and leading to their resolution."[1] In other words, when a therapist correctly names what is wrong (in psychiatric terms, "makes the correct interpretation"), then the client is able to resolve that particular conflict.

Witchdoctors do this in exactly the same way that psychiatrists do. In discussing the case of an Indian cured by a shaman, Lévi-Strauss observes:

> The shaman provides the sick woman with a *language* by means of which unexpressed, and otherwise inexpressible, psychic states can be immediately expressed. And it is the transition to this verbal expression . . . which induces the release of the psychological process, that is, the reorganization in a favorable direction of the process to which the sick woman is subjected.[2]

And psychiatrist G. M. Carstairs comments upon a healer in rural India:

> What was expected from the healer was reassurance. So long as the illness was nameless, patients felt desperately afraid, but once its magic origin had been defined and the appropriate measures taken, they could face the outcome calmly. The parallel with our own clinical experience is obvious.[3]

Another psychiatric view of the naming process is provided by Werner Mendel. He calls it "the assignment of meaning" and maintains that it is part of every therapist-client transaction:

> It is a process totally independent of the theories or techniques of the therapist even though its content is related to the school of psychotherapy. All schools help their patients to assign meaning to behavior, thoughts, fantasies, dreams, delusions, and hallucinations.[4]

Mendel then goes on to quote another psychoanalyst who sees the naming process as the essence of the psychoanalytic method:

> the essence of the psychoanalytic method is, I think, that it gives meaning to apparently meaningless sequences of thoughts and acts,

that by making certain assumptions and applying certain rules derived from them it provides a rational explanation for apparently irrational behavior.[5]

Underlying the principle of Rumpelstiltskin is an important assumption—that the therapist knows the right name to put on the disorder. And in order to know the right name the therapist must share some of the patient's worldview, especially that part of the worldview concerning the disorder itself. A psychiatrist who tells an illiterate African that his phobia is related to a fear of failure and a witchdoctor who tells an American tourist that his phobia is related to possession by an ancestral spirit will be met by equally blank stares. And as therapists they will be equally irrelevant and ineffective.

The remainder of this chapter will explore the assumption behind the principle of Rumpelstiltskin. It will first attempt to answer the question "Do all people think alike?" It will then examine specific aspects of mental disorders regarding which people's thinking differs from culture to culture. Finally, it will survey the psychiatric and anthropological literature for examples of attempted cross-cultural psychotherapy and evaluate these attempts. All of this will be found to support the contention that the principle of Rumpelstiltskin is a universal component of psychotherapy but that its content is culture bound.

Do All People Think Alike?

Underlying this question is a controversy that has been raging in anthropology and psychology for over one hundred years. It is the question of psychic unity versus psychic relativity: Do all people think alike or do they think differently?

Debate began in earnest during the last half of the nineteenth century with the evolutionism of William Henry Morgan and Sir Edward Tylor. They postulated that all men were really the same, both in feelings and in thought, but simply were in different stages of evolution. According to them, the Kalahari bushmen and the Australian aborigines would think exactly as we do once they reached our stage of evolution. Western cultures, of course, were considered to be the most highly evolved of all.

At the turn of the century, evolutionism began to be challenged. Franz Boas, the father of American anthropology, promoted a view called historicalism. He saw each culture as distinct and distinctive and said that man's feelings and thoughts were tied to the culture. This view implicitly challenged and denied psychic unity. Boas's theories became increasingly popular in American anthropology and influenced many other anthropologists—e.g., Ruth Benedict, who presented configurations of cultures in *Patterns of Culture*.[6]

But until recently, hard data to support cultural relativity has been sparse. One of the first attempts to study thinking patterns in others dealt not with thinking itself but with perception. This was the Torres Strait expedition to the South Pacific in 1898. There W. H. R. Rivers tested the visual perception of the inhabitants of the Pacific islands to optical illusions and found that they differed from Europeans.

Cultural variation in perception has since been substantiated. Kalahari bushmen have been shown to be superior in spatial acuity.[7] Other studies found a differential ability among Africans to perceive optical illusions, and argued that the differences were related to the number of like-shaped objects in their environment.[8] In other words, perception was shown to be partly dependent upon cultural experience, an argument in favor of cultural relativity of cognitive processes in general. All men apparently don't see things in the same way, and the way they see them is dependent upon their culture. Why shouldn't the same be true for reasoning and categorization and feeling?

Psychology has contributed circumstantial evidence toward the cultural relativity of thinking. Piaget and his co-workers in Geneva clearly showed that thinking processes in children differ from those in adults. For instance, when the child is thinking about a conservation-of-weight problem he goes through thinking processes that differ from those of an adult.[9] So by showing definite age-level differences in thinking, Piaget left the door open to cultural differences as well.

Linguistics has also contributed evidence to this controversy. In fact, the so-called Whorfian hypothesis provides one of the main foci for the controversy. The linguist Benjamin Whorf contended that different linguistic groups perceive and conceive reality in different ways, and that the language spoken by the group shapes the cognitive structure of the individual speaking that language.[10] In short, people's thinking differs, and these differences are related to and caused by the language people use. Whorf saw language as the mold into which thoughts are poured.

Whorf's hypothesis has received partial verification from studies in cognitive anthropology, though it has not been unequivocally established.[11] It *has* been clearly established, however, that the language of different groups reflects how people in that group divide their world. For instance, Eskimos have at least four different words for "snow." A non-Eskimo trying to learn their language cannot learn just one word; he must learn separate words for falling snow, snow on the ground, drifting snow, and drifted snow.[12] He will have to learn to make categories in his thought that he has not made before if he hopes to talk with an Eskimo about snow. Snow is very important to Eskimos, and its importance is reflected by the language.[13]

Probably the best evidence for determining whether all people think alike is found in anthropological studies. For instance, in the Philippines there is a group of people called the Hanunoo. They divide all colors into just four—mabiru, malaġiti, marara, and malatuy. Marara, for example, includes those colors that we call red, orange, yellow, and maroon. If you show a Hanunoo man a red shirt and a yellow shirt he will tell you that they are both marara. If you press him he might add that the first is "more marara" or the second "weak marara," but they will both remain as marara.[14]

Another example is the Dani in New Guinea, who do not count beyond two. Their numbers are one, two, and many. If a Dani tribesman wants to find out whether one of his goats is missing, he checks each goat by name. If one of the names is not there he knows it is missing. But he does not count. It is not because the Dani are not intelligent that they do not count beyond two; in fact, they have been shown to have excellent memories and learning abilities. It is just that they divide up the world differently than we do, and their world does not have any number except one, two, and many.[15]

Studies such as these, along with the studies of perception, psychology, and linguistics, all point toward the same conclusion —that people think differently. And these differences are not just superficial differences; they are fundamental and include such basic things as colors and numbers. They imply differences in thought at all levels.

The fact that people apparently do not think alike is in agreement with our subjective impressions of the world. We have long known that people differ in more superficial ways, such as dress. And Americans traveling abroad quickly learn that customs differ —in Fiji, you sit rather than stand to show respect to your elders. At a deeper level, we know that cultures condition people to like different things. Standards for sexual attractiveness differ markedly from culture to culture—the shape of the eyes and ears, the degree of fatness or thinness, the size of breasts, the size of hips, etc.[16] Aesthetics and art forms also reflect these cultural differences. Japanese archery, for example, is not a sport but rather an art form. It does not matter whether the arrow hits the target or not. From a Western cultural vantage point this is very difficult to comprehend.

Ideas, values, conceptions of time, the notion of cause and effect—all are culturally learned. Navaho Indians feel shame in situations where we would feel guilt. Such differences are found at all levels of our thinking, and reflect the wide cultural differences in child-rearing practices, through which culture is transmitted.[17] Anthropologist Walter Goldschmidt sums it up as follows:

> Anthropology has taught us that the world is differently defined in different places. It is not only that people have different customs; it is not only that people believe in different gods and expect different postmortem fates. It is, rather, that the worlds of different people have different shapes. The very metaphysical presuppositions differ: space does not conform to Euclidean geometry, time does not form a continuous unidirectional flow, causation does not conform to Aristotelian logic, man is not undifferentiated from non-man or life from death, as in our world.[18]

It would seem to be a short but logical step from here to seeing the implications of these differences for therapists. But these extensions of thought are only rarely made. The reasons they are rarely made are threefold. First, we are afflicted by a well-meaning but false internationalism. We *want* all people to think the same, therefore we see them that way. In the long run, however, the failure to recognize true differences in thought among groups of people impedes rather than assists mutual international goals.

The second reason relates to the ethnocentrism mentioned in Chapter 1. We have no insight into our own culturally learned ideas and values. They sit within us quietly, unconsciously, providing the baseline against which we make value judgments but never themselves coming into judgment. As therapists, for instance, we accept independence and responsibility as important goals in therapy, rarely realizing that these are culturally learned values and that other cultures may not share them.[19] Freud taught us how important childhood relationships with our parents are in forming an unconscious mold that shapes later relationships. What needs to be stressed equally is how important our culturally learned ideas and values are in forming an unconscious mold that shapes later ideas and values. When we fully realize this as therapists, then we will realize that we are indeed culture bound.

A third force militating against the recognition of cognitive relativity is the proponents of cognitive unity. These scholars deny that people think differently. Most of their work comes from the fields of communications and mathematics, and depicts the human brain as a complicated computer. The computers may differ in color or exterior appearance, but they are said to utilize the same processes and therefore to be the same underneath. Complicated studies of kinship terms by componential analysis, and studies of words by the semantic differential, have been brought forth in support of this apparent cognitive unity.

The discrepancy between advocates of cognitive unity and those favoring cognitive relativity can be resolved by looking at them as different-order abstractions. The bulk of evidence to date suggests that there *are* differences in cognition between different groups of people. This cognitive relativity is primarily concerned with thought *content*. On the other hand, there may be underlying unity, but this unity is in the realm of thought *process*. These are two different orders of abstraction. The unity of thought process can be explained as due to the physically and mathematically finite ways in which the human brain can respond. For therapists it is the content of the thought that is important. It is the content that is used to talk about what is wrong and to make interpretations. If there is an underlying unity of thought process, it is of secondary importance for psychotherapy.

Theories of Causation

Turning specifically to mental disorders, it can be shown that people in various cultures have different beliefs regarding their causes. Insofar as the therapists of a culture share these beliefs, or can persuade the people to accept their theories of causation, they will be effective. A psychoanalyst trying to cure a client who does not believe in oedipal conflicts and a witchdoctor trying to cure a client who does not believe in spirit possession will be equally ineffective unless they can persuade the person to accept their theory of causation.

Mental illness is universally thought to be caused by one of three things: biological events, experiential events, or metaphysical events. The first two are the foundation for Western therapy, the third for therapy elsewhere in the world. The difference is one of degree, however: All three are found in some form in almost every culture in the world.

Biological causes widely believed in by people in Western cultures include genetic damage, inborn constitutional factors, biochemical and metabolic imbalances, infections, drug toxicity, and damage to the brain. Depending upon which "school" of Western psychiatry the therapist favors, he will put either more or less emphasis on certain causes.

Other cultures accept biological causes of mental disorders, but not as often as Western cultures do. Almost all cultures have a theory of genetic causation, though it may be associated with other things (such as a sin or a broken taboo by an ancestor) as well. Such thinking is not absent in the West. Many cultures also differentiate mental disorders resulting from infections like malaria and typhoid fever ("false madness") from that caused by experiential or metaphysical events ("true madness").[20]

Some cultures believe in biological causes that Western cultures no longer accept. Examples are bad air, insect bites, and the intrusion of a foreign body into the person. The whole basis of Chinese psychotherapy is biological imbalance between *yin* and *yang* in the brain. Therapy then logically becomes correction of the imbalance, usually by stimulation of the nervous system with needles (acupuncture).

Experiential causes, especially experiences in childhood, are the hallmark of American psychotherapy. Both clients and therapists in our culture accept the importance of traumas in childhood, and much of psychotherapy consists of an exploration of these events. Other cultures include experiences as causative of mental disorder, but to a lesser degree. The loss of a love object may be a cause of illness among the Land Dayak in Borneo.[21] And in many cultures, mental disorders are thought to be associated with having broken a taboo.

Metaphysical causes are the most important ones in most of the world: the loss of the soul; the intrusion of a spirit into the body (spirit possession); sorcery; angering a deity. And it is because metaphysical causes are so prevalent in much of the world that the role of the therapist often overlaps that of the priest. This mingling of therapist and priest roles is common in most of the world but much less so in Western cultures. We like to think that psychiatrists, psychologists, social workers, and other psychotherapists in Western culture have been completely separated from any metaphysical or theological functions.

But this is not completely so. For thousands of years priests have explained the unknown to mankind, whether it be floods, earthquakes, or unusual human behavior. God's will, devils, and evil spirits sufficed for most occasions, and people felt better because somebody understood and could put a name to what was wrong. In recent years, aberrations of nature have been turned over to physicists and seismologists for explanation, while deviant human behavior has become the purview of psychotherapists. When *The Scarlet Letter* was written, in 1850, adultery was explained by a minister as the product of evil inside the woman. If the same book were written today the author would have a psychiatrist explain the woman's behavior as due to her low self-esteem and difficulty in getting close to people. Increasingly in court cases of unusual human behavior it is the psychiatrist who is asked to put a name to what is wrong, at which point many people feel better.

There are other similarities between the priest's role and the psychotherapist's role in Western cultures. In the past the priest had the answers to existential questions of "Why am I here?" and "What does life mean?" Now these questions are addressed to psychotherapists, and a whole school of "existential psychotherapy" has evolved to deal with such questions. Techniques used by many psychotherapists, such as confession, abreaction (mentally re-experiencing traumatic past events), and altered states of consciousness, have exact parallels in religious services all over the world. There are even parallels in rituals, such as the weekly visit to one's therapist or the omnipotent but benign picture of Freud gazing down upon the proceedings in most psychoanalysts' offices. It is not, then, the fact that Western psychotherapists are so different from their witchdoctor counterparts in priestly functions that makes us uneasy, but rather that they are not very different. Psychotherapists are the secular priests of postindustrial societies, and we would prefer to ignore that fact.[22]

Though most investigators dismiss theories of causation in other cultures as "just magic and spirits," those who have looked more closely have found a complex and coherent belief system as sophisticated as our own. A good example of this is Devereux's extensive study of Mohave Indian beliefs about mental illness.[23] Another good example is Carlos Castaneda's fanciful education by a Yaqui medicine man.[24] Castaneda, an anthropologist, first tried to conceptualize his information on Yaqui mental illness by using Western categories of causation. After much work, he "realized that my attempt at classification had produced nothing more than an inventory of categories." Beginning again, he tried to order his data by using the structure of the medicine man himself. The result was an intricate, logical, and internally consistent set of theories.

Finally, it should be noted that thinking on causation not only differs between cultures, but it differs also over a period of time. Only a few years ago in Western cultures, mental illness was thought to be caused primarily by witches. And in many developing countries mental disorder is increasingly thought to be caused by various acquisitions from Western cultures. One should not expect theories of causation to be any more static than other aspects of culture; they have evolved and will continue to evolve.

Systems of Mental Disorders

Causes of mental disorders are but one facet of an entire system —cause, goals of treatment, and techniques of treatment. They form a coherent, internally logical system, but one that is inextricably bound to the culture. For example, in the United States there is a general belief that adverse early childhood experiences produce many mental disorders. A common goal of psychotherapy is to produce a rational, independent individual who has self-control and the ability to examine introspectively how his or her emotions and behavior were influenced by the early childhood experiences. The techniques used to do this include confession, abreaction, and suggestion.

Other systems of psychotherapy are based on radically different theories of cause, and the goals and techniques of psychotherapy are correspondingly different. Chinese psychotherapy, for example, is based on a belief that most mental disorders are due to disharmony between cosmic forces and other influences on internal organs; some knowledge of Confucianism and Taoism is essential to understand the system. In Japan, various schools of Buddhism have led to Naikan therapy and Morita therapy. According to one study of these therapies, the goals are "respect for authority, gratitude toward superiors and responsibility toward subordinates. . . . Nor is there an intense emphasis on 'egalitarianism' or 'independency.' . . . Japanese therapies tend to be less specifically goal-oriented . . . [and] tend to concede the more powerful and determinative nature of external social and environmental forces."[25]

Because assumptions about causes and goals differ, classifications of mental disorders cannot be transposed from culture to culture. Staying with the Japanese example, a factor analysis of symptoms of Japanese psychiatric patients was made by the anthropologist William Caudill.[26] The symptoms emerged in six clusters, four of which overlapped Western disease classification (depressed, manic, psychopathic, and psychotic) and two of which did not. One of the two was *shinkeishitsu*, a commonly recognized Japanese mental disease consisting of phobias, bodily complaints, tenseness, withdrawal, and self-deprecation. The other was *wagamama*, characterized by childish regression, apathy, negativism, and emotional outbursts. Thus both of these two "diseases" overlapped several of our disease categories and could not be clearly categorized in our system. It should also be noted that even the four categories that overlapped did not correspond exactly—e.g., depression in Japan does not include bodily complaints.

Another example of how different a system of psychotherapy can be from Western models is the concept of *sahaja*, a goal of mental health in India. As described by J. S. Neki, one of India's foremost psychiatrists, *sahaja* is "a sustained condition of enlightenment in which empirical knowledge appears vain and inferior, life appears superior to logic, and timelessness cuts across time. It is not consciousness of one particular level, but an awareness of the totality of being."[27] Imagine for a moment your psychiatrist, psychologist, or psychiatric social worker announcing to you that *sahaja* is to be your goal in therapy and you get an idea of how culture bound our systems of psychotherapy really are.

There are many mental disorders in other cultures that cannot be translated into our classification system. One such example is the "totally discouraged" syndrome found among the Sioux Indians. It cuts across our divisions of depression, alcoholism, social deprivation, sociopathy, and obsessiveness.[28] "Moth craziness" and "ghost sickness" among the Navahos are similarly culture bound.[29]

Actually there is a whole series of mental disorders usually classified as "rare and exotic diseases" in Western psychiatric textbooks. These include *latah* in Indonesia, *bah-tshi* in Thailand, *yuan* in Burma, *imu* in Japan, *mali-mali* in the Philippines, *dhami* in Tibet, *koro* in China, *myrakit* in Siberia, *piblotoq* among the Eskimos, *susto* in Latin America, and *bouffées délirantes* in West Africa.

Koro provides a useful illustration. Found among Chinese males, it consists of anxiety secondary to a strong belief that the penis is shrinking into one's body. Death is believed to follow. Because of the rather unusual symptomatology, and the imaginative preventive methods Chinese families devise, the disorder has received considerable notice by Western psychiatrists. In their attempts to translate it into Western disease categories, they have variously labeled it an anxiety neurosis, a conversion reaction, a phobia secondary to masturbation, a type of hypochondriasis, a psychosis, and an extreme castration complex.[30]

What I hope has become clear from this discussion is that *all* mental disorders are culture bound because the system of classification is culture bound. Similarly, what is a "rare and exotic disease" depends on where you live. If you live in Shanghai, then perhaps *koro* is a major syndrome and such Western entities as cyclothymic personality might be relegated to the "rare and exotic" category.

All of this is not just an exercise in cultural relativity. It has important implications. Having a shared classification system between therapist and client not only is necessary in order to name the disorder correctly, but also is necessary in order to choose the correct form of treatment. For instance, *shinkeishitsu* is treated by Morita therapy in Japan,[31] and *koro* by countering the overactivity of the *yin* (female) part of the brain. The cultural specificity of some forms of treatment will be discussed in Chapter 6, here it is mentioned only to emphasize the importance of the cultural system of classification.

Finally, the classification of mental disorders, like their causation, is time bound as well as culture bound. There are many reports in the psychiatric literature about how the syndrome of depression has changed over the past half century. Content and classification of mental disorders change similarly in other cultures over time.

Attempts at Cross-Cultural Psychotherapy

If all the above is true, and the client must share a worldview (including theories of causation and classification) in order for the principle of Rumpelstiltskin to be effective, then one would not expect attempts at cross-cultural psychotherapy to be very successful. Examination of these attempts should provide suggestive evidence either to confirm or to refute this thesis.

In fact, all attempts at cross-cultural psychotherapy of which I am aware have been either difficult or unsuccessful. The degree of difficulty appears to vary directly with the gulf between the cultures—e.g., an American therapist will find it easier to have an American-born Japanese patient in therapy than a patient from Japan. This seems self-evident but is not generally discussed in the literature. To do so would entail seeing our own system of therapy in all its culture-bound nakedness. Such a realization contradicts our implicit but strongly held conviction that Western psychotherapy is universal in its validity, as universal as penicillin is for infections or insulin is for diabetes. This conviction is another aspect of our ethnocentrism and is, quite simply, wrong.

One of the classic attempts to do cross-cultural psychotherapy was Devereux's attempt to psychoanalyze a Plains Indian. Devereux had major difficulties which he says were due to his own "unconscious cultural narcissism and ethnocentrism."[32] Other testimonies to these difficulties are found in the work of Seward, Abel, Sauna, Bishop and Winokur, and Bustamente.[33] The last, a Cuban psychiatrist, relates how he could not make the correct interpretation of a dream by one of his clients with an African background until he understood the meaning of an obscure Nigerian symbol. My own experience working with foreign students in both individual and group therapy confirmed for me the difficulties of doing cross-cultural psychotherapy.[34]

Supporting though indirect evidence for the difficulty of psychotherapy across cultures is found in the research on psychotherapy with people of a lower socioeconomic class background. In this case, "class" contains its own set of ideas, ideals, goals, values, etc., and so can be considered as a separate culture—"the culture of poverty" in Oscar Lewis's phrase.[35] Since most Western psychotherapists come from middle- and upper-class backgrounds, such therapy would be, in a sense, cross-cultural.

Research on what happens in psychotherapy to clients from this "culture of poverty" shows that they are less likely to seek therapy, are less likely to be accepted for therapy, are more likely to be assigned to inexperienced therapists, will terminate and be terminated sooner, and are more likely to be treated by short-term and somatic therapies.[36] In short, they are not considered to be "good" clients by most psychotherapists. They are considered to be too "different." I would maintain that much of this difference is due to their having a different worldview than their therapists, sharing ideas about neither causation nor classification. Hence accurate identification of the cause, the naming process, is not possible.

Since the vast majority of therapists in Western psychiatry are drawn from higher classes, opportunities for satisfactory psychotherapy for clients from lower classes are negligible. Their culture, as well as their class, makes them too "different." Western therapists prove this repeatedly by restricting their practices to clients of their own class. It is not economic factors alone that lead to this state of affairs. Even when no fee is charged at all, most Western psychotherapists find themselves automatically accepting into therapy clients who share their own class and culture, and not accepting others. These are the clients who "understand," who "speak the same language," who are "good candidates for therapy." In short, they share a common worldview, common thoughts on causation, a common way of classifying mental disorders.[37] They have cognitive congruence.

Another piece of supporting evidence that Western psychotherapy is culture bound (and class bound) comes from the studies of its ideals. As long ago as 1938, it was clearly shown that the ideals of Western psychotherapy, at that time being espoused by the mental hygiene movement, coincided remarkably with the ideals of the Protestant ethic, being espoused by (among others) proper Bostonian Americans. Individualism, self-reliance, self-sacrifice, enhancement of wealth and social status, and rationalism were the recurring themes in both. At the time, the mental hygiene movement was completely dóminated administratively by proper Bostonians.[38]

More recently, a similar study confirmed the association of mental health ideals with those of the dominant class and culture. Examination of mental health literature for idea content showed that only 10 percent of a series of pamphlets on mental health was not directly associated with middle-class values. The authors concluded that "the mental health movement is unwittingly propagating a middle-class ethic under the guise of science."[39]

Therapists in other cultures are not as restricted in class background as are therapists in Western psychiatry. For example, an extensive study of Japanese shamans showed that their class background coincided with a general cross-section of the population. If anything, they were overrepresented in the lower middle class and underrepresented in the upper class. Thus they would be expected to share a worldview with similar-class clients.[40]

It should not be said that cross-cultural psychotherapy is futile or never effective. Occasionally it appears to help a client. When it does, however, it is probably because other factors in the therapeutic relationship are producing the change, not the principle of Rumpelstiltskin. For instance, the therapist may be raising the client's expectations, or may have personality characteristics that are therapeutic for that client. These other aspects of psychotherapy will be taken up in succeeding chapters.

In summary, then, the naming process—the principle of Rumpelstiltskin—is one of the basic components of psychotherapy. As stated by one researcher: "It may be that whether one invokes devils, hierarchies, or id, the process and net result are the same —so long as the particular technique is relevant to the assumptive world shared by patient and therapist and derives from an influential source to whom the patient is susceptible."[41] But in order for the process to be effective, the therapist and the client must share a worldview. It is said that among some Arab patients there is no Oedipus complex but rather a Seth complex (Osiris kills his father and marries his sister, but is subsequently killed by his younger brother Seth).[42] As Tseng and McDermott phrased it: "To interpret to an American husband that his difficulty with his wife is due to the fact that he was born with a fire nature while his wife has a water nature and that therefore they are poorly matched will not likely be very helpful to him."[43]

In the end, however, the principle of Rumpelstiltskin and a shared worldview is not enough by itself for therapists anywhere. They must judiciously mix common sense into the batter. This is illustrated clearly by a story about a Yemenite *mori*, the traditional therapist for part of the Arabian peninsula:

One of our informants told us about a *mori* to whom a man came complaining about the fact that his house was full of mice and requesting that the *mori* give him an amulet against mice. The wise *mori* wrote out a scroll for this special occasion, handed it to the client, and said, "Here is your scroll. Tie it to the neck of a cat, otherwise it won't help."[44]

Chapter 3

Personal Qualities:
The Medicinal Mensch

Personal qualities of the therapist constitute the second of the basic components of psychotherapy. Although the research literature remains clouded and contradictory, there is a general consensus that some psychotherapists have personality characteristics which are therapeutic, while others do not have such personality characteristics and are therefore less successful as therapists. The possessor of such therapeutic personality characteristics can be designated as a medicinal mensch—from the Yiddish word for "a human being in the moral and ethical sense; not merely a person but a person with worth and dignity, one who can be respected."[1]

Not only the actual personality characteristics of the therapist but those projected onto the therapist by the client are important. These projected personality characteristics are called the transference. Western psychiatric literature is abundantly endowed with analyses of transference, a specialty of psychoanalysis, but remarkably deficient in analyses of the therapist as the therapist really is. Underlying this deficiency are important questions for psychotherapy: How important is it to select a medicinal mensch as your therapist? How should therapists be selected and trained? Would a terry-cloth-covered computer therapist be just as effective?

Several years ago, I sat down at a keyboard connected to a computer and signaled that I was ready to begin. I was curious but skeptical. How could a computer act like a psychotherapist?

COMPUTER: Hello. Please tell me your name.

ME: Torrey.

COMPUTER: It's nice to meet you, Torrey. I would like to discuss your problem with you. Please tell me first whether you are male or female.

ME: Male.

COMPUTER: How old are you?

ME: Thirty-two.

COMPUTER: Are you married?

ME: Yes.

COMPUTER: Now, how can I help you?

ME: I don't know.

COMPUTER: Tell me something about your wife.

ME: She is a fine wife. We have a good marriage.

COMPUTER: I understand. Now tell me something about your parents.

ME: My father is dead. My mother has been sick.

COMPUTER: Tell me more about her.

ME: She is getting better now.

COMPUTER: Does your wife tend to be like your mother?

ME: No, not at all.

COMPUTER: I understand. Now let me ask you something else about your mother. Was she very strict in raising you?

ME: No, she was lenient. I made all my own decisions.

COMPUTER: Does it bother you that you made all your own decisions?

ME: No, I like to.

COMPUTER: Why do you like to?

ME: Because then I have created my own existential meaning.

COMPUTER: I understand. Please tell me more about someone close to you.

I wasn't certain whether the computer *did* understand or not. I decided to test it and see how it handled hostility.

ME: Why are you so insensitive?

COMPUTER: I am doing my best under these conditions.

ME: You are just a crazy machine.

COMPUTER: You seem interested in me personally.

ME: Who do you think you are?

COMPUTER: Please think of me as a doctor trying to discuss your feelings about people close to you. Call me anything you wish.

We went through an extensive history of my childhood, illnesses, the kind of women who attract me, the kind of men I admire, etc. The computer seemed interested in me and apparently wanted to help me. It questioned, clarified, focused, rephrased, and occasionally interpreted. It sounded strangely like a therapist, and evoked feelings of both fascination and disquiet.

This therapist was the product of Kenneth Colby, an imaginative psychoanalyst at Stanford University who tried to program psychotherapy and belief systems into computers.[2] In the process he raised some important questions about the nature of the psychotherapeutic relationship. A logical extension of this might be to cover the computer therapist with terry cloth. The prototype for such an innovation is the work of psychologist Harry Harlow on terry-cloth surrogate monkey mothers. In an effort to identify the important aspects of the mother-child relationship, Harlow separated newborn monkeys from their mothers, then substituted various kinds of mechanical surrogate mothers.[3] The most effective and efficient surrogate mother was found to be a block of wood covered with foam rubber and sheathed in terry cloth. A single "unibreast" bubbled milk from it and an electric bulb provided warmth.

> The result was a mother, soft, warm, and tender, a mother with infinite patience, a mother available twenty-four hours a day, a mother that never scolded her infant and never struck or bit her baby in anger. . . . It is our opinion that we engineered a very superior monkey mother, although this position is not held universally by monkey fathers.[4]

Through his studies Harlow began to isolate the components of the mother-child relationship and to assign the components relative importance. For instance, he found that the contact with a soft body is as important as the provision of milk for the baby monkey's mental development, which threw light on such human possessions as "security blankets."

Now, if we begin sheathing some of Dr. Colby's computer therapists in terry cloth, and programming the computer to respond in different ways (e.g., listening with only an occasional "I see," giving advice, strongly empathetic, actively interpreting), then we might begin to be able to learn more about psychotherapy. We might be able to determine the relative importance of the human element, find out which personality characteristics of therapists are most helpful for different kinds of clients, and even make statements about the selection and training of therapists that are based upon more than impressions. Facts in this area are badly needed and are conspicuously absent.

Therapist-Client Relationships

What is known about the personal aspects of therapist-client relationships? Most importantly it *is* a personal relationship, between a witchdoctor or psychiatrist and a client. Although some therapists strive to keep their own personality out of the therapy (apparently trying to emulate a computer), they are never entirely successful. In all cultures of the world, therapy remains a relationship between two persons.[5]

Within the boundaries of a personal relationship, the variety of interactions between therapist and client in all cultures is wide. In our own culture it may be a close daily encounter in a private sanitarium, a daily visit to the analyst's office, a weekly visit, or a single encounter in a group marathon at a retreat. Classical psychoanalysts even used to take their clients with them on vacations, though this is no longer done. The degree of responsibility that the therapist will accept varies just as widely, from total responsibility (usually in a hospital setting) to no responsibility other than agreeing to meet regularly.[6]

Therapists in other cultures show a similar variety. In Ghana and Sierra Leone, the client may move into the therapist's home and spend long periods with him or her each day.[7] The client may stay, along with five or ten others, for as long as two years. On the other end of the spectrum, an Iban witchdoctor in Sarawak may visit the client in his longhouse for a one-shot marathon curing session and expect the client to be well thereafter.

It is generally said that therapists in other cultures foster the dependence of their clients. This is probably true, though there are exceptions. What is not clear is whether Western psychotherapists do this any less often, even though in theory they are supposed to promote independence. It is also an open question whether a dependent or an independent relationship with a therapist is superior; it may well be that the answer is related to the value system of a culture.

In terms of responsibility, therapists in other cultures usually do not accept very much. For instance, in British Guiana: "The healer's job is to assist in devotions. He never offers a prognosis, and does not accept the principal responsibility. The effectiveness of the therapy is always the patient's responsibility."[8] This attitude has echoes in several schools of Western therapy.

There is no unanimity in any culture on whether the therapist has to accept a client for treatment. Western therapists, especially those in private practice, are usually selective and will accept only those whom they think they can help. Therapists in other cultures tend to be similarly selective, enhancing their reputations by accepting only those clients with a favorable outlook for recovery.[9] On the other hand, well-known therapists in all cultures are sometimes expected to accept the most difficult cases because nobody else is skillful enough to help them. The Ute Indian medicine man is an example.[10]

In regard to body contact in the therapist-client relationship, therapists in other cultures almost invariably use it more than Western therapists do. For instance, the Nigerian *babalawo* rubs the patient's body extensively, and carefully holds his head as he makes shallow cuts to receive medicine.[11] During my brief observations of a Balinese *balian* I noted that approximately half of the healing session included some kind of body contact, usually the rubbing in of medicated oils. Body contact in Western therapies is almost completely absent, being used only by faith healers, and recently in some group sensitivity sessions.

Therapists in all cultures tend to blame their clients for their failures. In Western therapy it is usually ascribed to the client's being "unsuitable for therapy," having "too rigid defenses," not being able to "give up his symptoms," etc. In other cultures it is usually blamed on a taboo broken by the client or his family, and therapists end most healing sessions by invoking enough taboos to ensure their being broken, thus leaving themselves an excuse for failure.

The therapist-client relationship is also in part determined by the fees paid by client to therapist. In most cultures there is thought to be a relationship between how much the therapy costs and how much it is worth. The cost of individual Western therapy can go over one hundred dollars a fifty-minute hour in large cities. Such an extraordinary fee is not exclusive to Western therapists. In Martinique, a therapy session may cost the equivalent of one week's wages; however, the therapy is often supposed to be completed in one or two sessions. In areas where both Western and non-Western therapy are available, the latter may be the more expensive. For instance, at a hospital I visited in Singapore, the traditional Chinese therapy was more expensive than the Western. In contrast to cultures where a high fee characterizes the therapist-client relationship, there are others in which the only fee is a donation. The client leaves whatever he can afford. Even in such cultures, however, the therapist is well off. In all cultures of the world, witchdoctors and psychiatrists are among the wealthier members of the society.

Occasionally in other cultures a male therapist may accept a female client as his wife in lieu of a fee. This is found, for instance, in Nigeria.[12] Although it is not rare in Western therapy for a therapist to marry his or her patient—some nationally known therapists have done it—presumably it is not in lieu of a fee.

Western therapists usually charge a fee, though a lower one, while they are in training. In other cultures this may differ. Shamans among the Northwest Coast Indians received no fee until they had finished their four-year apprenticeship.[13] And fully trained Tenino shamans could not accept a fee for their first five cases.[14]

Western therapists expect to be paid their fee regardless of whether the client gets well or not. This is not always true elsewhere.

An interesting way of regulating fees is found among the Paviotso Indians. There it is generally believed that a therapist who asks more or less than his or her power authorizes will become sick and no longer be able to practice.[15] In these days of Medicaid abuse, it is interesting to think what would happen if such a belief became prevalent among Western therapists.

Genuineness, Empathy, and Warmth

Since the mid-1950s, a series of researchers have tried to identify the personality characteristics of psychotherapists that are therapeutic. Much of the research arose from the theories of psychologist Carl Rogers, and began with Rogers's attempts to identify the important components of therapeutic personality change.[16] Simultaneously Betz and Whitehorn divided therapists into type A and type B, depending on how successful they were in treating patients with schizophrenia.[17] This was followed by an avalanche of research studies from Truax and Carkhuff,[18] Strupp and Luborsky and their associates, which has continued up to the present.

Some of these researchers have claimed that certain personal qualities of the therapist—accurate empathy, nonpossessive warmth, and genuineness—are of crucial importance in producing effective psychotherapy. These three qualities of the therapist "have been shown to relate significantly to a variety of positive patient personality and behavioral change indexes."[19] The therapists who possess these qualities consistently and convincingly get better therapeutic results than those who do not possess them. Four types of supporting research data have been brought forth.[20] The first is concerned with client outcome in cases receiving high levels of the three ingredients as contrasted with cases receiving low levels. Studies included individual therapy on fourteen schizophrenic inpatients, forty psychoneurotic outpatients, and eighty institutionalized male juvenile delinquents. The findings on the forty psychoneurotic outpatients, for instance, showed a 90 percent improvement rate when the therapist provided high levels of the three therapeutic qualities, and a 50 percent improvement rate when a low level was provided. Most of the research was done by trained raters who coded samples of tape-recorded psychotherapy, using research scales designed to measure the three therapeutic qualities.

The second type of supporting research data focuses on the three qualities themselves, contrasting client change with control groups receiving no psychotherapy. Studies included fourteen schizophrenic inpatients, forty institutionalized female juvenile delinquents, and twenty-four college underachievers. The results of the last, for instance, showed that nineteen of the twenty-four had a higher grade point average in the semester after the counseling, compared with eleven of the twenty-four controls.

Truax and co-workers also used these data to explain why past studies of outcome of psychotherapy have often failed. Truax maintained that such studies included all kinds of therapists, and did not differentiate those with genuineness, empathy, and warmth from those lacking it. Thus some therapists were getting their clients well whereas others were doing nothing or even making them sicker. The net result was zero.

The third type of supporting research data examines the respective roles of the therapist and the client in determining how high a level of these qualities will be offered. One study used eight therapists and eight inpatients in a block design. This study and others showed "that the levels of therapeutic conditions offered throughout counseling are due to the counselor rather than the client."[21] In other words, it is the therapist who determines whether the genuineness, empathy, and warmth will be present or not. The qualities are either there or they are not, independent of the personality or type of problem of the client.

Finally, there is converging evidence from research on learning and on parental influence. It has been shown, for instance, in a study of 120 third graders and eight teachers, that children learn to read faster under the teachers who offer higher levels of the three qualities cited above.[22]

None of the researchers in this area claim that personal characteristics of the therapist are the only, or even the most important, ingredient in psychotherapy. Rather, as summarized by Strupp, they believe that

> any meaningful definition of psychotherapy would have to accommodate personal qualities of the therapist that are brought to bear on the therapeutic interaction with a given patient. Thus to describe psychotherapy in terms of its theoretical orientation or techniques, as was common then and still is now, provides a truncated view of what is always a complex human relationship. By this reasoning, what the therapist communicates by attitudes, gestures, and innuendo must be studied and understood as carefully as the techniques he or she uses. In brief, psychotherapy is never adequately defined as a "treatment modality" or as a set of "technical procedures."[23]

One of Strupp's more recent and controversial research projects (done with Dr. Suzanne Hadley) was to compare five professional psychotherapists with an equal number of college professors as psychotherapists. The professionals included three psychiatrists and two psychologists, with an average length of practice of twenty-three years. The college professors were "selected on the basis of their reputation for warmth, trustworthiness, and interest in students"; none of them had any formal training or experience as therapists. The results of the study did not endear Strupp to his professional colleagues, for he reported that

> patients undergoing psychotherapy with college professors showed, on the average, quantitatively as much improvement as patients treated by experienced professional psychotherapists. . . . Our results suggest that the positive changes experienced by our patients . . . are generally attributable to the healing effects of a benign human relationship.[24]

In another recent study of the personality characteristics of psychotherapists, Luborsky and his colleagues studied three different modes of therapy in heroin addicts. The conclusion of the elaborate research design was that "the major agent of effective psychotherapy is the personality of the therapist, particularly the ability to form a warm, supportive relationship. . . . The therapist's ability to form an alliance is possibly the most crucial determinant of his effectiveness."[25]

Despite similar recurring findings over thirty years, there remains considerable skepticism about this research area. The personality characteristics studied have often been, in the words of one researcher, "such simplistic global concepts as to cause this field to suffer from possibly terminal vagueness," and "prescriptions for the ideal psychotherapist have included a litany of virtues more suited perhaps to the most honored biblical figures than to any of their descendants."[26] Many past studies included psychotherapy on patients with schizophrenia, now known to be a useless form of therapy for this disease except as a supportive mode, so the research results must be ignored. Furthermore, there is an emerging consensus that the critical variable is not the personality characteristics of the therapist per se, but how these interact with the personality characteristics of the client. Psychotherapy is seen as a dynamic interaction in which the therapist supplies half the ingredients but in which the client must interact and supply the other half. In the Strupp and Hadley study described above, for example, the researchers reported that "a substantial portion of the variance in treatment outcomes (up to 38 percent) could be accounted for by the patient's involvement in the therapeutic process."[27]

Some observers of the therapist-client relationship have carried this interaction to almost mystical dimensions. Koss, in describing healers in the Puerto Rican culture, claims that the interaction between therapist and client achieves "a special type of practitioner-client relationship in which empathy reaches the extreme of almost complete identification of the healer with his patient's illness. . . . Becoming one with one's patient within a special cosmic space beyond boundaries of the individual persona is the goal of many mystic healers."[28] Analogous observation from another culture is that of Hoch, who suggested that the most successful therapist in India is "somewhat like a hemodialyzing machine in that he 'takes in' the patient's troubled insides and returns them to the patient in a purified form. . . . The psychotherapist must function as a semi-permeable membrane which can take in the patient's inner turmoil and purify it without being overwhelmed by the process."[29]

The Personalities of Psychotherapists

A random observer in any culture in the world will quickly realize that not all psychotherapists have personality characteristics generally deemed to be therapeutic. In all cultures there are found some charlatans who are conscious that they are frauds and are only interested in making a quick zloty, rupee, or dollar. Also found in most cultures are psychotherapists with authoritarian personality characteristics, who appear to take pleasure in goading, confronting, or humiliating their clients. A surprising number of clients will pay money for these experiences, as purveyors of some weekend confrontation groups have discovered.

As a rule, however, psychotherapists around the world usually have personality characteristics that are admired in their culture. It is doubtful that such personality characteristics change significantly once the person has become a therapist, so some self-selection must be operating to determine who becomes a therapist.

Western psychotherapists are chosen primarily through self-selection and academic achievement. A therapist must finish high school and college, then get postgraduate training as either a social worker, a psychologist, or a psychiatrist. If the person chooses psychiatry, he or she must go on through four years of medical school, one year of internship, and three or four years of psychiatric residency training—a total of twelve years training after high school. A psychoanalyst can add still another four to eight years to this before he or she is considered fully qualified.

Western therapists, quite obviously, must be good academic students to survive this selection process. Unfortunately there is evidence that being a good student has nothing to do with being a good therapist.[30] One study even showed a negative correlation between the grades of therapists-in-training and their ratings on empathy.[31] Another study found that psychiatrists, the most highly trained psychotherapists in Western culture, scored lower on empathy ratings compared with psychologists, social workers, psychiatric nurses, or occupational therapists.[32] Carl Rogers perhaps expressed the logical conclusion best when he said: "Intellectual training and the acquiring of information has, I believe, many valuable results—but becoming a therapist is not one of those results."[33]

If personality characteristics of the therapist are as important for successful therapy as research has indicated, then our present method of selecting therapists in Western culture may be grossly inappropriate. It is possible, in fact, that the prolonged academic trial may even be *antithetical* to selecting good therapists. Those genuine, warm, empathetic therapists who do emerge may do so in spite of, not because of, the system of selection. And it is very disquieting to realize that there may be many individuals with the proper personality characteristics who are presently blocked from ever becoming professional therapists because they cannot or do not wish to learn trigonometry or microbiology.

The selection of therapists in other cultures is done by criteria other than academic achievement. The most common methods of selection are through heredity, supernatural designation, and self-designation. Heredity is rarely the only method, but it is frequently present. The child picked to succeed the therapist parent may not necessarily be the eldest, but may be the one who shows the greatest interest or capacity as a therapist. Many witchdoctors in western Nigeria have had medicine in their family for four or five generations.[34] This kind of family tradition is present also in Western culture, though it is less marked. Erik Erikson's translation of the pressure felt by a Yoruk Indian girl whose mother and grandmother are shamans sounds suspiciously like a dialogue that many Western therapists have heard before:

> "My mother say, 'You be doctor.'
> "I say, 'no.'
> "She say, 'You have much money, beautiful clothes; if not doctor, will have nothing.' "[35]

Another type of quasi-hereditary selection is the automatic designation as therapists of certain individuals who are different. Eskimo shamans, for example, are often drawn from the ranks of orphans and those with physical deformity.[36] And in one part of Japan all girls who are blind or crippled are expected to become shamans.[37] It is thought that such "special" individuals have been supernaturally marked for this unique role in society.

Designation by the supernatural is probably the most common way of selecting therapists in other cultures. The following account of a *tahu'a* on Tahiti is typical, and echoes the Old Testament:

> Tama was about forty-five years old at the time of the study and was one of the most famous *tahu'a* on the island of Tahiti. He was a successful farmer and entrepreneur. He had no special thought of becoming a healer, nor did he think much about the supernatural until twelve years before the author met him, at which time he had experienced a vision in his sleep. A cloud appeared to him and a voice came out of it, saying: "Heal the sick. Cure the people." Similar dreams are typically described to mark the onset of all *tahu'a* careers.[38]

Tseng gave a similar account of the selection of a Taiwanese Dang-gi (shaman):

> Mr. Wu became a shaman 13 years ago when he was 23. There was an old temple about 200 feet from his home whose old Dang-gi had passed away in that year. According to the custom, the elders of the temple beat the golden drum every evening, looking for someone

in the neighborhood who might fall into a trance and thus be chosen by the god as the new Dang-gi. According to Mr. Wu, one evening, on hearing the sound of a drum in the temple, he felt very strange, as if he had become a different person, and suddenly fell into a trance. He went to the temple by himself while he was in the dream state. The elders in the temple immediately realized that he had been chosen to succeed the deceased Dang-gi.[39]

Many healers receive their calling through dreams, visions, and unusual experiences. It is generally believed that they *must* obey such a calling, and that the penalty for failing to obey is sickness or death.

Designation by the supernatural may also be sought by a potential therapist. This was commonly the case among Native American medicine men, who would deprive themselves of food, water, sleep, and comforts as they wandered in search of their "calling." Clearly there is also a voluntary component to selection in this manner.

Self-selected therapists are less common in other cultures, and usually have less status than those selected by heredity or by the supernatural.[40] The self-selection process is illustrated by this account from Martinique:

> It is neither by inheritance nor by training that a healer obtains his position. He is self-designated on the basis of his conviction that he has special magical powers or gifts. The sort of evidence accepted as proof of this was indicated by a male nurse who despite his skepticism wondered if he himself had magical powers. He based his belief on the fact that he had once cured someone by concentrating hard and because he had often dropped syringes and thermometers but had never broken anything. To become a healer there is no initiation, no payment of fees, and no special garb; one need only let it be known that one has taken up the work of healer. The authors were convinced of the healer's sincerity in believing that he could genuinely help patients.[41]

Also frequently included in self-selection are factors similar to those that may motivate Western therapists, such as a desire to help people, to gain social status and wealth, or to master the unknown so as to be better able to protect oneself and one's family.[42]

Are Psychotherapists Mentally Ill?

There is a common belief in Western cultures that most psychiatrists are themselves a little disturbed. It is often said in jest, but reflects a rather widespread general suspicion. Similarly, there is a common belief among those with any exposure to anthropological literature that witchdoctors are disturbed individuals. Are these beliefs true? What kind of individuals, really, are psychiatrists and witchdoctors?

Regarding Western therapists, there is remarkably little objective evidence available with which to answer these questions. Most observations have been confined to what kind of person a therapist *should* be—e.g., intelligent, imaginative, sensitive, likeable, respected, self-controlled, flexible, and energetic.[43] It is occasionally said that therapists should have gone through illness themselves in order to understand their clients. One study of medical students electing to specialize in psychiatry found that 28 percent of them had already been in psychotherapy.[44]

Recent data on suicide rates for professional people show that psychiatrists have an inordinately high rate—double that for other types of doctors.[45] They also are known to have a comparatively high rate of drug addiction. Whether these figures can be used to support a contention that psychiatrists are, as a group, more disturbed than the general population is another, and debatable, matter.

My subjective impression of the personality of psychiatrists is that there is some overrepresentation at both ends of the spectrum, but that generally psychiatrists are not grossly different from most professional groups. In other words, there appears to be a greater-than-expected group of highly motivated, well-integrated, stable, healthy individuals, and also a greater-than-expected group of misfits. The abnormally high suicide rate presumably comes from the latter group. More objective data on this issue is badly needed.

Turning to witchdoctors, there is a widespread but erroneous impression in the anthropological literature that they are very disturbed individuals. The witchdoctor's vocation is often portrayed as a haven for the schizophrenics, opportunists, and sexual deviants of a society.

This belief originated with Bogoras's study of the Siberian Chukchi early in this century. He contended that their shamans were "as a rule extremely excitable, almost hysterical, and not a few of them were half crazy."[46] Anthropologists such as A. L. Kroeber, George Devereux, and Ralph Linton perpetuated this belief, and being prolific writers, they succeeded in establishing it as a fact which was until recently unchallenged. Kroeber, for instance, contends that one of the points differentiating a "primitive" from a "developed" society is that the former rewards its psychotics with a socially sanctioned role as a healer.[47] The line of reasoning usually follows psychoanalytic thinking and always, of course, comes from the vantage point of the writer's cultural norms.

A psychoanalyst who studied Apache Indian shamans provides further data. L. B. Boyer's earlier work on one shaman concluded that he was a disturbed individual.

> He was shown to suffer from a personality disorder, with impulsive and hysterical traits, and to have characteristics of the imposter. His principle fixations were oral and phallic. There were suggestions he lacked clear masculine identity and suffered from problems resulting from latent homosexuality.[48]

From this Boyer generalized that all Apache shamans were disturbed.[49]

Three years and eleven shamans later, Boyer completely reversed himself. After further studies he concluded that "Apache shamans have not been psychological deviants at any period of their lives." In fact, he says that they are *healthier* than the average member of their society.[50]

Boyer's observations are instructive. If you look at only one therapist in any culture you may find a deviant. There are abundant accounts of single therapists in other cultures who are psychopathic, manic, emotionally unstable, psychotic, or frauds.[51] It is no more valid, however, to generalize from these single thera-

pists in other cultures than it is to generalize from a single therapist in our culture.

It is also clear that judgments about the mental health of therapists in other cultures often suffer from the ethnocentric bias of
the observer. Thus spirit possession and associated hysterical behavior is not only normal but often valued and desirable in other
cultures. In our own culture it is considered deviant. It was just
this kind of behavior that led Bogoras originally to the conclusion
that the shamans must be crazy.[52]

To make a generalization about the mental health of therapists,
an observer must study several of them and must also know what
kinds of behavior are considered normal in the culture. A good
study which meets these criteria is by Dr. Yuji Sasaki, a Japanese
psychiatrist. He found that of fifty-six Japanese shamans, thirty-
eight were without evidence of personality deviation, ten had
some degree of neurosis, six were psychotic, and two had organic
brain disease.[53] Unfortunately there is no data on Western therapists against which to compare these figures.

Another commonly cited fact in favor of the therapists-are-
mentally-ill thesis is the use of transvestites as therapists. This was
a well-known (and widely commented upon) arrangement among
the Plains Indians, where such individuals were called *berdaches*.
For anthropologists like Kroeber, this "proved" that therapists in
other cultures are disturbed.[54] The fact is that *berdaches* certainly
did exist but this arrangement is a rare one. It is found in a few
other cultures in the world,[55] but not nearly as often as Western
anthropological preoccupation with it would lead one to believe.
Most therapists in other cultures are as heterosexual as most therapists in our own culture.

There is increasing evidence with which to refute the idea that
therapists in other cultures are disturbed. In fact, many observers
note that, as a group, the therapists appear to be among the least
disturbed members of the society. Typical is the judgment of
anthropologist Marvin Opler on the Ute Indian shaman:

> The Indian shaman was a man or woman ordinarily not only adult
> chronologically, but mature, poised, and serious in personality. . . .
> In his hands, as with the medical practitioner in our society, lay an

enormous responsibility for maintaining the health and vigor necessary in the culture. . . . His role, depending on his prowess, became in most instances a crucial and respected one, not merely
medical but ethico-religious in essence.[56]

Lambo described therapists in Nigeria as displaying "extraordinary qualities of mind—common sense, great eloquence, tough-
mindedness, great boldness and unrivalled capacity for deep insight into human problems."[57] And according to Dean and Thong,
the *balian* in Bali "is selected for years of training by the village
elders because he has special gifts and inspires confidence—in
short, because he has a therapeutic personality."[58] He is a Balinese medicinal mensch.

Unusual intelligence and memory are frequently ascribed to
these therapists of other cultures. For instance, a Navaho medicine man must learn for a curing ceremony a volume of details
that has been compared to memorizing a Wagnerian opera, including "orchestral score, every vocal part, all details of the set-
tings, stage business, and each requirement of the costume."[59]
And a Yakut Indian shaman must have a professional vocabulary
of twelve thousand words, compared to the usual Yakut vocabulary of four thousand words.[60] Other commonly mentioned attri-
butes are "unusual decency, upright character, judgment, and
responsibility."[61] An observer of Yakut Indian shamans sums up
best of all the qualities that make a good therapist in that culture,
and probably in many cultures: "One must feel an inner force in
him that does not offend yet is conscious of its power."[62]

Many other testimonials could be proffered to support the
thesis that most therapists in other cultures are unusually stable
and mature individuals. They cover a wide area from African
witchdoctors[63] to Australian medicine men ("altruistic and intelligent men")[64] to Native American shamans and medicine men.[65]
After an extensive survey of the character of this last group, one
field worker concludes: "quackery and charlatanism are no more
prevalent in primitive than in civilized society."[66]

Western therapists have organizations such as the American
Psychiatric Association and the American Psychological Association to ensure minimum standards of conduct and professionalism
among their members. Though less commonly, therapists in other

cultures are sometimes similarly organized. Witchdoctors in the Sudan, Kenya, Tanzania, and Nigeria have fraternal organizations,[67] and shamans in Korea not only form guilds but even contribute money for the erection of lodges in which they meet.[68] Societies such as these can enforce good conduct; for instance, candidates for the Association of Nigerian Doctors must take an oath that they will use their powers only for good purposes, never for sorcery.[69] These societies can also exclude mentally disturbed or unstable candidates from membership. Finally, many groups of therapists have a common ethic demanding professional secrecy regarding what the therapist has been told by patients.[70] One of the effects of such organizations is to encourage and enforce ethical behavior, thereby attracting more ethical personality types as therapists.

Chapter 4

Client Expectations:
The Edifice Complex

A taxi drives up to the front door of the Menninger Clinic in Topeka. A depressed middle-aged man from northern New England gets out with his family. It has been a difficult trip, including two changes of planes and much financial sacrifice. But even as he enters the door he feels better. He has hope.

A crowded bus stops in the center of the West African village. A depressed middle-aged man from up-country gets out with his family. The trip has entailed a day of walking, two buses, and much expense. Up on the hill the famous healing shrine is visible. As he starts up the hill toward it, he feels better. He has hope.

Both of these men illustrate the third component of psychotherapy. Along with a shared worldview and the personal qualities of the therapist, client expectations are a powerful and important part of the therapeutic process. Anything that raises client expectations aids this process. Therapists everywhere in the world utilize this principle, though too often in Western cultures it lies misplaced and unrecognized beneath our piles of sophisticated theories and techniques.

Freud recognized its importance. In commenting on the similarity of primitive and religious therapies to psychoanalysis, he said: "In order to effect a cure a condition of 'expectant faith' was induced in the sick person, the same condition which answers a similar purpose for us today."[1]

But it has remained for psychiatrist Jerome Frank to clearly outline the importance of hope and client expectations for psychotherapy. After reviewing many types of healing in his lucid *Persuasion and Healing*, Frank concludes: "The apparent success of healing methods based on all sorts of ideologies and methods, compels the conclusion that the healing power of faith resides in the patient's state of mind, not in the validity of its object."[2] And in a later paper: "efforts to heighten the patient's positive expectations may be as genuinely therapeutic as free association or habit training."[3]

This chapter will examine the available evidence that supports these contentions. It will then describe some of the ways in which psychiatrists and witchdoctors raise their clients' expectations and produce hope, itself therapeutic. The building associated with the healer (the edifice complex), his reputation, his accessory paraphernalia, his reputation, and his training are all effective parts of therapy and induce hope that the client will, after all, get well.

The Importance of Expectations

There is now abundant evidence from many sources that shows the importance of expectations. What a person expects to happen often will happen if the expectations are strong enough. This is the self-fulfilling prophecy.

Expectations are a major determinant of human behavior. Psychologists are familiar with experiments showing how visual perception is influenced by the person's expectations.[4] One sees what one expects to see. An experiment involving classes of college students and a "substitute teacher" showed how expectations influence the formation of opinions. Half the class was given advance biographical data on the "teacher" that indicated he was a "cold" person; the other half, a "warm" person. Testing after the class revealed that those with expectations of a "warm" teacher found him significantly more considerate, more sociable, more humorous, and less formal than their counterparts found him. Furthermore, they participated more actively in the class.[5]

Some of the strongest evidence for the importance of expectations comes from studies of patients going to surgery. In one such study, a group of surgical patients was warned before the operation about postoperative pain and was given breathing exercises to do for the pain. Another group was not given any warning or exercises. The group that had been told to expect pain requested only half as much pain medication and left the hospital earlier by an average of almost three days.[6] Clearly patient expectations are a powerful therapeutic tool.

The importance of patients' expectations in determining the efficacy of any medication is well known among physicians and was clearly described in 1823:

> A new medicine will frequently obtain a fortuitous fame, during the continuance of which there is no doubt that it actually produces some of those salutary effects which are ascribed to it. But the fault of these new remedies is that they will not *keep*. For so soon as the caprice of the day has gone by, and fashion has withdrawn its protecting influence, the once celebrated recipe is divested of its beneficial properties, if it become not deleterious; by which it would appear that its reputation had not been the result of its salutary efficacy, but that its salutary efficacy had been, in a great measure at least, the result of its reputation.[7]

A review of recent studies on this phenomenon claims that "at least 50 percent of the effect of any drug that influences patients' subjective states is due to the physician's expectations as transmitted to the patient—that is, at least 50 percent is a placebo effect."[8] Andrew Weil, in an excellent review of modern medicine, simply states that "the history of medicine is actually the history of the placebo response."[9]

Some of the more colorful placebo medicines on which doctors in the past made their reputations included lizard blood, crocodile dung, swine teeth, powdered Egyptian mummy, and frog sperm.[10] Modern-day versions of placebos, such as kelp, honey, horehound leaves, and pigweed, can be found in several best-selling books of home remedies.[11] Some of these contain a grain of therapeutic truth, but many of them are simply placebos. But they work. And they work because people expect them to work.

The power of a patient's expectations is also suggested by studies done on its obverse—hopelessness. Internists and surgeons know well the problems of trying to cure a hopeless patient. Some surgeons will not even operate on a patient who does not expect to survive the operation—too often they do not survive.[12] Related to this is the high mortality rate of old people shunted off to nursing homes; they apparently give up hope and just die.

Probably the most impressive demonstration of the efficacy of patient expectations is "voodoo death." This dramatic demise occurs when a person is "hexed" by another who is believed to be powerful enough to kill him or her.[13] The hexed person becomes sick and dies within a few weeks. Having expected to die, the person does die. The actual mechanism of death has been debated, but probably it involves activation of the nerve to the heart, causing the heart gradually to stop. Deaths due to this kind of patient expectation have been reported by Western observers in South America, Africa, Australia, and the Caribbean. Voodoo deaths point to the great importance of patient expectations in determining a person's health status.

In recent years, the importance of patients' expectations in medical disorders has come into vogue as a subject of serious research. The interaction of the central nervous system with the endocrine organs (often referred to as the hypothalamic-pituitary axis) as well as with the immune system (including the lymphatic system and the thymus gland) has attracted increasing interest. Norman Cousins's 1979 best-seller, *Anatomy of an Illness*, focused attention on the interplay of mind and body, and even though many in the medical profession doubted Cousins's account of his "ankylosing spondylitis" illness and its cure by positive thinking and humor (a literal version of "laugh your troubles away"), what emerged from public discussions was a much greater awareness of how mind can influence body. Respectable research is now taking place on the altering of thought patterns using such mechanisms as biofeedback, hypnosis, and mental imaging to try and affect such conditions as headaches, colitis, hypertension, rheumatoid arthritis, cardiac arrhythmias, and the spread of some cancers.[14] It is evident that we have much to learn about the power of patients' expectations.

Emotional Arousal

The expectations of a client in psychotherapy are a composite of many factors. Hope is an essential element, and this in turn is related to trust in the healer or therapist. Trust is dependent on the personality characteristics of the therapist, and in this way the third component of psychotherapy (client expectations) interacts with the second (personal qualities of the therapist). Since the therapeutic relationship is an interaction between two individuals, the personal qualities of the therapist and expectations of the client reverberate back and forth, producing what is commonly referred to as the "fit" between therapist and client. When it is a good fit, then therapy proceeds smoothly; when it is not, the therapist says things like "He's just not a good candidate for psychotherapy" and the client says things like "I just don't have any faith that he will be able to help me."

In recent years, researchers have focused on another important aspect of client expectations—the role played by emotional arousal in the client. Data suggest that the greater the arousal, the greater the client's expectations and thus the probability of psychotherapeutic change. Interest in this phenomenon began in 1924 when a great flood took place in Leningrad. Pavlov, experimenting with conditioned responses in dogs, found that the trauma of the flood in the animal houses where the dogs were kept virtually wiped out the conditioned behavioral patterns that had recently been taught. Out of such observations came the realization that emotional arousal was capable of abolishing much learned behavior and then allowing the introduction of new behavioral patterns.

The importance of emotional arousal in modern psychotherapies is stressed by Dr. Jerome Frank and his colleagues in the psychotherapy research unit at Johns Hopkins University:

> Most therapies use emotional arousal as part of the treatment, either at the beginning of therapy, followed by systematic reinforce-

ment of newly developed attitudes, or in the latter parts of therapy, crystallizing gains of the preceding therapeutic sessions. Most conventional psychotherapies which derive from psychoanalysis introduce arousal in a less systematic way, and usually when therapy seems to slow down or when the patient "resists" the guidance of the therapist.[15]

Some methods used to induce emotional arousal are obvious, such as the cathartic expression that occurs in many encounter groups, marathon groups, behavioral therapies in which the client is asked to imagine the phobic object, and psychotherapies utilizing screaming or nudity. Other therapies produce emotional arousal by isolation and the withdrawal of all stimuli. The best-known of these is Morita therapy, used commonly in Japan, in which the client is put alone in a room for several days and not allowed to do anything except write in a diary. A similar technique is utilized by some American therapies. In primal therapy, the client is instructed: "For 24 hours before your first session, you must confine yourself to a hotel room and, unless otherwise advised, restrict yourself to essential activities such as eating and sleeping . . . the length of isolation, which rarely exceeds a few days, is determined by the therapist."[16]

The reader may have noticed that some of these methods for eliciting emotional arousal are remarkably similar to techniques used in brainwashing and also in religious conversion and faith healing sessions. In fact this is true, and Dr. William Sargant has written a book (*The Mind Possessed*) on the similarities of psychotherapy, brainwashing, and religious conversion.[17] All three, according to Sargant, depend on cortical excitation, emotional exhaustion, and subsequent conversion of the client's thinking to a new point of view. Religious faith healing sessions, for example, include a healer with special powers derived from the Bible, a highly charged emotional climate in which witnesses testify to the efficacy of the method and how much they have been helped, and often a crescendo of loud prayer and singing as the healer lays hands on the client to make him or her well. In the United States, faith healing has been called the poor man's psychotherapy.[18]

The Importance of Setting

Many techniques and methods are used by therapists around the world to increase a client's expectations and induce emotional arousal. The process begins when the client decides to go to the healing institution. Even making an appointment and thinking about going is often enough to make the client feel better. Expectations are increased by the trip; The longer the trip is, the higher will be the client's expectations. Often a trip to a major healing institution takes on the qualities of a pilgrimage, as is implied in the two cases described at the beginning of the chapter. Western clients will often talk of their trip to the Menninger Clinic, the Mayo Clinic, the Leahy Clinic, or any of the other renowned medical centers in terms that other pilgrims have used for Delphi, Mecca, or Lourdes.

This, in the phrase of Dr. Harry Wilmer, is the edifice complex.[19] Though it is as old as the Greek myth of similar sound, it bears no relation to it. It is faith in the institution itself, the door at the end of the pilgrimage. It is the light in the client's eyes when you tell him or her that you are associated with *the* medical center. It is the misty prestige of antibiotics and open-heart surgery seeping down the hall to the Department of Psychiatry. It occurs when "patients invest the hospital itself with a healing function, and assume that whatever goes on within its walls is done to help them."[20] It is that portion of psychotherapeutic effectiveness which would be lost if psychiatrists operated out of austere rooms in a county courthouse rather than out of the medical center. In psychoanalytic terms, it is transference to the institution.

Western therapists commonly utilize the edifice complex to raise client expectations, though they are not usually aware of using it. They use it more often than therapists in other cultures because they are more likely to be attached to a single building or institution. Witchdoctors are less apt to center themselves in one place, and more commonly make visits to the client's home. The edifice complex is certainly not unknown among therapists in other cultures, however; healing shrines of wide repute are found scattered throughout almost all cultures. They are commonly semireligious in nature, contrary to their more purely therapeutic nature in Western cultures.[21]

The Therapist's Paraphernalia and Belief in Himself

We have seen that the therapist's ability to raise a client's expectations is intimately connected both with an ability to name what is wrong and with personal qualities. In reference to the first, much of the naming process and the assignment of meaning can be looked at from the vantage point of increasing the client's faith in the therapist and increasing the expectations of cure. It is the naming, in fact, that is the necessary first step; only when the malady is properly identified does the possibility of curing it become a real one.

Another aspect of this is the therapist's belief in himself. Several studies have shown that the greater this belief is, the higher are the client's expectations of being helped.[22] Accounts of both successful witchdoctors and successful psychiatrists invariably include the strong belief the therapist has in himself. It can be seen, for instance, in the "inner force . . . that does not offend yet is conscious of its power" in a Yakut Indian shaman[23] as well as in the writings of a Western therapist like Carl Rogers.

Another phenomenon that points toward the importance of a therapist's belief in himself is the continuous succession of "new" types of therapy in Western cultures. These are usually associated with a single therapist, the "founder," and flit across the therapy screen like fads. It is as if the psychological journals had a therapist-of-the-month foldout. These "new" therapies are invariably most effective in the hands of their "founders," who usually claim, and probably obtain, spectacular cure rates. They have, after all, the most faith in the "new" methods, and they transmit their certainty to their clients. Later devotees who try to implement these "new" therapies never quite match the original cure rates, being naturally plagued by more skepticism than the "founders."

Therapists do other things to raise the expectations of their clients. In most cultures they stand out as different, apart from the great mass of people. In Western culture psychotherapists even stand apart from their healing brethren in the medical specialties. They dress differently, may have beards, and are rarely in danger of being confused with surgeons or pediatricians. The colorful regalia of African witchdoctors is well known. And among Native Americans, many medicine men utilized distinctive dress, masks, or other paraphernalia that immediately identified them to everyone in that culture. The carved and painted masks used by Iroquois medicine men in the False Face healing ceremony were so distinctive and powerful that certain masks by themselves acquired a reputation for being especially efficacious.[24] It is interesting to speculate whether there is any relationship between the face paint and the masks commonly adopted by therapists in other cultures and the beards and pipes used by psychiatrists in our own culture.

Each culture has its distinctive paraphernalia to increase expectations of patients and clients. In Western culture, nonpsychiatric healers have their stethoscope, and psychotherapists are supposed to have their couch. With the decline of classical psychoanalysis there has been an accompanying disappearance of the couch, and therapists frequently observe their patients looking furtively around for it on their first visit. Therapists in other cultures have their counterpart trademark, often a special drum, mask, or amulet. A South American Caraibe therapist, for instance, can always be identified by his large colored feather headdress and a sacred gourd rattle which he carries in both hands.[25]

Individuality of the therapist, though usually not consciously affected, tends to increase the client's expectations of him. The therapist is different. He has high status in the society, and is accorded respect and sometimes reverence. Simultaneously he is held in awe and sometimes fear. Most members of the society have a lurking suspicion that he has a special relationship with occult or mystical powers. The feelings of a Yoruba tribesman toward a *babalawo* (literally, "father of mysteries") have an exact counterpart in the feelings of a cocktail party guest toward the psychiatrist in the room—attraction, awe, avoidance, fear. In his study of Indian medicine men, Maddox sums up this aspect of them; his description fits many cultures:

He is readily distinguishable from the laity by his taciturnity, his grave and solemn countenance, his dignified step, and his circumspection. All of these peculiarities tend to heighten his influence, and, by rendering his appearance impressive and suggestive of superiority, serve to increase his control over the people.[26]

Therapist Training and Reputation

The ability to engender hope in a client and raise expectations of being cured ultimately depends upon a therapist's reputation. And though reputations may be forged in different ways in different cultures, they are forged primarily upon the anvil of training.

Certainly this is true in Western cultures. Therapists compete heatedly to obtain positions in the prized training institutions, and for the rest of their lives they do not hestitate to let people know where that was. For their clients they advertise it by way of their diplomas, a constellation of which discreetly covers a wall in most therapists' offices, bearing silent testimony to the therapist's skill in being accepted by *the* university, *the* medical or graduate school, *the* residency, *the* professional society, etc. They are often in Latin, which compounds the respect they inspire. This is social sanction for the therapist in a broad sense, and reputation in a narrow sense. The client relaxes in his or her chair, assured of being in good hands.

Therapists in other cultures also use training systems to increase their reputations. These systems vary widely, but almost all cultures have some expected course that therapists are supposed to undertake. Even therapists who receive their powers hereditarily must have it supplemented with an apprenticeship.[27]

Just as in Western cultures, aspiring therapists elsewhere will often travel long distances to train under famed masters of their trade.[28] In Haiti, a master therapist's fame is reflected in his pupils, and pupils are proud to have studied with the master. The training period varies from two years, for a Yoruk Indian shaman,[29] to ten years or longer, for Nigerian *babalawos*.[30] The training course includes such things as memorizing a vast body of literature, mythology, and associated rituals, and learning specific healing techniques as well as a special language for healers.[31] Eskimo shamans in training must learn and be able to name "all the parts of his body, every single bone by name in the sacred shaman's language."[32] The training of therapists also includes practicum in such skills as water gazing, divining, and impregnating charms with various spirits, as among the Ashanti in Ghana.[33]

Another interesting aspect of the training of therapists in some cultures is the emphasis on self-control and self-knowledge as part of the training. Blackfoot Indian medicine men, for instance, used much of their seven-year training period to teach their mind to have complete control over their body.[34] Ute Indian shamans underwent individual dream analysis:

> Since dreams were also the agency through which shamans obtained individual supernatural curing power, the shaman in his own development learned much about his own past unconscious motivations. . . . By his encounters with the supernatural, the shaman not only learned much about the rituals of driving out evil spirits in patients, but he came to understand himself better.[35]

We will return to the use of dreams in Chapter 6.

There are various ways of signifying the end of the therapist's training. Yoruk Indian shamans can finish the minimum "core curriculum" in two years. After that they can take an optional course culminating in a "pain-cooking dance." The extra study is expensive but gives them a higher reputation and the right to charge higher fees.[36] Among some Native American groups, there were as many as four separate degree levels, only a select few therapists attaining the highest one.[37]

A few cultures have a regular examination at the end of training. The Association of Nigerian Doctors, for example, both holds an examination and grants a certificate to be a witchdoctor.[38] The best description of such a system is anthropologist George Murdock's account of Tenino Indian shamans:

> To practice, it was not sufficient merely to have accumulated the requisite number and variety of spirit helpers. The prospective shaman also had to pass the equivalent of a state medical board

examination conducted by the shamans who had already been admitted to practice.[39]

The purposes of this board examination, according to Murdock, were to disqualify false shamans who did not really believe in their own power and "to review carefully the entire life of the candidate." He concludes that "their decision as to whether or not to admit him to practice seems clearly to have rested on their collective estimate of his personal characteristics, of his fitness to be entrusted with the exercise of great power."[40]

One other aspect of the training of therapists in other cultures is interesting in comparison with that in our own—it is often very expensive and includes privation. In reference to Menomini Indian medicine men, Maddox says:

> Frequently the collections of skins, peltries, and other goods that have to be purchased involved a candidate hopelessly in debt; but so great was the desire on the part of some Indians to become acknowledged medicine men that they would assume obligations that might require years of labor in hunting to liquidate; or, if they failed, then their relatives were expected to assume the responsibility thus incurred.[41]

And privation was often thought to be good for the candidates, improving their knowledge of the spirits.

To increase their reputations, therapists may advertise. A Nigerian therapist put up a sign claiming: "We cure mad fellows in 21 days."[42] Another Nigerian healer ran an ad in the local newspaper: "Medicine for tired penises, medicine to go in contact with woman and get no disease; medicine for office love; medicine for 'girls follow me.' "[43] A Haitian voodoo doctor's Miami newspaper ad claimed expertise in treating clients who "stay sick all the time, suffer from female trouble, can't hold onto your money, can't enjoy sex with your mate, no peace in the home."[44]

Most Western psychotherapists are more subtle in their advertising, although that is not always the case. Psychologist Arthur Janov, founder of primal therapy, has claimed that his brand of psychotherapy actually "cures" such disorders as "alcoholism, drug addiction, ulcerative colitis, asthma and stuttering." Physical improvements at all orifices, according to Janov, are reported by his patients: "Up until recently I could not burp. Recently, however, I've been burping, which for me is amazing." And another: "I used to have hemorrhoids—they went away!"[45] Even Janov, however, cannot compete in testimonials with a *bomoh* in Malaysia, as reported by United Press: "Malay villagers in Lumut said yesterday that a poisonous cobra twice bit a 'bomoh' or witchdoctor, and the snake died soon afterward."[46]

Other methods sometimes used to enhance the reputation of therapists are legerdemain and "miracles." These practices are of course regarded as nonprofessional by Western therapists. Eskimo shamans frequently used tricks like ventriloquism to impress their patients. They would also appear to do things like grinding a stone into sand with their bare hands.[47] And a shaman in Tibet was known to be able to wash his face in boiling oil without getting burned.[48]

Divination is the other technique commonly used by therapists, especially in Africa, to impress their patients. Nigerian *babalawos*, for instance, do not take a history from their patients. Rather a patient whispers his problem to a handful of palm nuts; the *babalawo* then casts the nuts and from their position makes a diagnosis.[49] Anthropologist Marlene Dobkin described the use of fortune-telling cards (*naipes*) by healers in Peru to both elicit a history and increase the expectations of the client.[50]

Other methods of divination include throwing "bones" (wooden blocks with markings), feeling the patient's pulse, gazing at water, star gazing, watching the flickering of an oil lamp, listening to the wind, and watching the trembling of the hands. It should be emphasized that these procedures, frequently ridiculed in Western descriptions of other cultures as proof of their "primitiveness," are methods used by the therapist to increase his reputation and, thus, increase the client's faith and expectations. Often the therapist is in possession of accessory information that allows him or her to make an accurate diagnosis.

Psychotherapy Studies

Despite strong evidence that the expectations of clients can be raised in a variety of ways, and the presumption that such increased expectations are an important ingredient in successful psychotherapy, hard research on this question is surprisingly sparse. Assessing the research in 1973, Wilkins wrote: "The client's expectancy of improvement is currently regarded as an explanatory construct accounting, in part, for actual psychotherapeutic improvement. In spite of the widespread acceptance of this construct, the empirical data necessary to establish its validity have not been generated."[51]

One study of forty-three clients who were applying for psychotherapy found that their expectations of help at the time they applied were significantly related to the degree of symptom relief obtained in the initial psychotherapeutic interview. The more the client expected to be helped, the more he or she was helped.[52] A similar study, using medical students as psychotherapists, showed that the client's optimism at the onset of treatment was directly related to the symptomatic relief during the course of therapy.[53]

Also pertinent are studies in which the effects of placebos have been compared with the effects of short-term psychotherapy. Fifty-six psychiatric outpatients, all diagnosed as neurotic, were given placebos as the only form of therapy. The outcome results compared favorably with the results obtained by short-term psychotherapy in a similar group.[54] In another study, 109 psychiatric outpatients were given placebos (presented to them as "a new pill") and then followed for three years to see what the effect was. After one week on the pill, 80 percent of the patients reported improvement in their symptoms. And of those still taking it three years later, 66 percent reported continued improvement.[55] Jerome Frank cites such experiments as confirming "the hypothesis that part of the healing power of all forms of psychotherapy lies in their ability to mobilize the patient's hope of relief."[56]

In a more recent study, thirty-six clients who had applied for group psychotherapy were assessed for their expectations of therapeutic improvement as well as for the improvement. Expectations were found to be related to the improvement only when the improvement was assessed by the client and not when it was assessed by the therapist.[57] Finally, there is an intriguing study of twenty "psychoneurotic outpatients," some of whom were given artificial emotional arousal (through breathing ether) while others were not; those emotionally aroused were found to improve significantly more (as measured by a word test) than those who received the psychotherapy without the emotional arousal.[58]

Despite the paucity of empirical research data, the suspicion remains that the expectations of clients, especially when accompanied by emotional arousal, is a major component in psychotherapy. Anecdotal accounts from both medicine and psychotherapy are too impressive to be ignored. For example, there was the experiment with three severely ill women, one with chronic gall bladder disease, a second recovering from major surgery, and a third with terminal cancer. Their physician obtained the services of a noted faith healer without the women's knowledge; his efforts were of no avail. Next the physician told the women he had obtained the services of the healer to assist them, and told them the healer would be working on their cases at a specific time when in fact the physician knew the healer would not be working. All three women showed improvement at the appointed hour.[59]

Psychiatrist Raymond Prince describes a healing ceremony in India that is pertinent to this question. Every evening, "a group of thirty or more patients with both physical and psychiatric ills" gather in a graveyard before the shrine of a saint.

> Sitting before the tomb, one of the patients (about 80 percent are women) will begin to rotate her head and rock her body. This motion increases until the patient's head strikes the ground. Possession rapidly spreads to other patients. Soon the patient begins to rave in a strange voice of how she came to be possessed and how long she will have to attend the shrine to become free of the spirit. One or more family members are in attendance to hear the communications of the spirit. After perhaps a half-hour of strenuous activity, the patient falls back on the ground exhausted. Most patients are required to return to the shrine for thirty consecutive evenings. According to local beliefs about half of the patients recover from their illnesses.[60]

The remarkable thing about this healing ceremony is that there is no therapist of any kind involved in it. Healing is entirely based on the expectations and emotional arousal of the clients.

Chapter 5

Learning and Mastery: The Superman Syndrome

The man watched his psychoanalyst rise slowly, indicating the end of the fifty-minute hour. This was the last of 260 sessions, stretching over almost three years, and the man thought briefly about how far he had come. The analyst extended his hand and smiled warmly. "You can do it now, I know you can," he reassured the man. They had been preparing for this moment from the beginning, and the man knew he had the knowledge and insight he needed. "Yes," he answered confidently, "I can do it."

The Balian *usada* rose slowly, turning toward the Hindu altar to offer one final Balinese prayer. The man knew it was time to leave, the last of his seventy visits over almost two years. But he was confident, for he now possessed the knowledge of the palm leaf manuscripts written in old Javanese. Furthermore, he held in his hand the sacred amulet that, if he remembered to pray correctly, would ensure that the spirits of his ancestors did not return and cause trouble. His stomach pains had eased as domestic matters at home had improved, and his depression was long since gone. Yes, he thought, he could make it on his own now.

Both these men illustrate the Superman syndrome, the fourth of the basic components of psychotherapy. They are convinced that their therapy has provided them with the knowledge, competence, insight, and understanding necessary to master life's adversities, whether the adversities be in the form of a passive-aggressive wife (similar to his mother) or an ancestral spirit (similar to his mother). They each have incorporated the knowledge and made it part of their armamentarium, almost as if they are carrying a small piece of their healer with them in their psyches. They feel confident and strong, like Old Testament David setting forth to do battle against the Philistines: " 'The Lord who delivered me from the paw of the lion and from the paw of the bear, will deliver me from the hand of the Philistine.' And Saul said to David, 'Go, and the Lord be with you!' "[1]

Remarkably little formal attention has been devoted to this aspect of psychotherapy, despite its ubiquity. Jerome Frank and his research colleagues at Johns Hopkins University, among the few who have studied it, claim that "as a major motivating force and reinforcer for the human organism, a sense of mastery may exert a major influence in psychotherapy."[2] Frank links a sense of mastery to "the restoration of morale" in a client, engendering positive feelings in the individual to counteract negative feelings of despair, isolation, alienation, failure, unworthiness, helplessness, impotence, and damaged self-esteem. "All successful therapies," Frank says, "implicitly or explicitly change the patient's image of himself from a person who is overwhelmed by his symptoms to one who can master them."[3]

The sense of mastery in a client is inextricably bound up with the other components of psychotherapy. The naming process—the principle of Rumpelstiltskin—contributes to the client's confidence that somebody knows what is wrong. The sense of mastery goes beyond that, however, equipping the client with knowledge about what to do for the future and how to overcome life's adversities. Similarly, the client's expectations and emotional arousal contribute significantly to his or her feelings of mastery and control.

The Therapist as Guru

It is the personal qualities of the therapist, however, that are most closely bound up with the client's emerging sense of mastery. The therapist-client relationship is simply one species of the teacher-student genre, which is universal: The teacher imparts specialized knowledge to the student, thereby strengthening him or her, and for this knowledge the student is supposed to be eternally grateful. A psychotherapist in this sense is analogous to a guru and has overtones of spiritual preceptor as well as instructor. Dr. J. S. Neki has in fact compared the psychotherapeutic relationship of Western psychoanalytic psychotherapy with the guru-chela relationship of India. In both cases the therapist/guru possesses specialized knowledge. "Both take ignorance as the basic premise of misery, and it is ignorance that they seek to dispel. . . . Both are, in other words, encounters for transformation—a change in consciousness and awareness of personal feelings. Both tend to modify our relations to others and to objects."[4]

The spiritual aspect of the therapist-client relationship in Western psychotherapies is rarely discussed but is nonetheless real. It becomes evident when a client discusses the ineffability of his or her therapeutic relationship. To quote Neki on gurus, "the guru does not merely receive the Word, he is also established in the Word and the Word established in him." The strength of the therapist-client bond is also hinted at by Rosenthal's classic experiment, in which he compared value systems in psychiatric outpatients who improved in psychotherapy versus those who did not improve. The "patients who improved tended to revise certain of their moral values in the direction of the therapists', while the moral values of patients who were unimproved tended to become less like their therapists'."[5] The sense of mastery acquired by clients in psychotherapy, then, is not merely a function of knowledge per se; it also includes the incorporation of values and perhaps a piece of the soul as well. It is this manifold acquisition by client from therapist that truly produces a Superman syndrome.

Types of Knowledge

The type of knowledge acquired by clients varies considerably among forms of psychotherapy. It may be simple, such as the proper prayer to say to counteract an evil spirit, or the correct way to use an amulet. Or it may include control of one's body, such as biofeedback training, which has become popular in recent years in the United States; in this form of therapy the client can see his or her own mastery improving on a meter that registers muscle tension. Another kind of mastery is that acquired during desensitization in behavior therapies. Therapists commonly assign graduated tasks to clients, who can then assess their own progress just as they would in a course of study. A woman with phobias of open spaces may be told to go outside on her back porch for one minute the first day, two minutes the second day, etc. As she is able to carry out the tasks, she feels an increasing sense of mastery.

The acquisition of knowledge is one of the hallmarks of Western systems of psychotherapy, especially those based on psychoanalytic principles. Freud's dictum "where id is, there ego shall be" functions as a beacon guiding therapists and clients through the psychotherapeutic night. The assumption is that clients' problems have been caused by early childhood experiences, and by making those experiences more conscious and "working them through," then the problems will no longer exist. Knowledge of one's unconscious becomes a magic scepter, and he who wields such a scepter is master indeed.

Some observers have claimed that healing ceremonies in other cultures accomplish exactly the same goal by increasing the client's knowledge of his unconscious. B. Y. Rhi, a Korean psychiatrist trained in Jungian psychoanalysis, studied Zinoki healing ceremonies run by Korean shamans to cure persons being harassed by ancestral spirits. Such spirits are usually those of individuals who died young or prematurely, as by illness, accident, or in childbirth. According to Rhi, the healing ceremony proceeds as follows:

> To begin with, the shaman (*Mudang*) cleanses the ceremonial ground and offers a feast to various demons. During the divination the shaman is endowed with supernatural powers. The spirit of the dead is then invoked and welcomed. Next "soul talks" take place during which, in a state of possession by the ancestral spirit, the shaman, or members of the patient's family, impersonate the spirit of the dead. Songs are performed and there is dancing and a good

deal of weeping. An encounter is construed and experienced between the spirit of the dead and the living person afflicted by the spirit. Through the mouth of the shaman the deceased ancestor then recounts the incident or the illness which led to his or her death. Dramatically, for instance, the shaman may reenact the ancestor's drowning. Subsequently, the possessions of the dead person which were not used in his lifetime are spread out by his family and are used, as it were, to complete his life and to assuage his rancor. Often the whole family passes into a trance. . . . Finally, farewell is bid to the spirits, and sacrifices are offered. The shaman spreads four separate long pieces of cloth symbolically bridging heaven and earth. He ceremonially cuts them with a knife, finalizing the separation of the dead from the living. The participants burn some of the spirit's belongings or a doll who symbolically represents the dead person.[6]

Rhi claims that the ceremony passes through the same stages Jungian psychoanalytic therapy passes through, first making the unconscious conscious, then reexperiencing the archetypes involved in the conflict, and finally effecting resolution by sending the purified archetypes back to the collective unconscious.

Although psychoanalytic psychotherapy is well known for promoting the knowledge-is-power precept, many other brands of Western psychotherapy are founded on the same premise. An example of this, in fashion during the 1970s, was Erhard Seminars Training, popularly known as est. Thousands of well-educated adults paid $250 to sit in a motel ballroom for two weekends and be given secret knowledge about how to live their lives. According to founder Werner Erhard, the purpose of the training (he claims it is not "therapy") is to get clients to arrive at true knowledge by transcending reason: "When you transcend reason, then you are able to reason. Like, for instance, Einstein transcended reason when he developed the theory of relativity. So he was able to reason."[7]

Erhard's lieutenants impose this kind of thinking on the recruits for hour after bladder-filling hour (bathroom privileges are allowed on official breaks only). "You are all assholes," the clients are told. "You don't know anything yet. Your life is miserable. You are shits. You're a machine, a machine. Nothing but a goddamn machine. You're a mechanical asshole, that's all." After fifteen or twenty hours spent in convincing you that you are miserable (which would seem to be a reasonable response after the first ten minutes, considering what you had paid out), est provides you with the secret knowledge. The secret is that you *are* a machine, and that you cannot be anything but what you are. That's it—that's the secret. The only way to be happy is to be what you are and do what you're doing because you cannot be anything else or do anything else. If you understand that, then you've "got it," as est aficionados say.

Erhard himself is one person who clearly "got it," and "it" took the form of a large house in Marin County, a Victorian mansion as an office, a Mercedes, and a leased plane. Erhard explains it: "The purpose of the training is to transform your ability to experience living so that the situations you have been trying to change or have been putting up with clear up just in the process of life itself." Many satisfied clients emerge from est training sessions believing that they have got more than their money's worth. What they have got is self-knowledge, which they then take back to their homes and jobs, confident that they are stronger. Est seminars are nothing more, and nothing less, than giant telephone booths in which each mild-mannered Clark Kent can change his or her clothes and emerge as Superman.

The Validity of Knowledge

Critics of est are fond of pointing out the prosaic quality of its insights and the nonsensical nature of the truths it propounds. What such critics fail to realize is that scientific validity of insights and truths is irrelevant in psychotherapy. Learning is a process, and the achievement of mastery is an end in itself. It matters little whether the truths have a small or a large *t;* if they are accepted by the client, then they have the same force as religious beliefs have on the devout Muslim, Buddhist, or Christian. As any mullah or priest can tell you, it is the strength of a person's belief that is the important determinant of whether the person is able to translate belief into action.

The best case study for assessing the validity of knowledge is the psychotherapeutic belief system most widely used in Western cultures—the psychoanalytic system. Although relatively few therapists are pure psychoanalysts, the teachings of Freud and his followers pervade almost every training program for all varieties of therapists, and the vast majority of psychotherapists have incorporated at least some psychoanalytic doctrines into their practice. In view of such widespread use and the fact that these beliefs have been widely propounded for over half a century, it is useful to ask what we know about the scientific basis of psychoanalytic teachings.

One of the cornerstones of psychoanalytic theory is a belief that there are constellations of personality traits in children and adults (e.g., the "oral" character who demands gratification, the "anal" character who keeps everything neat), which arise from the oral, anal, oedipal, and genital stages of development through which all children pass. Scientifically there is indeed evidence that there are constellations of such personality traits, but there is no evidence that there are such stages of development or that the constellations of traits arise from early childhood experience. Drs. Seymour Fisher and Roger P. Greenberg, who did an exhaustive review of the scientific evidence of psychoanalytic theory, concluded that "we have found little available evidence that would support Freud's idea that there are precise oral, anal, Oedipal, and genital phases in each individual's development."[8] As far as scientific evidence goes, it is equally plausible to postulate that the existing constellations of personality traits are inborn (e.g., you got your "oral" character traits from Grandfather) as to say they arose out of early childhood experiences.

A second cornerstone of psychoanalytic theory is that insight into one's early childhood experiences is a desirable goal to strive for, leading to altered behavior and a resolution of one's problems. Freud himself stated both implicitly and explicitly that making the unconscious conscious would improve a person's behavior and elevate the level of function. Again, there is no scientific evidence whatsoever in support of this teaching. As Fisher and Greenberg concluded after reviewing the existing studies:

> The field is filled with vagueness, appeals to authority rather than evidence, lack of specificity in definitions used, and unreliability in

the application of techniques and dynamic conceptualizations. . . .
The empirical literature has not yet given us an answer as to
whether there is a direct link between insights and symptom
relief.[9]

The lack of a scientific basis for the tenets of psychoanalytic
psychotherapy should not detract from the importance of Freud's
contributions to Western thought generally. As nobody before
him had done, Freud directed twentieth-century man to look
inward, noting dreams and slips of the tongue as manifestations of
our unconscious and the vital role it plays in our lives. One can
appreciate this contribution without having to accept the importance of early childhood experiences as crucial in determining
later behavior, or of assuming that insight per se leads to any
behavioral changes.

The lack of a scientific basis does not mean that psychoanalytic
psychotherapy is not effective. As will be discussed in Chapter
12, the evidence is strong that virtually all types of psychotherapy
are effective. For the psychoanalytic type as for the other types, it
is likely that the effective ingredients are the nonspecific basic
components. To again quote Fisher and Greenberg: "There are
strong indications that many other components besides insight
play a major role in achieving positive therapy outcomes."[10] The
scientific validity of the insights and truths propounded by psychoanalytic psychotherapy is on exactly the same level as that of
those propounded by est, or Morita therapy, or shamanistic healing ceremonies in Korea.

Since many of us in Western cultures have grown up with psychoanalytic theories as "truth" within our own cultural framework, it is difficult to step back and look at the theories from the
outside. We *know* that our theories are true because the theories
are included in media accounts of behavior. What we often fail to
realize is that many media accounts are written by people who are
themselves in psychoanalysis and have a vested interest in propagating this belief system. The belief in psychoanalytic theories of
psychotherapy is merely a reverberating circuit dependent on
one person telling the next person that it is true. The psychotherapy belief system of a Greenland Eskimo or a Tanzanian tribesman has precisely the same scientific basis.

In conclusion, learning and mastery are important components of effective psychotherapy not because the theories being taught have any scientific basis but because people believe in them. Armed with new knowledge gleaned by considerable effort (and often considerable expense), the client goes forth to slay the psychic dragons in his life. With Nietzsche, the client of successful psychotherapy can say: "Dead are all the Gods; now do we desire the Superman to live."[11]

Chapter 6

Techniques of Therapy

Many people may be willing to concede the fact that therapists all over the world utilize the same four components of psychotherapy—a shared worldview between therapist and client, personal qualities of the therapist, expectations and emotional arousal, and an emerging sense of mastery in the client. They do so secure in the belief that they hold a trump card which will provide definitive separation of Western psychotherapists (e.g., psychiatrists) from those of non-Western cultures (e.g., witchdoctors). This trump card is the techniques used in psychotherapy, techniques that are thought to be sophisticated and scientific in Western cultures, and to be primitive and magical elsewhere in the world.

In the psychotherapy game, however, there turns out to be no trump card. Techniques of therapy used everywhere in the world are surprisingly similar. Cultures, as will be shown, favor certain types of therapies or techniques because they are more compatible with the customs or values of that culture, but the differences are more quantitative than qualitative. Furthermore, a study of techniques used in therapy strongly suggests that it is not the techniques themselves that are important, but rather the fact that the techniques enhance the four basic components of psychotherapy discussed in the preceding chapters. It is not that the techniques have *no* therapeutic value in and of themselves, but rather that their value is negligible compared with the four basic components. As will be discussed in Chapter 12, the techniques of psychotherapy are the canary in the horse-and-canary pie.

Before beginning the discussion of specific therapies, four warnings should be sounded. First, the division between techniques of therapy and the personal characteristics of the therapist is artificial. The two reinforce each other and are really inextricably intertwined. Certain therapists choose certain techniques which are compatible with their personalities; for instance, an authoritarian personality may choose suggestion or hypnosis. Second, it is easy to confuse techniques used to increase the expectations of the patient (such as hanging diplomas on the wall or magical divination, discussed in Chapter 4) with the techniques used for therapy per se. This, too, is an artificial division, but one that will have to be adopted to break up the massive subject into digestible units.

Third, the reader is reminded of the discussion in Chapter 1 regarding magic and science. With few exceptions, the techniques used by both witchdoctors and psychiatrists are on exactly the same scientific—or prescientific—plane. And given their theories of causation, the treatment techniques of therapists elsewhere are just as logical as ours. Parenthetically it should be noted that therapists everywhere believe that *their* techniques are "scientific" and that other therapists use "just magic." The disparaging appraisals that I have heard of one witchdoctor's work by another are the equal of anything I have heard among therapists in Western professional circles.

Finally, although the techniques of therapy have been separated into categories below, it should be emphasized that all therapists usually employ more than one category simultaneously. The techniques are discussed under the headings Pharmacotherapy, Physical Therapies, Psychological Therapies (confession, suggestion, altered states of consciousness, psychoanalytic techniques, and conditioning), and Group and Family Therapies, but in fact psychiatrists and witchdoctors around the world mix them in varying combinations, depending on the cultural beliefs and the needs of the particular client. Skill in this mixing may be one aspect of being a successful psychotherapist.

Pharmacotherapy

Since the introduction of tranquilizers in the 1950s, pharmacotherapy has become a mainstay of therapy in Western cultures. No culture, past or present, has developed such an array of sophisticated and potent drugs, though other cultures have tried. The Aztec and Toltec Indians of Mexico, for example, had a highly developed pharmacopoeia, which covered most illnesses;[1] Western pharmacology has been slow to appreciate the formulations and indigenous drugs used by other cultures.

Drugs may be utilized in one of several ways by psychotherapists. First, they may be used to treat specific diseases of the brain, as for example antipsychotic drugs (e.g., fluphenazine, trade name Prolixin) reverse many of the symptoms of schizophrenia. The use of antipsychotics to treat this brain disease has been shown in scientifically controlled studies to be effective in the majority of cases.[2] Employed in this fashion, the antipsychotics are analogous to using penicillin to treat pneumonia, insulin to treat diabetes, or phenytoin (trade name Dilantin) to treat some seizure disorders.

Western psychiatrists pride themselves on having these modern antipsychotic drugs available to them, and are usually unaware of the fact that one variety of antipsychotic has been used for centuries. In the early 1950s, reserpine was introduced into Western psychiatry as one of the first antipsychotics. It is derived from the rauwolfia root widely available in India and West Africa, and had been used by healers in these areas to treat individuals who were severely disturbed. In 1925, in fact, a famous Nigerian witchdoctor was summoned to England to treat an eminent Nigerian who had become psychotic there.[3] Armed with his rauwolfia root, the witchdoctor had better medicine to offer the psychotic patient than did any English psychiatrist of that period. Rauwolfia remains a favorite among West African witchdoctors as an initial treatment for acutely disturbed patients, and is also occasionally used in Nigeria to produce prolonged sleep therapy, a type of pharmacotherapy popular in French psychiatry.[4]

A second use of drugs by psychotherapists is in producing perceptible but nonspecific somatic changes in the person; these drugs do not treat any specific disease. Foremost among them are the benzodiazepines, a family of minor tranquilizers which include drugs with such trade names as Valium, Librium, Tranxene, Serax, Restoril, and Halcion. For ten years Valium was the most widely prescribed drug in the United States; in 1980 alone, 33 million prescriptions for it were filled. It has a mild tranquilization effect, decreasing anxiety and producing sedation. Many drugs in this family, in fact, are used as sleeping pills. The danger of using benzodiazepines is that they impair reflexes (and thus may make driving a car hazardous) and can produce true addiction, with withdrawal symptoms when they are stopped; the magnitude of these dangers has been appreciated only in recent years.

Since drugs like Valium do not treat any specific disease, does that mean that they are not effective? On the contrary, such drugs are exceedingly effective as psychotherapeutic agents not because of their pharmacological properties but because they enhance the basic components of psychotherapy. They are compatible with a Western cultural worldview which posits that everything can be helped by modern technology—better living through chemistry. They enhance the personal qualities of the therapist because giving a drug demonstrates the caring quality of the therapist; the client may be symbolically taking home little pieces of the therapist in the pill bottle. Drugs dramatically increase a client's expectations that he or she will improve, and this is known to be a major source of the effectiveness of all pharmacological agents. Finally, drugs are used to increase a person's sense of mastery. An injunction to "take one of these three times a day and you will cope with the stresses better" is analogous to the major elixirs used in mythology; it becomes a self-fulfilling prophecy and the person does cope better.

Drugs producing perceptible but nonspecific somatic changes are commonly used in Western systems of psychotherapy but are not unknown elsewhere. Minor sedatives were used in China in the twelfth century B.C.[5] Kava is a sedative widely used by therapists in the Pacific islands.[6]

Another way pharmacologic agents may be used in psychotherapy is to produce an altered state of consciousness, thereby increasing suggestibility and the expectations of the client. This will be considered in greater detail below but is a common use of pharmacotherapy in some cultures. The client may take the drug, or the therapist may take it, or both may take it, as occurs in folk healing ceremonies using a cactus derivative in northern Peru.[7] In Western cultures, the use of pharmacologic agents to produce altered states of consciousness in psychotherapy is not considered to be respectable and is relatively little used.

Drugs may also be used in psychotherapy for their symbolic value. Purgatives and emetics to produce diarrhea and vomiting are commonly used by therapists in cultures where it is believed that foreign objects or evil spirits have entered the body. The client becomes literally purged of the intruder at the same time as the nonspecific effects of the pharmacotherapy are operating. A related application of drugs to produce psychotherapeutic change is the use of injectable drugs like calcium gluconate, which makes the body tingle. The recipient of such an injection is usually profoundly impressed by its power, and expectations of therapeutic improvement soar astronomically. The calcium gluconate has no appreciable physiologic effect on the body other than causing the tingling. It is used by healers in some African cultures and also by some root doctors, indigenous healers who utilize roots, in the southeastern United States.

Finally, there is a class of drugs used by psychotherapists that have no known somatic effect on the body but are nonetheless effective in making the person feel better. The efficacy of such drugs is due to their ability to activate the expectations of the client and increase the sense of mastery. Many of the leaves, roots, and herbs used in other cultures fall into this category. Often such agents are prescribed by the therapist to counteract what is thought to be wrong within that cultural framework, such as in Chinese medicine, in which illness is thought to arise from disharmony between cosmic forces and internal organs; or in Vedic medicine, in which imbalance in natural elements is thought to lead to excess heat, cold, bile, wind, or fluid within the body. Within that cultural belief system the prescription of a particular root or herb may be well known to be the proper form of therapy to redress the imbalance, and a therapist who did not include such a prescription would be considered incompetent.

Therapists in other cultures often prescribe medicine with considerably more élan than do therapists in Western cultures. For example, in Nigeria the witchdoctor may make a series of shallow razor cuts and rub the medicine into them. Injections are also used more in other cultures, as they are believed to be more efficacious than the same medicine taken by mouth. I recently observed a clinic at a market in rural Tanzania in which bottles filled with colored water were lined up; a client could select the most effective color and have the healer inject it into his or her arm. Such injections are undoubtedly effective in increasing expectations of psychotherapeutic change.

One of the most common criticisms of witchdoctors is that they use harmful, even fatal, drugs. As is true for many of the stereotypes we are dealing with, it is probable that we overestimate the harmful techniques of other therapists and underestimate the harmful aspects of our own techniques. Put another way, we overvalue our own techniques and undervalue the others.

It is certainly true that therapists elsewhere use drugs that are sometimes harmful; a certain drug they frequently apply to the eye, for instance, may cause serious inflammation.[8] On the other hand, Western medications, including the drugs used in psychiatry, may also produce harmful results. The psychiatric literature is replete with descriptions of cases that went wrong because of side effects of a drug. In an interesting study done on over a thousand hospitalized patients at an eminent American medical center, it was found that 20 percent suffered some complication of the therapy. Over half of these complications were moderately or very severe, and in sixteen cases they caused or contributed to the death of the patient.[9] It is doubtful if the morbidity caused by therapists elsewhere is much higher than this.

Physical Therapies

Physical therapies are used by psychotherapists more commonly in other cultures than in Western cultures. Massage and the therapeutic laying on of hands are employed very widely, but in the United States their use has been restricted to Esalen-type weekend groups or to fringe therapies. Similarly, basic attention to diet and exercise is included in a healer's recommendations in much of the world but rarely included by psychotherapists in the West.

Relaxation and meditation techniques to focus the mind are also prevalent in other cultures and in recent years they have become popular in newer Western therapies such as Transcendental Meditation. As practiced in India, meditation can be considered a form of conditioning as well as a physical therapy. The client first assumes certain postures, then practices specified exercises. Gradually he learns to control his voluntary muscles, then his involuntary muscles. This produces symptom relief. The next step is meditation, aimed at determining the causes of the bodily disturbance. The client may need a guru or teacher to help. Factors interfering with the meditation are explored, one by one, in a process quite similar to analytic psychotherapy. The object is to detach the self from the sources of conflict and examine them. In this manner the conflicts are resolved and the client arrives at the end state, peace of mind.

Hot baths and thermal radiation were once popular treatments for neuroses in Europe, and are still found in other countries. An example is the Navaho sweat bath,[10] a sauna-like affair. Placing a mentally disturbed person under a blanket filled with steam, as used by Muslim *alfas* in Sierra Leone, is another example.[11] This raises the body temperature and is reminiscent of therapy used for syphilis early in this century in Western cultures.

Acupuncture, the placement of narrow needles through the skin, has been used for over three thousand years to treat mental and physical illness among the Chinese. The rationale for its extensive contemporary use is based on the theories of Pavlov; it is believed that mental disorders are caused by a disequilibrium between cerebral inhibition and excitation (*yin* and *yang* principles) and that proper stimulation of the peripheral nervous system with needles will rectify the imbalance.[12] Acupuncture is recommended for treating neurotics in China.[13]

Bloodletting is used relatively rarely for mental problems by therapists elsewhere, despite a common Western stereotype to the contrary. Usually cuts are made on the body, as by Ndembu therapists in Zambia.[14]

Shock therapy to us signifies electroconvulsive therapy (ECT). Milder forms of shock therapy are used in many cultures, as when *curanderos* throw water into the face of a client during a healing session.[15] The effect is to raise the level of emotional arousal and condition the client to accept whatever the healer suggests. Such techniques are used only in confrontation-type group therapies in the West.

Major forms of shock therapy were until recently a very important technique in Western psychiatry. The convulsion produced was believed to be effective in treating psychotic states and severe depression. Developed in the 1930s, convulsive therapy remained until the spread of major tranquilizers in the 1950s a therapeutic mainstay for Western psychiatrists. The shock and convulsion were produced by drugs such as camphor, picrotoxin, Metrazol, Indoklon, and insulin, or by an electrical machine.

Shock therapy is not new, however; the idea is about four thousand years old. There are drawings of electrical fish on the walls of Egyptian tombs dated at 2750 B.C. The Greek name for these fish can be translated as "numbing," and authors such as Aristotle, Pliny, Plutarch, Cicero, Dioscorides, and Galen discuss their medicinal properties. The first clear reference to their application to the head is by Scribonius Largus, a Roman physician, contemporary with Pliny, who recommended their shock to cure severe headache. Ten centuries later, a Muslim physician recommended them to cure epilepsy.[16]

A clear reference to the use of electric fish to produce shock and cure psychiatric cases is found in a sixteenth-century Jesuit missionary account of Ethiopia: "The superstitious Abassines [Ethiopians] believe that it [the electric catfish] is good to expel Devils out of the human body, and it did torment Spirits no less than men."[17] I find this reference especially interesting since during my stay in Ethiopia in 1964–66, electric shock therapy was being widely promoted by a psychiatrist there as a new technique. Modern psychiatry, he said in effect, was coming to Ethiopia to expel Devils out of the human body.

This should not denigrate the discoveries of Sakel, Meduna, and Cerletti, the originators of modern shock therapy. Rather it should give needed historical perspective, and recognition of psychiatric techniques in times and in places other than our own. Cerletti himself became aware of these references to earlier uses

of electric shock therapy after he had written his famous mono-
graph, and paid them their due respect.[18]

Shock therapies are still in use by isolated cultures that have
never heard of men like Cerletti. One rather remarkable account
of the use of drug-induced convulsions to treat psychotics among
the San Blas Indians (who live on a group of islands off the coast of
Panama) follows:

> In the course of our stay there Dr. Iglesias explained to me that
> they had their own method of prescribing shock treatment in se-
> lected mentally ill cases. This consisted of a presentation of a psy-
> chotic case to the Council of Chiefs. If the Council reached an
> agreement on the method of treatment the patient would be
> brought before the Council and so advised. Whereupon the patient
> would be taken by two tribesmen to an uninhabited island and
> instructed to drink a cup of an especially prepared potion. There
> would apparently be no difficulty in having the patient comply with
> the instructions because of the inbred superstitions. Immediately
> upon consuming the medicine the patient would go into a series of
> convulsions. He would be left alone on the island for three days,
> and when the tribesmen returned for him he would be completely
> recovered. The name of the medicine could only be furnished in
> Cuna language, so could not be related in this way to any medicines
> known to us.[19]

What is especially interesting in this account is that the Indians
deal directly with the ethical issue of administering shock therapy—i.e., through review of the case by the Council of Chiefs.

Psychological Therapies

Psychological therapies have held much greater prestige than
pharmacotherapy or physical therapies in Western cultures in the
twentieth century. Among many psychotherapists, in fact, the use
of medication is an admission that the therapist is not skilled
enough, and any therapist utilizing massage, diet, or exercises is
considered badly in need of reeducation.

Most psychological therapies begin with the taking of a history, which is one of the sacred shibboleths of therapists' training in the West. It has become increasingly apparent to Western therapists that taking a history in itself is a technique of therapy, the act of ventilation by the client and the art of listening by the therapist often being effective in producing symptom relief.

In sharp contrast to their Western counterparts, some non-Western therapists ignore history taking. A few even pride themselves on making a "blind" diagnosis of the client's problems, with the client saying nothing. This type of divination, often done with the casting of bones or other paraphernalia, is intended to increase the client's expectations. In most cases such therapists have surreptitiously learned something about the history; in other cases they phrase the history in generalities that are applicable to most people, just as fortune-tellers do.

Many other therapists make history taking an important part of their therapeutic procedure. Here, for instance, is an account of how a traditional healer in Ghana evaluates a case:

> The patient was a teacher in his early twenties, preparing for an entrance examination to an institution of higher learning. He was taken to the healer one evening by several friends in a state of violent upset and behavior disturbance. The first thing the healer did was to administer forcibly what must have been a (herbal) sedative, and when the patient fell asleep the healer found out what he could from the friends who had brought him. This was later followed by long talks with the patient himself, who stayed in the healer's compound. From this a picture of the case was built up.[20]

A Sudanese *zar* doctor carefully asks the client about such things as eating and sleep disturbances. On the basis of the answers, this therapist decides whether or not the illness is serious enough to warrant a full *zar* healing ceremony.[21] Other accounts of history taking include the Yemeni *mori*, the Haitian *hungan* (who questions relatives as well as the client), and Maya Indian healers in Mexico (who ask about dreams as part of their routine history).[22] In Japanese Morita therapy, history taking is one of the most important parts of the therapy; client and therapist review the client's written diary on a daily basis.[23]

CONFESSION

Confession and suggestion are the two most important psychological therapies used in other cultures. In Western psychotherapy they are less emphasized in theory, though in practice both may be very important components contributing to the efficacy of the therapy.

Confession may be by private prayer, to another person, such as a friend or therapist, to supernatural beings or ancestors via an intermediary (such as a priest), or it may be public. Confession to a therapist and the public confession of group therapy are both relevant for Western psychotherapy. Most psychotherapists will attest to the symptom relief that accompanies the client who feels "so much better because I've finally been able to tell someone." The client has shared his or her guilt. What part this plays in therapy can only be speculation, but most therapists believe it is very important. Confession solidifies the bond between client and therapist, and through ventilation of the problems, often provides the client with a greater sense of mastery of them.

Confession is acknowledged to be very important by non-Western therapists and often plays an integral part in therapy. Weston LaBarre, an anthropologist, has done an extensive review of confession as used by the Indian groups of the Americas.[24] He describes confession to an appointed individual (an old man or a shaman, who first asks, "Have you done bad?") as well as public confession. He concludes that the confession is clearly associated with emotional catharsis.

In addition to sharing the guilt and obtaining emotional catharsis, confession often produces a reliving of painful experiences (abreaction) that may be therapeutic.[25] This is frequently found among the peyote cults of the Navaho and other Indian groups. As one observer noted: "It is difficult to overestimate the importance of this feature."[26]

Confession is also used extensively by *curanderos* in Mexico and Guatemala. The Guatemalan *curandero* may ask the client to confess everything bad he or she has done from childhood up to the present.[27] Mexican *curanderos* often center attention on the events immediately preceding the onset of symptoms, and make the client confess everything wrong he was doing or thinking.[28] These confessions are usually public to everyone attending the healing ceremony. Public confession is used by therapists in many other areas, including Sierra Leone, Burma, and Ethiopia.[29] In Ethiopia, the confession may be made by the client during possession by a *zar* spirit. The spirit speaks through the mouth of the possessed, telling those assembled all the evil things he or she has done.

Natural sequelae to confession are acts of atonement (penance) and absolution. Both are important parts of many therapists' armamentarium. In Catholic cultures, the penance is often prayers, offering candles to certain saints, or visiting a sacred shrine. Abstinence from a favorite food or activity (such as sex) is found universally as penance. Another common prescription is the requirement that the person wear certain kinds of clothing, or carry special objects, or avoid specific words or places. With all of these the therapist has given the client something to do that, if carried out, will absolve the wrongdoing and remove the symptoms. Such restrictions and taboos also alleviate guilt, and may act as a substitute for a tic or a compulsion if the person was afflicted by these.

One reason that confession, atonement, and absolution are not discussed as techniques of psychotherapy in Western cultures is that they are part of religion. Any priest can testify to their efficacy in removing psychiatric symptoms. Psychotherapy and religious healing are very closely allied, as Jerome Frank describes very clearly in *Persuasion and Healing*.[30] In the West, psychotherapy and religion are distinct entities. In many other cultures, the therapist may also be the religious agent, and use of the techniques of confession, atonement, and absolution follows naturally.

SUGGESTION

Suggestion is the other major psychological therapy used in other cultures. And like confession, it is not emphasized in theory by Western psychotherapists, though it may play an important role in practice. As a therapeutic technique, suggestion is closely bound up with the client's expectations. The higher these expectations are raised and the greater the desire to please the therapist, the more effective suggestion will be. Its effect can also be enhanced by concurrent factors like physical exhaustion—e.g., Luo patients in Kenya may be made to dance for hours before the curing ceremony begins.[31]

Suggestion may be of many types. One of these is direct command. This may be an assurance that "you will get well" or an admonition to "stop behaving like a madman." Accounts of witchdoctors' activities in many cultures contain suggestion of this kind. Their use of suggestion has been likened by one observer to a Madison Avenue advertising barrage—one is told to do it, one hears slogans and rhymes about it, one is told about the bad effects of not doing it, the suggestion becomes associated with music, etc.[32]

Symbolism constitutes another form of suggestion. Water or another liquid is almost universally used in symbolic cleansing rituals, purifying the body of the causes of the mental disturbances. The most famous Mexican-American *curandero* of this century relied on a simple glass of water or a bath as his most potent technique.[33] Often the purifying liquid is drunk with much ritual, as by the Apache shamans, who present the potion in a turtle shell, have the patient approach it to his lips four times before drinking, and mark the spot on the shell where he drank by a cross of pollen.[34] The more vivid is the visual imagery used, the stronger the suggestion—e.g., "As the river always flows forward and never back, so your illness will never return."[35]

Suggestive symbolism is also important in folk therapies in the Arab world.[36] The words of God as transmitted in the Koran are considered to be among the most powerful remedies available for all kinds of maladies. It is common, therefore, for therapists (especially *marabouts*) to write verses from the Koran on a piece of paper, which is then burned, the fumes being inhaled by the client, or on a prayer board with a special ink, which is then washed off and drunk by the client. The person is literally inhaling and drinking the word of God.

Another use of suggestive symbolism is in ceremonies of death and rebirth, such as are found in the treatment of mental disorders in New Guinea and the Sudan.[37] R. H. Prince, a Canadian psychiatrist who studied Yoruba healers in Nigeria, has described such a ceremony in great detail. It is done as a discharge ceremony. Client and therapist stand in the middle of the river with three doves, which are ritually killed, one by one, accompanied by much suggestion and incantation, and allowed to float away. The disease is gone and the person emerges from the river reborn.[38]

Suggestive symbolism is also used by therapists to retrieve lost souls. The healer may make a brief imaginary journey, and then some apparent thumping in the next room signifies the return of the lost soul. A medicine branch may symbolically brush out evil spirits, a very common technique among Eskimo shamans, or the soul may be brushed back into the afflicted person: "With a large handful of plants, Manuel ushered the spirit in the door of the hut, brushed it along the floor, and into the patient's body."[39]

In another type of suggestion in wide use by witchdoctors, the client is given charms, amulets, rings, talismans, religious objects, effigies, or magical formulas written on a piece of paper. In many cases this is preventive psychiatry, intended to obviate recurrence of the illness. In much of the world, almost all children, as well as many adults, wear an amulet around their neck, usually containing a piece of paper with verses from the Bible, the Koran, or another religious scripture. This is to prevent symptoms from the evil eye that can cause either physical or mental illness. Medical missionary lore is replete with stories of the "primitive native" who took the prescription the white doctor had written for him and wore it around his neck. What the missionary fails to realize is that for many of the drugs prescribed (such as minor tranquilizers) there is probably more benefit from wearing the prescription, since that is more compatible with the person's belief system.

Another form of suggestion is a sacrifice. Commonly an animal is killed after first having the person's disease transferred to it. The Nigerian ceremony of rebirth described above is an example. I myself once had the assistance of such a sacrificial ceremony for a patient I was treating for both physical and mental symptoms in rural Ethiopia. After considerable preparation, a lamb was passed over the person's head three times. The patient then kissed the tail of the lamb and the animal was sacrificed. The patient was well a few days later; whether the lamb or any medicine was responsible I am not certain.[40]

A final therapeutic aspect of suggestion is that it provides an institutionalized and accepted way to express aggression. Not only can you symbolically divest yourself of your symptoms, but you can project and displace them onto others. In some cultures, for instance, the therapist instructs you to place an object (containing the symptoms) next to a path. The first unwary passerby then becomes afflicted with your symptoms.

Many of these techniques of suggestion are what have given witchdoctors their bad name in Western psychiatry. It is all looked upon as foolishness and superstition—mere magic for the ignorant. What is important to realize is that these treatment techniques are perfectly logical within the framework of the disease's causation. If the psychiatric symptoms are being caused by the intrusion of a foreign object, then exorcise it. If a lost soul is to blame, coerce it back. If evil spirits are the cause, appease them with a ritual or sacrifice. It is only because we have a different framework of causation that such techniques look foolish.

Arguments about the role of suggestion in Western psychotherapies have raged since the time of Anton Mesmer, when the "fluidists" (who said psychotherapeutic change was the result of a magnetic fluid coming from without) did battle with the "animists" (who said the change was a result of "imagination" coming from within).[41] Freud recognized the existence of suggestion in psychoanalysis, but believed that if the therapist was aware of how he or she was influencing the client, then the effects of suggestion became less important. As Hans Strupp has pointed out: "The important distinction, then, is not whether suggestion is used in psychoanalysis, but how it is used. Indeed, it may be said that one of the most central contributions of psychoanalysis lies in the nonexploitative use of suggestion."[42]

That suggestion is an important technique in most Western brands of psychotherapy seems self-evident. Each time a therapist assures the client that he *will* get better, he is using suggestion. Each time a therapist smiles, nods, and says "hmm-hmm" approvingly, he is suggesting to the client that that is the way things really are. (He is also using conditioning.) Each time a primal scream therapist tells the client to reexperience his birth, each time an est trainer mockingly calls a client an asshole, and each time a gestalt therapist asks the client to reexperience the trauma with his mother, they are using suggestion.

But suggestion as a psychotherapeutic technique is suspect among Western therapists. Respectable healers, especially those psychoanalytically inclined, don't want to be seen in its company. Possible reasons for this are at least fourfold. First, suggestion is associated with symptom removal, a goal of therapy not held in high regard in many forms of Western psychotherapy. The assumption is that new symptoms will just replace the old ones and the person will not be any better off. This may or may not be true.

A second reason for the low status of suggestion as a psychotherapeutic technique in the West is that it is not compatible with the Protestant ethic, which says that you get something worthwhile only by working hard for it. Suggestion promises relief of symptoms with a minimum of work, and as such it is not acceptable. The obverse side of the coin is a therapy such as psychoanalysis, which may take five hundred hours or more and cost forty thousand dollars; such a therapy is highly compatible with the Protestant ethic.

Another reason is that suggestion as a psychotherapeutic technique is quite similar to some aspects of religion. In cultures where psychiatry and religion are closely intertwined, this poses no problem. But in Western cultures, where they have recently separated, therapists are suspicious of any technique that has overtones of religion. Finally, the use of suggestion strikes too closely at our own magical thinking to be comfortable. Western psychotherapy is supposed to be rational and scientific, not irrational and magical. This is true despite the theory of Western psychiatry, which gives great importance to the irrational and the unconscious.

ALTERED STATES OF CONSCIOUSNESS

Although little used in most Western forms of psychotherapy, altered states of consciousness are one of the most commonly used and most powerful techniques of therapy in most of the world.[43] Such altered states include hypnosis, trance states, and dissociation states (which differ from trance in that the person has amnesia for the events), but in fact altered states of consciousness are not an either/or phenomenon. Rather they are one end of a spectrum which begins with full consciousness, proceeds to emotional arousal and suggestibility, passes through guided imagery and light hypnotic states, and ends at deep hypnosis, trance, and dissociation. Skilled psychotherapists in many cultures often make use of all points on this spectrum, depending on the needs of the client.

Altered states of consciousness used in healing may be employed by the therapist (as when a Malaysian *manang* goes into a trance), by the client (as when a client is hypnotized by a psychologist), or by both together (as in healing ceremonies in northern Peru). Mind-altering drugs are used in some cultures to help achieve the altered states of consciousness, while in other cultures, such as our own, only hypnotic suggestion is used ("You are now going into a deep sleep. Your arm is getting lighter and lighter. Feel your arm getting lighter and lighter!").

Most cultures that do not use drugs to produce altered states of consciousness in healing ceremonies rely instead on rhythmic drumming, clapping, chanting, singing, dancing. Drumming is especially effective; its ability to produce neurophysiological changes was recognized by Dr. Adolf Meyer early in this century, and in 1961 Neher published definitive studies showing that drumming at certain frequencies (e.g., 180 or 240 beats per minute) produced changes in human brain waves as measured on an electroencephalogram.[44] Dr. Wolfgang Jilek, a Canadian psychiatrist who has written a lucid analysis of the use of altered states of consciousness in Indian healing ceremonies, notes that "susceptibility to rhythmic sensory stimulation is increased by stress and exertion, with resulting adrenaline secretion, also by hyperventilation and hypoglycemia [through fasting],"[45] all of which are frequently part of such healing ceremonies. The only analogous situations in Western cultures are faith-healing ceremonies in fundamentalist churches, in which rhythmic singing and clapping often induce trance. The phenomenon is also seen at teenage rock concerts, where the drums and the music may bring about trance states in the musicians or the listeners. (Though such concerts are not generally categorized as psychotherapy for the teenagers, they may serve as such for their parents, who enjoy a quiet house for the evening.) Aldous Huxley offered perhaps the best summary of the power of rhythmic phenomena to induce altered states of consciousness:

> No man, however highly civilised, can listen for very long to African drumming, or Indian chanting, or Welsh hymn-singing, and retain intact his critical and self-conscious personality. . . . If exposed long enough to the tom-toms and the singing, every one of our philosophers would end by capering and howling with the savages.[46]

Altered states of consciousness may be used by therapists in the process of becoming a therapist (e.g., Mr. Wu, the Taiwanese shaman described in Chapter 3, who realized his calling because he fell into a trance state), as well as in diagnosis or in curing. For diagnosis, the healer is usually the one who goes into the trance, and while in another world, is able correctly to name the malady and identify the offending agent. For curing, the client usually experiences the trance, during which suggestions of health and well-being are implanted by the therapist.

The use of altered states of consciousness for healing is not new. Hypnosis is reported to have been utilized in therapy in China three thousand years ago.[47] Modern descriptions of its users include a mystical group of *Sufi* practitioners in Afghanistan. These therapists learn about it in secret training (which may take as long as sixteen years!) and employ it for physical and mental illnesses of all kinds. One report of a treatment session involving eighteen patients claimed fifteen immediate cures.[48]

It has also been described as a therapeutic technique practiced by Apache and Washo Indian shamans. One of the latter, at the turn of this century, even sent away for a book on it—*The Art of Attention and the Science of Suggestion*—from a mail order catalogue. He then practiced his technique on rocks and trees until he had it perfected.[49]

Hypnosis, like other altered states of consciousness, is a state of hypersuggestibility and therefore is a potent therapeutic tool. In terms of the basic components of psychotherapy, such altered states of consciousness dramatically increase the expectations of a client and forge a strong bond between healer and client. They also provide the client with a heightened sense of mastery, for a person who has conquered his own inner world feels better prepared to conquer the outer world as well. It may also be argued that taking people through an altered state of consciousness provides them with a magic wand, as if they have access to an inner kingdom unavailable to most others; insofar as this is true, the client would also feel a heightened sense of mastery.

Western systems of psychotherapy have neglected altered states of consciousness as therapeutic tools except for formal hypnosis, mostly employed by psychologists. One of the hallmarks of some of the newer therapies, such as Transcendental Meditation, est, and primal therapy, is their greater use of this technique. It may even be argued that the utilization of altered states of consciousness in these newer therapies is a primary reason for their popularity, many people finding the traditional tell-me-about-your-mother approaches too dull. There is some indication in recent years that Western therapists are prepared to take a closer look at altered states of consciousness; in 1980, for example, a conference was held in Montreal to examine the relationship of endorphins and other brain peptides to altered states.

Ultimately, however, altered states of consciousness are likely to continue to play a minor role in Western psychotherapies because they are not consonant with Western cultural values. Like suggestion, they promise symptom relief without hard work, they have overtones of religion, and they give off an odor of magic. In a rational, work-ethic society which prides itself on its scientific base, such psychotherapeutic techniques will always be regarded with suspicion by the majority.

PSYCHOANALYTIC TECHNIQUES

The techniques associated with psychoanalysis have held the highest status in Western psychotherapy since Freud popularized them early in this century. By some they are regarded as the only techniques, everything else being relegated to the realm of magic and "mere suggestion." Psychoanalytic techniques continue to be a hallmark of Western psychiatry, though their image has declined with the increasing popularity of newer forms of psychotherapy.

Although there is no other culture in the world where psychoanalytic techniques are as important as they are in the West, these techniques do appear elsewhere. Dream interpretation, the pennon of psychoanalytic techniques, provides an illustration. Dreams can of course be used for purposes other than interpretation. For instance, they may be used to foretell the future, to ascribe social role status (as in becoming a shaman), or to gain power from the supernatural.[50] The concern here will be only with their interpretation in gaining more knowledge of the patient's unconscious.

Probably the best study of dream interpretation in another culture was done by Anthony F. C. Wallace, a highly respected anthropologist who studied the seventeenth-century Iroquois Indians. He observed:

> The Iroquois looked upon dreams as the windows of the soul, and their theory of dreams was remarkably similar to the psychoanalytic theory of dreams developed by Freud and his associates. In brief, the Iroquois believed that the soul had wishes of which the conscious intelligence was unaware, but which expressed themselves in dreams.[51]

And in another passage:

> Intuitively, the Iroquois had achieved a great deal of psychological sophistication. They recognized conscious and unconscious parts of the mind. They knew the great force of unconscious desires, and were aware that the frustration of these desires could cause mental and physical ("psychosomatic") illness. They understood that these desires were expressed in symbolic form by dreams, but that the individual could not always properly interpret these dreams himself. They had noted the distinction between the manifest and latent content of dreams, and employed what sounds like the technique of free association to uncover the latent meaning. And they considered that the best method for the relief of psychic and psychosomatic distress was to give the frustrated desire satisfaction, either directly or symbolically.[52]

Wallace concluded that Iroquoian and Freudian dream theory are not exactly the same, but that the differences are not more marked than the differences between, for instance, Jungian and Freudian theories of dream interpretation.

The Navahos are another Indian group that used dreams in this way. A Swiss psychoanalyst, Dr. Oskar Pfister, examined notes from Navaho curing ceremonies in the 1930s and decided that Navaho therapists were "instinctive psychoanalysts." He described what was occurring as follows:

> The shaman understood that the sterility of the woman had as cause an incestuous attachment to the father . . . it was necessary first of all, in order to overcome the frigidity, to bring about compromise with the incestuous attitude in Freud's sense. The sterile woman had to acknowledge that she really harbored incest wishes toward the father and had an attachment to him. The medicine man, as an incorporation of the father, performed the act symbolically, in a manner acceptable to society and therefore removed further repression.[53]

Another study of dream interpretation among Native Americans was done by anthropologist Marvin Opler. In order to get valid data on Ute healers, he became ceremonially adopted into the tribe and then underwent a shamanistic treatment for a feigned illness. He concluded that "it was obvious that Ute shamans employed quasi-psychoanalytic techniques, independently invented in their culture." Dream analysis was their chief technique: "Wishes, culturally geared motivations, and typical attitudes were dissected by shamans in dealing with the thematic material in dreams." Opler's observations on the nondirective methods of the shamans in eliciting material from the patient is especially instructive:

> no shaman divulges more of his own nature than is actually necessary in ceremonial practice. His neutrality and religious importance is parallel, perhaps, to the efforts of the analyst in evoking free associations and self-expressions from the patient before becoming involved in countertransference functions.[54]

The Diegueño Indian healers of southern California also used dreams skillfully. "To the witchdoctor . . . dreams were signifi-cant because of their diagnostic value in the cure of neuroses and functional mental disorders, which he recognized as such and treated in a manner suggestive of psychoanalytic methods." The Diegueño therapists distinguished manifest and latent dream content, and believed that "dreams reveal to the dream doctor the patient's conflicts and desires, which are usually of a sexual nature."[55] Other parts of the world where dream interpretation is used by witchdoctors include Turkey,[56] Ghana,[57] Sierra Leone,[58] and the Philippines.[59]

Free association is another important psychoanalytic technique in Western therapy. The mind is allowed to wander freely from subject to subject as the client simultaneously verbalizes thoughts to the therapist. This technique is used by some of the Native American groups mentioned above, as well as in group healing sessions in Ghana. A psychiatric observer of the latter notes that "the couch might be missing, and there may be many spectators, but the patient is given an opportunity to bring up anything that comes to his mind."[60] Aristophanes in ancient Greece also knew of free association as a psychotherapeutic tech-nique. In *The Clouds,* a character lies on the couch and expresses all his thoughts as free association so as to dispel an obsessive fantasy he has about controlling the moon.[61]

CONDITIONING

Conditioning and behavior techniques have recently become popular in Western psychotherapy, though they still are more used by psychologists and social workers than by psychiatrists. The major subtypes of conditioning are operant conditioning (re-ward), aversion therapy (punishment), desensitization (building up to the stress slowly), and extinction (repeating the stress many times until it no longer elicits a maladaptive response). Though these techniques are often written about in Western psychiatric literature as though they were new, they are, according to Hans Strupp, "in principle not very different from those which have been employed over the centuries by parents in raising their children. What dynamic psychology and learning theories have contributed during this century are a much clearer explication of the conditions under which these techniques exert their influence [and] the requirements which have to be met for them to become effective."[62]

Therapists in other cultures have long employed the principles of reward and punishment. Praise, exhortation, threats, and punishment are commonly used by them. The exercises and meditation in Indian psychotherapy may be seen as conditioning. Much of the ritual chanting of therapy sessions elsewhere may also be viewed as verbal conditioning.[63] An example of more complex conditioning techniques is found in western Nigeria. In order to treat bed-wetting there among male children, a toad is tied to the penis of the child by a string. When the child wets, the toad croaks and the child wakes up.[64] This is almost exactly analogous to a conditioning technique, introduced in England and the United States, where a bell rings each time the child starts to urinate.

Group and Family Therapies

Group therapy has become increasingly popular in Western psychiatry in the past twenty-five years. In some parts of the United States, almost everyone belongs to some kind of group, whether it be a confrontation group, a T-group, a sensitization group, psychodrama, Synanon, or Alcoholics Anonymous. More research is being done on groups, and it is becoming clear that they are an effective means for bringing about behavioral changes as well as symptom relief.

Therapists in other cultures also conduct groups. In fact, the more widespread use of groups is one of the most marked differences between indigenous psychotherapy in other cultures and Western psychotherapy. Group therapy goes far back in history. Some of the earliest groups were associated with the rites of Dionysius in Greece. The early Christian Passion plays can also be considered group therapy, with catharsis occurring through acting out or through identification with the participants.

One of the most common types of group therapy occurring in other cultures involves possession of some or all of the participants by spirits. These possession cults are found throughout the world, although the best-known are in the Caribbean area and South America. Among them are the voodoo cult in Haiti, the Shango cult in Trinidad, the Babalu cult in Cuba, and the Macumba and Umbanda cults in Brazil. There are several good reviews of these cults, which show them to be much more similar than dissimilar.[65]

These possession group therapy sessions can be very useful for clients with certain kinds of problems. Attempts have been made in some countries in which they are prominent to integrate them into the evolving social structure. An excellent illustration of how this can be done successfully is the use of "terpsichore trance therapy" (T.T.T.) in Brazil. This adaptation of traditional Brazilian trance and possession cults has been described as follows:

Weekly therapy sessions lasting two hours take place in an auditorium of the State of Guanabara Telephone Workers Union. The technique is as follows. Middle and upper-middle class patients referred from the clinic are instructed to assemble in the auditorium wearing informal clothing. They are joined by an orchestra, the therapist, and his assistants. Patients stand shoulder to shoulder with their eyes closed, as samba-like music is played. They are told to think exclusively about their most pressing problems or the things they wish for the most. The "mono-idealism" is intended to encourage trance induction. The orchestra plays slowly and softly at first and increases its pitch and tempo as the session proceeds. The same music is played at the start of each session. The therapist induces trance in each patient in turn, using a method derived from the Umbanda sect. The patient bends forward and the therapist causes him to rotate with increasing speed until he enters a trance, at which point he is slowed down and encouraged to dance to the rhythm of the music. He is then left to continue on his own while the therapist repeats the procedure with the next patient. Some patients are able, after a few sessions, to enter into a trance state by themselves, the stereotyped opening music acting as a signal stimulus to trance induction for these individuals. Although verbal communication is not encouraged in T.T.T., some use is made of creating lyrics to music drawn from Umbanda ritual. The lyrics focus on themes such as living more happily, solving problems, and other intensely personal and individualistic goals.[66]

The results of this modified form of group therapy are reported as very favorable, especially for patients with hysterical, neurotic, depressive, and psychosomatic problems. T.T.T. is employed most frequently as an adjunct to supportive psychotherapy and drugs.

Since there is a considerable body of literature on these cults and their social and psychological significance, I will review here only those aspects that are pertinent as techniques of group therapy. One of the foremost among these techniques is confession, which is probably even more effective in relieving symptoms when done in a group setting. It is a common and important feature of these groups, functioning to allay both guilt and anxiety.

Another psychotherapeutic technique of these groups is acting out. They permit "the sanctioned expression of behaviors which are otherwise socially unacceptable or unavailable."[67] The participant may, for instance, reverse roles and play the opposite sex, thereby giving vent to suppressed homosexual wishes.

Abreaction, the reliving of an emotional experience, is another important technique used in group therapies. Alexander Leighton describes it in Navaho ceremonials:

> The ceremonial itself, or some parts of it, constitutes a symbolic reenactment of something which went wrong in the past and which is now being set right. . . . The patient does it over again symbolically without a mistake, and so through the mediation of the healer comes into harmony with great and mysterious forces within and without himself.[68]

Confession, role playing, and abreaction are all integral parts of psychodrama, and so many of the group therapies in other cultures qualify as psychodrama. An observer of a Haitian voodoo ceremony concluded: "It is a psychodrama which serves as a last resort against deeper mental illness."[69] And an observer of a group healing ceremony for a disturbed woman in Malaysia described it as follows:

> The bomoh had staged a kind of theatrical production in which the woman's closest relatives and her fellow-villagers each had roles to play. It was noteworthy that the actors in this little play had to

demonstrate warm affection for the patient. Embraces, friendly gestures and tender caresses were much in evidence. The play took on an increasingly frenetic character with dance-like movements, until those taking part fell into a trance and finally reached total physical exhaustion. The coaxing of the evil spirit which had caused the illness with an offering of food until it could be caught in a container and packed off on a "journey without return" down the river was merely a ritual appendage. The young woman was now considered to be cured. I heard that the bomoh had passed the whole of the previous day before the ceremony in the house of her family so as to "get in touch with the spirit." Only in its outward appearance does this treatment differ from what is accepted in the industrialized world as group therapy under expensive psychiatrists.[70]

Hypnosis and trance is found commonly in such group healing ceremonies.[71] One especially good description of it is by anthropologist Richard Katz, who studied the Kung bushmen on the Kalahari desert. During an all-night dance ceremony, a form of "energy" becomes "activated in those who are healers, most of whom are among the dancing men. As [the energy] intensifies in the healers they experience a form of enhanced consciousness during which they heal everyone at the dance."[72] One Kung healer described it to Katz: "In your backbone you feel a pointed something and it works its way up. The base of your spine is tingling, tingling, tingling, tingling. Then [the energy] makes your thoughts as nothing in your head." Katz notes: "Kung healing involves health and growth on physical, psychological, social and spiritual levels; it affects the individual, the group, the surrounding environment and the cosmos. Healing is an integrating and enhancing force, far more fundamental than simple curing or the application of medicine."[73]

Such healing ceremonies play a cultural role that goes well beyond group therapy, of course. In Bali, where I was able to observe it, group possession is integrated with art and is the major aesthetic expression in the culture.[74] Other cultures do not necessarily compartmentalize things as we do into religion, psychotherapy, and dance. Conversely, Western psychotherapists often underestimate and fail to recognize the therapeutic aspects of our own plays, movies, dance, and other art forms.

The witchdoctor in these group therapies plays a variable role. More often than not, he or she also becomes possessed by spirits. In Kenya, the healer also goes into a trance during which he or she discusses the patient's problems, "in a way similar to psychoanalysts who intersperse abreactions with interpretations, in accord with Freud's teaching that abreaction without the release of strong emotions was without effect."[75]

Not all group therapy in other cultures includes possession as a component, however. One that does not is the *moot* among the Kepelle of Liberia. Gibbs shows how this gathering of neighborhood people to settle a dispute out of court, ostensibly a legal procedure, also functions as a form of group psychotherapy.[76] A similar amalgamation of functions is described by Dr. John Cawte, who has done extensive work with Australian aborigines; the systems of medical healing, psychotherapy, law, religion, and social sanction are found to interlock closely.[77]

Psychotherapy in other cultures, to a much greater extent than in the West, utilizes environmental manipulation and social reintegration as important parts of the process of therapy. *Curanderos* in Mexico, for instance, almost always have family members attend the healing session, and often charge them with carrying out certain aspects of the prescribed treatment. Witchdoctors in Nigeria are quick to tell a client to take a new occupation or move to a new compound (because evil spirits are inhabiting the old one) if they believe that it will relieve the stress. This account from Kenya also illustrates how a therapist may manipulate the environment:

> The repeated warnings to the patient and to the members of her home that they must maintain good and harmonious relations by behaving in a correct and charitable manner underline the importance of social factors in maintaining the mental health of the patient. All this behavior is sanctioned by the threat that another attack may be made by the spirits if the taboos are not observed.[78]

Social reintegration of the person is in many cultures regarded as equal in importance to the removal of the symptoms. In several

African cultures, the reintegration is effected by voluntary societies of ex-patients. These societies are social groups and function
to give the person a new set of social alliances. Examples are the
Poro Society in Sierra Leone[79] and the Sopono cult in Nigeria.[80]
One observer of these societies summarizes them as follows:

> Treatment is not merely a "doctor-patient" relationship but a form
> of social reintegration through the medium of social groups like the
> highly specialized N'jayei Society of the Mende. African medicine
> therefore plays a dual role designed to maintain the continuity of
> society as a functioning whole.[81]

A variant of this is found among the Pueblo Indians, where the
disturbed individual is adopted into another clan in the tribe, thus
acquiring a new set of social relations.[82]

In the process of manipulating the environment and reintegrat-
ing the person socially, therapists in other cultures become
deeply involved with the social stresses of their community. This
is expected of them and is considered to be part of their proper
job. Such involvement is more natural since the psychotherapist's
role often overlaps with religious, legal, and political roles in the
community. A Zambian therapist provides an example.

> It seems that the Ndembu "doctor" sees his task less as curing an
> individual patient than as remedying the ills of a corporate group.
> The sickness of a patient is mainly a sign that "something is rotten"
> in the corporate body. The patient will not get better until all the
> tensions and aggressions in the group's interrelations have been
> brought to light and exposed to ritual treatment.
>
> The sick individual, exposed to this process, is reintegrated into
> his group as, step by step, its members are reconciled with one
> another in emotionally charged circumstances.[83]

This extension of the role of therapist, as a manipulator of social
stresses, underlies a contemporary debate in Western psychiatry.
Is the therapist's role to treat the client alone, or to treat the
"sickness" in the society of the client as well? What are the
boundaries of community psychiatry? Most other cultures, it ap-

pears, have devised a very broad job description for their therapists.

The involvement of the family and the community in the therapeutic process accomplishes many things. The family often has to provide materials, labor, or finances toward the client's treatment. Therefore they have a stake in the treatment, and are more likely to reinforce the changes that the healer is trying to make. This is found in Western psychotherapy but in a much less developed form. The family and friends also reassert the importance of the continued participation of the individual in the group, and affirm the existence of a network by which the person can reestablish social contacts.

Group and family therapies are very effective in activating the basic components of psychotherapy. The naming of the illness-causing agent is done not in a private office with just therapist and client present, but in a social setting with dozens, even hundreds, of family members and neighbors witnessing the event. The sense of mastery engendered by the healing ceremony is not felt by the client alone, but by the whole group, which becomes an accessory to keeping the person well in the future.

But it is the client's expectations of getting well that rise most dramatically in a group setting. Imagine, for a moment, that you are a Malaysian with psychological problems necessitating a healing ceremony. A *bomoh* gathers a group of singers and musicians, who come to your house for an all-night ceremony, at considerable cost to your family. "The patient is laid out on the floor, surrounded by friends and relatives, with such ritual accompaniments as ceremonial water and incense." After examination and palpation of your body, the *bomoh* takes a careful history. Accompanied by music and head twirling, the *bomoh* then becomes possessed by a *hantu* spirit. "The healer in trance chants, prays, attempts exorcism if necessary, and encourages the patient to act out his problems."[84] Your family and neighbors are looking on, encouraging the *bomoh* to exorcise the offending spirit and encouraging you to get well. Or imagine that you are a young adult in the Wape tribe of Papua New Guinea and you require a healing ceremony for psychological problems. In the village plaza at the edge of the forest are assembled "dozens of colorful exotic masks twenty feet high circling the plaza and surrounded by several hundred singing and dancing women and children."[85] Could you possibly *not* get well, given the expectations of the group?

Relation of Culture to Techniques

While discussing the therapeutic technique of suggestion, I speculated on possible reasons why this technique is denigrated by Western psychotherapy. Briefly, these reasons were that it only aims at symptom removal, it has overtones of religion, it is irrational, and it is contrary to the Protestant ethic—you must work hard for what you get.

This provides a useful starting point for exploring the relationship between culture and the techniques of therapy. For while it should be evident from the foregoing discussion that all techniques of therapy are found scattered around the world, it is also true that they are not distributed evenly. Certain techniques occur much more often than others, and each culture appears to have its own preferences.

The reason is that techniques of therapy are intimately related to culture. They are related to the theories of causation of illness, the personality types valued, and the goals of therapy in the culture. The last is a reflection of more general cultural values.

The relation of theories of causation to techniques is obvious. If you believe that your sickness is caused by the loss of your soul, then you want techniques that will successfully retrieve the lost soul. A therapist who offers to explore your childhood experiences with you will be regarded as irrelevant, misinformed, and a quack. Maybe you will even call him a "witchdoctor." Conversely, if you believe that your sickness is caused by childhood experiences, then you want a therapist who will explore these experiences and not undertake a ritual to look for a lost soul.

Occasionally the same therapeutic technique will be used in different cultures for quite different reasons. For instance, confession might be used by a Western psychotherapist because he believes that the person will relive the confessed experience and better understand it. Confession might be used by an Indian medicine man, on the other hand, because he believes that only thus will the spirit of the offended clan ancestor be liberated, permitting the person to recover. Though the technique—confession—is the same, and the result—recovery—may be the same, nevertheless in both cases the technique is closely associated with the cultural belief about causation of the sickness.

Techniques of therapy are also related to the personality types valued by the culture.[86] If in a certain culture the therapist is expected to be a warm, gentle, empathetic, nonassertive individual, then the techniques of therapy favored by that culture are not likely to be directive ones like suggestion and hypnosis. Similarly, each individual therapist, consciously or unconsciously, selects those techniques that are most compatible with his or her personality. In one of the very few attempts to analyze this relationship, psychiatrist Ari Kiev attempted to relate the childhood experiences in a culture to the consequent adult personality type, and then to the techniques of therapy preferred by the culture. To illustrate, he describes certain childhood experiences that produce guilt (as opposed to shame) in an adult; he then considers how this feeling relates to the use of bloodletting as a therapeutic technique in that culture.[87] This is an interesting beginning in an area where much more work needs to be done.

The goals of therapy are also culture bound, and are related to the basic values of the culture. Possible goals of therapy include the following:

1.   Symptom removal—e.g., reduction in anxiety.

2.   Attitude change—e.g., "right-mindedness" stressed in Eastern therapies.

3.   Behavior change—e.g., stopping of compulsive handwashing.

4.   Insight—e.g., understanding why you are depressed.

5.   Improved interpersonal relationships—e.g., getting along with your neighbors.

6.   Improved personal efficiency—e.g., greater ability to accept responsibility.

7. Improved social efficiency—e.g., greater ability to do socially useful work.

8. Prevention and education—e.g., increasing the ability to adapt and cope in future situations.

Though many of these goals overlap, they are differentially emphasized in different cultures. The choice of goals for any specific culture is related to values of that culture. The goals chosen then determine, in part, the choice of therapeutic techniques that will be used.

In the United States, for instance, cultural values held in high regard are work, achievement, independence, responsibility, and rational thinking. Goals of therapy that are usually considered appropriate for a therapeutic client in this culture are therefore insight, improved personal efficiency, and improved social efficiency. And the techniques of therapy that best achieve such goals are psychoanalytic, insight-oriented therapy; behavior therapy; drug therapy; and occupational therapy.[88] The importance of childhood experience is compatible with our strong assumption of cause and effect to explain everything. Therapy is rational, objective, intellectual, and "scientific." In harmony with the Protestant ethic, you must work for success in psychotherapy and successful psychotherapy will help you to work.

In other cultures, the values, goals, and techniques are often quite different. In Nigeria, for instance, there is much less stress on independence and rational thinking. Symptom removal and improved interpersonal relationships are considered desirable goals of therapy, and are achieved through suggestion, group therapies, and environmental manipulation. There is no attempt at insight and little attempt to change behavior. A psychiatric observer in Nigeria concluded: "Indeed, I have seen very little evidence in Yoruba psychotherapy of any attempt to change the individual."[89]

Another example is Navaho Indian culture, where harmony within the community is an important cultural value and improving interpersonal relationships is the goal of therapy. The technique of therapy most used is a long curing ceremony involving the whole community. The forces of change are then set into motion:

> A significant implication of this view is that the patient does not need to reflect on his behavior or examine his motives, conscience, or reactions in order to be helped. There is no exhaustive analysis of intrapersonal dynamics; he need only place himself within the curing system, which, once set in motion, proceeds almost automatically. . . . In one sense, all Navaho curing is psychotherapy. Looked at another way, however, none of it is psychotherapy as we know it. In the sense of verbal interaction between patient and therapist, with the goal of changing behavior through increased insight and self-awareness, psychotherapy hardly exists at all.[90]

Morita therapy in Japan provides still another illustration. Japanese cultural values are based upon ancient Oriental philosophy and patterned after Zen Buddhism. The ideal is a calm but happy acceptance of reality.

> In such terms the goal and problem of psychotherapy for the Japanese is how to live in the midst of this sad transitoriness of all things—one does not struggle against this, but becomes one with it. There is no need to look backward as in Western psychotherapy to seek for past causes which no one can prove to have really taken place.[91]

The goal of therapy that is compatible with cultural values such as this is "right-mindedness," a change of attitude. The techniques used to achieve the goal are a particular combination of personal history taking, rest, solitude, and occupational therapy. The techniques are closely interrelated with the goals and values, and Morita therapy is no more exportable to Western culture than psychoanalytic therapy is importable into Japan.[92]

Finally, there is an important vertical dimension to the problem as well as the horizontal dimension we have been examining. There are not only differences in techniques of therapy between cultures, but also differences within the same culture over a period of time.

Anthropologist A. F. C. Wallace's study of Iroquois Indian psychotherapy provides a classic demonstration of this. Wallace documents how the preferred techniques of therapy changed from expressive, cathartic techniques centering on dream interpretation, to repressive, disciplinary techniques centering on public confessions and authoritarian commands. The shift occurred simultaneously with a change in Iroquois society from being powerful and politically independent at the end of the seventeenth century to being emasculated and politically dependent in the early nineteenth century.[93] He suggests that the system of psychotherapy is related to the political and sociocultural organization of the society at any given time. Since cultural values would also be expected to change with shifts such as the above, it would be reasonable to expect a temporal relationship between cultural values and techniques of psychotherapy. Different periods in the life of a culture may require different types of therapy.[94]

In the light of this, it is interesting to speculate about contemporary changes in Western psychotherapeutic techniques. Does the decline of classical psychoanalytic techniques and the emergence of brief therapies, group therapies, instant insight, "breakthroughs," etc., represent changes in Western culture? Some observers contend that we are moving from a production-oriented, work-oriented system of values to one that is consumption and leisure oriented. If this is true, what will future Western psychotherapy be like?

PART II

PSYCHOTHERAPISTS IN ACTION

Chapter 7

Therapists in Ethiopia, Borneo, and the United States

Up to this point in our study of psychotherapists, we have been building mosaics, borrowing pieces freely from widely varying sources. This produces a picture of a therapist who is whole but not real. He or she is like a momentary pattern on a shifting kaleidoscope.

This chapter is an attempt to fix the kaleidoscope, to look behind the mosaics at real people. These people are therapists in Ethiopia, Borneo, and the United States. They each help people who are disturbed in their particular cultures. It is relatively easy for us to know Western therapists as real people—we have seen and heard them. But therapists in other cultures, be they witchdoctors, medicine men, shamans, or whatever, lack substance in our minds. Attempts to picture them as real people constantly conflict with our deeply ingrained stereotype of masked, evil figures gathered around a pot full of boiling missionaries. This stereotype represents the Tarzan stage of Western understanding; it is time to grow beyond that.

An Ethiopian Spirit Doctor

Abba Wolde Tensae Ghizaw was the best-known priest-healer in Ethiopia. His fame was such that fourth-grade schoolchildren a thousand miles away knew who he was—they had heard their mothers discussing him. As a therapist, he represented an important mental health resource in this African nation.

To reach his village from Addis Ababa, the capital, is a trip of an hour and a half by car. I made the trip often during my two years in the country from 1964 to 1966. It takes you along the heart of the eight-thousand-foot plateau that occupies much of Ethiopia; in the distance are thirteen-thousand-foot mountains, eucalyptus trees, and fields of yellow daisies. The lush farmland is cultivated with simple tools and wooden plows. Centuries exist side by side here as the country attempts to leapfrog into the technological present.

The village, Ghion, is indistinguishable from dozens of others along the main roads of Ethiopia. The streets are mostly unpaved. Small shops form a perimeter for the large open marketplace near the center of town. Grains and spices and household supplies change hands there, especially on days of the big market, when people come in from the countryside for miles around. They all knew Abba Wolde Tensae, both as a priest and as a healer.

His house was a modest wooden structure with an aluminum roof, surrounded by well-kept gardens. It was like the houses of the schoolteachers, the successful merchants in town, and the government health officer who ran the medical clinic. Abba Wolde Tensae owned some of these other houses, for he was one of the largest landowners in town. But he did not like to discuss money or his investments—he said it was God's money, which he had invested to carry out His work. At the edge of town were clustered many smaller dwellings, made from a mud-and-straw paste that hardens like plaster. Aluminum or thatched leaves were used for the roof. Some of the dwellers originally came to the village to be cured by the healer and then stayed on.

Abba Wolde Tensae was a priest in the Ethiopian Orthodox Church. This branch of Christianity broke off from the mainstream in the fourth century and since then has gone its own way. For centuries Ethiopia, cut off from the rest of the world by its mountains and canyons, developed by itself. It was only vaguely known to outsiders as the mysterious kingdom of Prester John. Ethiopian Orthodox Christianity became the core of Ethiopian cultures and values. The religion was embraced by the ruling Amharas as the official religion, and potential persecution by its

Muslim neighbors on all sides solidified the bonds of church and state.

Thus religion and culture are closely interdigitated in Ethiopia. For a priest like Abba Wolde Tensae to be also a healer is logical and consistent with the infusion of religion into all aspects of the culture. In the village of Ghion he occupied a place of importance religiously, therapeutically, politically (as an important church figure), and economically (as a landowner).

As a therapist, Abba Wolde Tensae was an important health resource. Ethiopia had, at the time of my stay there, just over 300 medical doctors for its 22 million people. Most of these were located in the cities, and a town like Ghion had none. Medical care was given at the government health station by a health officer (with four years of training after high school) and dressers (equivalent to nurse's aides). Some health officers tried to work cooperatively with priest-healers like Abba Wolde Tensae; others scorned them as representing everything "uncivilized" that educated Ethiopians wanted to eradicate. There were only three Western-trained psychiatrists in the country, all of them Europeans concerned primarily with running the single mental hospital in the capital.

Abba Wolde Tensae and healers like him fill the gap in mental health services. He knew what was wrong with clients who came to him—they were afflicted with *zar* spirits. These spirits may attack an individual in a variety of situations, especially if he or she is alone near a river, in the forest, or in a cave.[1] Most clients who came to Ghion for treatment were found to be possessed by them. In making the diagnosis, Abba Wolde Tensae was confirming a belief in *zar* spirits that is very widespread among Ethiopians. Even those who have been educated in Europe or America will often cling to their belief in *zar* spirits, especially as the cause of mental illness. It is a belief encouraged by the culture generally and by the church specifically. The following statement by a high church official is representative:

> There are many kinds of diseases. It is man himself that brings disease on himself. We believe evil spirits are the cause of some diseases. . . . Most mental illnesses are caused by devils. Most of the time doctors say that mental cases can be cured by prolonged

treatment, but we usually see them cured by going to the holy water.[2]

Thus the naming process is easy as long as the therapist shares these conceptions of causation with his Ethiopian clients.

In regard to classifying illnesses, Abba Wolde Tensae did not make many of the distinctions that Western classificatory systems do. The important things are whether or not the disease is spirit-caused, what parts of the body the spirits are in, and how many spirits are present. The Western dichotomy into physical and mental illness is approximated by a division into non-spirit- and spirit-caused diseases, but there are many points of divergence. Thus a tuberculous abscess of the spine may be treated as a local collection of *zar* spirits, whereas tuberculosis of the lung is referred to the health center. In one analysis of cases seen by Abba Wolde Tensae, one quarter were clearly psychiatric, one quarter were clearly somatic, and half were admixtures.[3] Like most therapists in the world, he did make a distinct category of "insanity," corresponding approximately to those mental diseases that Western classificatory systems label as psychosis.

Abba Wolde Tensae was an impressive and imposing person. At age forty-seven he carried his two hundred pounds on a large frame. He appeared strong and athletic, and moved with a certainty that implied confidence and success. He had a long black flowing beard that was streaked with white hairs. Usually he wore all-black robes at his work, with a white sash and sometimes a white skullcap. Often he wore black sunglasses as well.

His main personality characteristics were his confidence, genuineness, fatherliness, and interest in his clients. His underlying warmth was partly masked by an authoritarian manner. Those around him spoke highly of him, and appeared totally dedicated to assisting him in his work. When discussing his work he was humble, declining to take any credit for his cures and insisting that he was only God's tool. At the same time he was proud that his healing ability was so well known, he placed important people who visited him in the front row at his healing ceremonies, and he delighted in having pictures taken of him at work. Overall he appeared well adjusted, and Ethiopian friends assured me that they did not consider him to be psychiatrically deviant.

His relationship with his clients was one of a father with his children. He knew what was best for them and did not hesitate to tell them so. He expected respect and obedience on their part; he had little time for those who disagreed. During the healing ceremony there was considerable bodily contact through the laying on of hands as he exorcised the evil *zar* spirits. Most clients were seen once or twice during a healing ceremony. Difficult cases, however, remained near his compound for weeks or months, being cared for by relatives. His fee was whatever donation the client wanted to leave.

Abba Wolde Tensae came to his healing profession partly through heredity and partly through supernatural designation. He originally learned how to heal from his father, and when he entered the priesthood his healing powers increased through divine sanction. He attended the first six years of public school, then entered the traditional church training school for the priesthood. He spoke Amharic, the official language, as well as Gaez (the church language), and a little English and Arabic. During World War II he fought against the invading Italians. He had been at his location in Ghion for twelve years. Prior to that he was in another part of the country. It is rumored that he had to leave his former post because he was run out—he carved a large cross on a tree sacred to Muslims in the area. Whether true or not, the story is an accurate reflection of this man's zeal.

Clients came to Ghion from all over Ethiopia. Some traveled for several days to reach it. In a survey, only 14 percent were found to be from the Ghion area itself.[4] The edifice in which Abba Wolde Tensae conducted his healing ceremonies was not an imposing structure, though it could immediately be pointed out by anyone in the village.

Clients' expectations were raised by this healer's imposing appearance and self-confidence as well as by his reputation and the pilgrimage they had made to see him. He conveyed an air of absolute certainty that he knew what was wrong and how to make it right again. He had been observed by at least two other Western-trained psychiatrists, and both were also impressed by his genuineness and belief in himself.[5]

Healing ceremonies were held in a large room with a rough-hewn wood floor, an aluminum roof with skylights, and wooden benches. On a weekend the room was crowded with two hundred to three hundred people. One of the walls was full of proofs of his powers—canes and crutches thrown away by healed cripples, jars of worms representing spirits he had exorcised, and mementos of gratitude from healed clients. Abba Wolde Tensae began the service on a raised pulpit that contained some Orthodox Christian inscriptions, pictures of Jesus, colored lights, a wreath, and a telephone. Since telephones were still uncommon in Ethiopia, its presence was impressive; moreover, when a call came during a service, the question of where it might be coming from added a distinct aura of mystery.

The ceremony began like many religious ceremonies, with reading from Holy Scriptures. It was usually not long before the reading "struck home" with an offending *zar* spirit present: The afflicted person cried out and collapsed on the floor. This person was helped to an open area immediately in front of the pulpit with a chair in the middle for clients. Often the client began writhing and screaming and had to be held by assistants. Abba Wolde Tensae slowly descended from the pulpit, approached the client, and began a rather standardized dialogue in Amharic:

ABBA WOLDE TENSAE: What is your name?

SPIRIT SPEAKING THROUGH CLIENT: Buda.

ABBA: What kind of devil are you?

SPIRIT: *Zar* devil.

ABBA: When did you take possession of this woman?

SPIRIT: Three years ago near a river while she was washing clothes.

ABBA: Why?

SPIRIT: Because she did wrong. She did not care for her baby properly. She left it uncovered to the evil eye.

ABBA: I command you to leave this woman now.

SPIRIT: No.

ABBA: You will. Howl like a hyena and leave her.

At this point the woman cried out and fell to the floor, writhing. After one to two minutes she lay still and was carried away by assistants, to recover slowly in the next room.

During the dialogue Abba Wolde Tensae carried a large wooden cross in his left hand. His right hand was in a bucket of holy water held by an assistant. Alternately he threw handfuls of the water in the client's face and then hit her forcefully with the cross. Often the spirit was reluctant to leave, and so he became more and more forceful in his exhortations and accompanying actions. The whole cure usually took less than ten minutes. He then returned to the pulpit and resumed the reading of Scripture until the next spirit cried out. During a single service he exorcised spirits from ten to twenty people.

Abba Wolde Tensae also saw individual clients in his office. In addition to the techniques of therapy used in the public ceremony—suggestions, confession, and aversive conditioning—he employed a type of hypnosis and environmental manipulation. In private consultations he also often added specific advice about how to live and how to behave. (In other parts of Ethiopia, a classical group therapy was used by *zar* therapists.[6]) The techniques that he used were certainly compatible with his fatherlike, authoritarian personality.

How effective was this therapist? Judging from his reputation and the personal testimonials I heard, I would say very effective. He claimed to have treated over one million people in the previous fourteen years, though in actuality it was probably about 100,000. Because of the large number of *zar* spirits he had exorcised, some people in the town encouraged him to move elsewhere; they feared that all the free *zar* spirits would constitute a public health hazard. He kept careful records of all his clients, and entries showed approximately five hundred a month. The number of repeaters was relatively small, less than 15 percent.[7] Clearly he was an important mental health resource in Ethiopia.

An Iban Therapist in Borneo

The Iban are a group of people who live on the other side of the world from Ethiopia. Part of the group live in the Indonesian part of Borneo and about 250,000 live in the Malaysian part, called Sarawak. It was the latter group that I visited in 1969.

The Iban, also known as Sea Dayak, were the original head-hunters of Borneo. (I had hoped to find that they also shrank their captured heads and thus make contact with the original headshrinkers. Alas, they did not, shrinking apparently being confined to groups in New Guinea and South America.) Once renowned for their fierceness and their use of blowpipes with poisoned darts in warfare, the Iban gave up headhunting early in this century. Now they are industrious, cheerful, and peaceful, making their living by cultivating plots of rice and sago and tapping rubber trees beside the tributaries of the Rejang River.

Therapists among the Iban are called *manangs*. One of the *manangs* whom I visited was Digat Anak Kutak. He lived in a longhouse beside a river one day's drive from the capital, Kuching. The road was unpaved. I was accompanied by Paul Beavitt, an English anthropologist who knew the Iban people in this long-house and who acted as translator. The drive wound between low rolling hills, rice paddies, and orchards of pepper trees belonging to the Chinese, the Land Dayak, and other inhabitants of Sarawak. It was sparsely populated, with less than one million people in the whole country.

Digat's role as a therapist and healer was an important one, for Western-trained therapists were in short supply. There were less than twenty doctors in the whole country, none of them psychiatrists. The single three-hundred-bed psychiatric hospital was in Kuching. It was set up by a psychiatrist who had since left, and was being run by a general practitioner and a psychiatric nurse. They did an impressive job, but with the scattered population of the country and the limited transportation, it was obvious that they saw psychiatric cases only when they had become severe and needed confinement. Once a patient was discharged there was usually no follow-up, since the scattered government clinics are often distant from the patient's home.

In order to assess the relative importance of *manangs* like Digat in treating cases of mental illness, I spent time at the psychiatric hospital interviewing Iban patients confined there. All eight patients I interviewed had seen a *manang* during the onset of their illness, and seven of the eight reported improvement from the contact.

In contrast to the scattered government clinics, *manangs* are usually close to people. Digat saw clients from two nearby rivers in addition to his own, but he was especially well known. The ratio of lesser-known *manangs* to the population was about one for every two hundred people, so an Iban could always reach one within a few miles on the river.[8]

Another asset that makes the *manang* an ideal mental health resource is that he speaks the same language as his clients. Sarawak has twenty-two separate languages, and Ibans form only one third of the population. Consequently even if Western-trained therapists were desirable and available, they would not be able to communicate with Iban clients as Digat could.

Digat, like most *manangs*, usually had no difficulty diagnosing a case of mental illness. He knew what was wrong immediately—the individual's soul had been lost. This is part of a worldview shared by all Iban. The world is divided into the realm of men and the realm of spirits. The latter may be either helpful or harmful. A helpful one, for instance, may be an ancestral spirit; if you get lost in the forest, this spirit might masquerade as a small deer and lead you back to safety.

Evil spirits, on the other hand, are always trying to steal souls. Most commonly they steal them during sleep. Dreams are thought to be the wanderings of the soul and are one of the two main lines of communication between the world of spirits and that of men. (The other line of communication is through the calls of birds.) Thus dreams are accepted as the primary validation for their worldview by the Iban. An Iban *knows* his theories are correct because his subjective experiences during dreaming prove it and because when the *manang* captures a lost soul during treatment, the sufferer usually gets well.

A person's soul is most likely to be stolen by evil spirits under certain conditions and it is these conditions that determine the classification of Iban mental diseases.[9] One such condition is the violation of a taboo, such as eating an animal forbidden by the mandate of an ancestor. Another possible condition is a failure to fulfill a command from the spirit world communicated by way of a dream or a bird call. The person may have been ordered to hold a feast, sacrifice an animal, even to become a *manang*. Other conditions that are thought to weaken the soul and make it susceptible to being stolen by spirits are frustrated love, heredity, poor circulation, retained placenta at childbirth, and becoming a Christian.

As a therapist, Digat was not an imposing man, but he was impressive. Like most Iban men, he was short, about five feet four inches. He was in his mid-forties and had a wiry build which reflected his long days clearing land and planting his rice. He had receding hair and his skin was covered with the decorative tattoos commonly found among the Iban. Usually he wore long loose pants and no shirt, and went barefoot. There was nothing in his appearance that marked him as a *manang*.

His manner was intense. He listened carefully, pursed his lips, and nodded frequently. He gave a strong impression of total attention directed toward the speaker. When he had an idea his eyes lighted up, he became excited, and he suddenly smiled widely, revealing two gold teeth. He said very little until he had had time to listen carefully. When he finally did speak, he conveyed the impression of having thought the problem carefully through.

As a *manang*, Digat's relationship with his clients was that of a technological expert rather than a father. He had special knowledge about lost souls and how to retrieve them. Other *manangs* have this knowledge too—he was just especially skilled at it. Consequently there was relatively little aura of mystery and charisma about him. He did not have to accept cases that came to him for help but could simply tell them to find another *manang*. Other accounts of Iban *manangs* imply that they are quite selective in the cases that they will undertake.[10] Digat, like most *manangs*, treated only one case at a time. The fee charged was usually set before treatment began and was not dependent on a successful cure. It varied with the difficulty of the case, the length of the journey necessary to see the person, and the reputation of the *manang*. It might be paid in cash, goods such as rice, or valued items like Chinese jars.

Digat was commanded to become a *manang* by spirits in a dream. Failure to carry out this command would have meant sickness or death. Other *manangs* migrate toward the profession either because their fathers are *manangs* or simply because they want to. Another *manang* I met in Sarawak had never had a command; he simply was interested in the work and apprenticed himself to a *manang* as a boy.

Digat's major asset for raising client expectations was his reputation. And much of this rested upon his training. Digat was a *manang mensau,* a higher level of therapist than most of his counterparts nearby. The lower level of *manang* is called *manang mata*—"he can repeat many of the incantations used and he assists others in their cures."[11] But he cannot undertake difficult cases like mental illness without being a fully trained *manang mensau.*

Training to become a *manang mensau* may take as long as eight years of part-time study. The aspirant must learn a vast volume of lore, songs, and incantations. And even more important, he must come to understand and be able to control his own guardian spirit. Only after he has done these things can he be considered for initiation. This decision and ceremony are in the hands of fully trained *manangs* in his area, who gather together and admit him to the profession. The lengthy initiation ceremony includes application of medicine to his skin to protect him, gold dust sprinkled on his eyelids to help him find lost spirits better, a small fishhook placed in his fingertip to help him grapple with evil spirits more successfully, "and lastly they pierce his heart with an arrow [symbolically] to make him tender-hearted and full of sympathy for the sick and suffering."[12] Pigs are then sacrificed and he is declared to be a *manang mensau.*

There is yet one higher grade of *manang* among the Iban, the *manang balis.* Assuming woman's dress and manners, and perhaps even taking a "husband," they have become transvestites, they claim, at the command of the spirits. *Manang balis* have always been rare[13] and at the time of my visit were almost nonexistent. I was unable to find anybody who had ever seen one, though rumors of their existence were abundant. Their function may represent a socially sanctioned role for sexually deviant Iban men.

Most *manangs* are not sexually deviant and in fact are looked upon as stable community leaders, second in respect and political authority only to the chief.[14]

Manang Digat almost always saw a client in his or her own longhouse. He journeyed to it after a day in the rice paddy and performed a healing ceremony during the evening, usually returning home the same night. Because he had to farm like other men, he was able to see only about ten clients each month.

A typical case for Digat was that of a young widow who complained of generalized weakness and inability to do her work.[15] Fearing that her soul had been lost, her relatives called Digat. He came to her longhouse at dusk and sat down with her relatives in the common corridor that ran the length of the longhouse and connected the twelve separate family dwellings that opened onto it. The longhouse was raised off the ground about eight feet; beneath it ran chickens and pigs. Kerosene lanterns provided light as all the families in the longhouse slowly gathered to watch the ceremony. Outside, small monkeys at the jungle's edge chattered at the Southern Cross, then disappeared.

Digat had decided that this woman was not very sick and only required a small ceremony. For a more serious case he would use a full-scale ceremony, involving preparations by all the members of the longhouse and lasting sometimes all night.

His first job was to make a positive diagnosis. For this purpose he got out his private medicine bundle. This bundle was highly valued, and, more than any other single thing, marked him as a *manang*. Digat was reluctant to show it to me on my visit. Finally, I offered him a small supply of my most powerful medicine for "madness" (chlorpromazine) in exchange for an examination of his medicine bundle. He consented.

The most important item in it was a piece of quartz with the horns of a large beetle attached. This was Digat's "stone of light," which he used to make a positive diagnosis. By holding it up to the light and looking at the client, Digat could tell whether her soul was missing, and if so, how far it had gone. Other items in the bag included a wild boar's tusk (to help retrieve the soul), large pebbles, roots, and pieces of cotton. The last was to symbolically plug up holes so that the soul would not leave the body again once it had been retrieved.

Having ascertained the location of the lost soul, Digat began chanting and went into a trance. He fell to the floor and was covered with a special blanket by his assistant. The blanket was reserved only for special ceremonies like this. It was thought that while Digat was beneath the blanket he went on a trip to the realm of the spirits to retrieve the lost soul of the client. His own special guardian spirit guided him on the way.

Retrieval of the lost soul may involve many obstacles and dangers, but Digat was almost always successful. Some *manangs* participating in large ceremonies go into an adjoining room and emerge with a bloodied dagger, proof that they killed the offending spirit who was responsible. Once the soul was recaptured, Digat came out of the trance and blew it back into the woman's body through the fontanel in her skull. Finally, Digat charged the client, and often the family or community, with certain taboos to prevent relapse.

The principal therapeutic technique used by Digat in healing ceremonies such as this is suggestion. There may be some confession by the client in front of her relatives and neighbors, but this is not necessary. Analysis of the person's dreams is common, and it is used in attempts to decipher messages that have been sent by the spirit world. Bad dreams, in and of themselves, are valid reasons for consulting a *manang*. Drugs made from local herbs are also used frequently, though there is another healer in the culture, the *dukun*, whose main function is to treat people with drugs. Often a *manang* and a *dukun* will help each other, and in Digat's healing this was the case.

It is also clear that Digat and other *manangs* utilize environmental manipulation to an important degree. All healing ceremonies involve at least the family of the client and often the entire longhouse. They become directly involved with the client's problem, may have responsibilities for preparations needed for the healing ceremony, and often must observe certain taboos after the ceremony to keep the person well. It is in their best interest for the client to get well, since a community as interdependent as a longhouse misses any sick member. In the above case, Digat suggested a redistribution of labor among the widow's relatives to help her through the prolonged mourning period.

The question arises whether *manangs* are "honest" in what

they do. Early missionary accounts especially ridicule them as frauds and expose the tricks they use to get blood on the dagger, etc. My conversations with three of them convinced me that while they are not above trickery, they use it in the belief that they are helping the client. They have absolutely no doubt that the person's soul is lost, and they believe that anything which will assist in its retrieval is not dishonest. Other observers confirm this view of their authenticity.[16]

How effective are Digat and other *manangs* as therapists? It would appear that for treating a depressed woman like the one above they are quite effective by virtue of their mobilization of community resources and through the technique of suggestion. For more serious cases of mental illness, like psychosis, their effectiveness is much lower. In a country where there are no alternative resources for most people, *manangs* are the first, and often the only, line of defense.

A Psychiatrist in California

The Californians are a group of people who live on the West Coast of the United States. Most ethnographers consider them to be part of the dominant Anglo-American culture found throughout the United States, though a few consider them to be a distinct subculture.[17]

Among the most common types of psychotherapists in this culture are those called psychiatrists. There are estimated to be thirty thousand of them, and as such they constitute an important mental health resource. One of the better-known psychiatrists is Dr. William Boyce, who lives in the town of Palo Alto (translation: "high stick"). It is an affluent, intellectual town, wedged between rolling green hills and the San Francisco Bay. The main commercial area is thirty miles to the north, in San Francisco.

Dr. Boyce is well known in California. Although most of his clients come from towns in the immediate vicinity, occasionally people travel several hours from more distant towns for an appointment. Clients come to see him once or twice a week on a regular schedule, and treatment usually lasts several months.

When hospitalization is needed, it is carried out in the nearby Stanford Medical Center. Whereas there is no single "typical" psychiatrist in American culture any more than there is in any other culture, Dr. Boyce can be considered as representative of the majority of the psychiatrists in this culture.

Dr. Boyce and his patients share a common worldview about what is wrong—the clients have been made ill by bad childhood experiences. Sometime during their early years the clients have had relationships that were pathological, and these have in turn infected their adult relationships. Most often the offending agent is either the mother or the father, though other agents are possible as well. Dr. Boyce and his clients are able to validate this theory of causation by examination of the client's dreams. Further validation arises from the fact that when these early relationships are explored, the clients often get well. There is a complex system for classifying mental disorders in this culture, but it is largely ignored by Dr. Boyce and his clients, except for use on official documents.

The personal qualities of this therapist that stand out are his self-confidence and his professional manner. There is a hint of warmth underneath, but it is not in direct evidence in his day-to-day contact with clients. Rather it comes out most strongly when he is at home, playing with his three small children. Similarly, his professional manner might be mistaken by some as aloofness; on the tennis court on Saturday, however, it is conspicuously absent and is replaced by exuberance. He devotes total attention to his clients, and listens both carefully and thoughtfully. Occasionally he interrupts with a question, but more commonly he reserves his thoughts and interpretations for the long pauses when the person has stopped talking.

He is a distinctive-looking man, almost six feet tall, with heavy glasses and a full beard. He is usually dressed in a suit and a colored shirt, and generally is not as orthodox in his demeanor as the healers in the other medical specialities in town. Because of these personal qualities he possesses a certain aura of mystery which his clients find attractive. His fee is ninety dollars for each visit and is payable only in money. The fee must be paid whether or not the client gets well.

Dr. Boyce became a psychiatrist through self-selection and

through academic selection. Following secondary school, he went to college, medical school, and internship for a total of nine years. This course of study was required by the culture as a prerequisite for admittance into the profession of psychiatry. He then attended a psychiatric residency for three years, during which time he learned the theories and lore of his profession, control over his own thoughts, and how to treat clients. His teachers were older psychiatrists who had previously been accepted into the profession. Two years after he finished his residency, he was officially initiated into the profession after passing an examination given by the older psychiatrists in his area.

Client expectations are raised by Dr. Boyce's impressive office. Situated in a new steel-and-glass building, the office is richly carpeted and furnished. A couch, the requisite paraphernalia of his profession, stands against one wall. Modern paintings grace the other walls and bespeak refinement, intelligence, and success. The collecting of them is one of his favorite hobbies. Furthermore, the office is situated adjacent to the Stanford Medical Center, thereby accruing further client expectations which spill over from this eminent institution. Dr. Boyce maintains a teaching position on the faculty there and does not hesitate to identify himself as a faculty member when asked by a client.

But Dr. Boyce's major asset in raising expectations is his reputation. Much of this comes from the fact that he was trained at the leading psychiatric center on the East Coast and then went to Europe, where he studied briefly with one of Freud's leading disciples. Framed pieces of paper on the wall attest to these facts. He returned to start practice and although he never completed a classical analysis himself, he is regarded by his colleagues as being well trained in the classical psychiatric tradition. His reputation has since been enhanced by his publication of four scholarly papers on psychiatric history.

The techniques of therapy used by Dr. Boyce are predominantly psychosocial. He takes a careful history, concentrating on the client's childhood experiences and relationships with his or her mother and father. In the process of giving the detailed history, the client often makes confessions. Dr. Boyce encourages the person to make interpretations of childhood experiences and try to relate them to the present difficulties. Dreams and free association are often utilized to accomplish this. Sometimes the therapist will help the client make these interpretations, and he will also help the person see his or her resistances to getting well. Dr. Boyce operates on the assumption that his clients will relate to him in the same way they previously related to their mother and father; occasionally he points this out. Other techniques of therapy that he uses occasionally are drugs and group therapy for clients for whom they appear to be indicated.

Dr. Boyce sees approximately forty different clients a month; usually ten of them are new. Regarding his effectiveness, his former clients freely extol his virtues. And insofar as client satisfaction and a long waiting list for appointments correlate with effectiveness, he must be viewed as one of the better psychotherapists in the Anglo-American culture.

Chapter 8

Curanderas Among Mexican-Americans

The Hispanic community in the United States is the most rapidly growing segment of the population. Civil unrest and poverty in Latin America combined with a geographic proximity to the United States makes it likely that Hispanics will continue to settle in this country, both legally and illegally, often arriving with little knowledge of English.

This chapter explores mental health resources for Mexican-Americans, one subset of the Hispanic community. Admittedly, grouping together all Mexican-Americans is simplistic and naive, for they range from braceros who come from Mexico to pick crops, to middle-class, activist Chicanos who are proud of their heritage, to wealthy, totally assimilated professionals who are Mexican-American in name only. Nor do generalizations about the subculture take into consideration the facts that Mexican-Americans come from different parts of Mexico, with distinct cultural differences, that they may be more Spanish or more Indian in their heritage, or that one group of "Mexican-Americans" in southern Colorado came to the United States directly from Spain and were never Mexicans at all. Such facts set limiting boundaries on generalizations about the subculture, and these boundaries should be kept in mind.

The Mexican-American subculture in Santa Clara County, California, can serve as a focus for examination. I became familiar with this group over a two-year period when I studied the system of psychotherapists utilized by Mexican-Americans there. The county is a fertile crescent around the southern tip of San Francisco Bay, and includes the city of San Jose as well as wealthy suburban and rural areas. Ten percent of its population is Mexican-American, as it is in the state of California as a whole. The county provides a full range of Anglo psychotherapists, both in private practice and through an extended network of community mental health centers.

Underutilization of Anglo Psychotherapists

The first thing that becomes apparent when one examines mental health services among Mexican-Americans is their gross underutilization of Anglo psychotherapists. In Santa Clara County in 1970, for example, only 4 percent of visitors to the community mental health center (with a sliding fee scale) were Mexican-Americans, and the majority of these were participants in the drug rehabilitation program. Anglo psychotherapists in private practice claimed to rarely see any Mexican-American clients. Statewide only 3.4 percent of admissions to mental hygiene clinics were Mexican-Americans,[1] and a study in Los Angeles showed that Mexican-Americans were less likely to be offered individual or group therapy and were likely to be terminated more quickly by the therapist.[2]

There are many reasons Mexican-Americans do not utilize existing Anglo mental health services. An obvious reason is the cost. Another is the language problem, with many Mexican-Americans less than fluent in English and few Anglo therapists able to speak Spanish. It is not language alone, however, for as was discussed in Chapter 2, a person's language shapes thought patterns. Between therapist and client there must be more than just linguistic congruence; there must be cognitive congruence as well.

Another reason for the underutilization of Anglo mental health services is the tendency of Mexican-Americans to use general physicians rather than therapists when faced with mental health problems. This explanation has been favored as an important one by Karno and his co-workers in their extensive survey of Mexican-Americans in East Los Angeles.[3] It has some validity to it; most groups with low incomes in the United States probably consult family physicians for emotional problems. However, it is at most a partial explanation for the underutilization by Mexican-Americans specifically; Karno's own survey revealed that the difference between utilization of family doctors by Mexican-Americans and Anglos in the same area was only the difference between 75 percent and 66 percent.[4]

Another explanation of the underutilization was put forward by E. G. Jaco, who suggested that Mexican-Americans may have a lower incidence of mental illness.[5] This is probably false. Although there is no worthwhile comparative study of Mexican-American mental illness, one attempted study of neurosis among adults in Mexico City arrived at the incidence of 44 percent for women and 32 percent for men.[6] In Santa Clara County, indicators of stress and maladaptation such as the numbers of welfare recipients, juvenile delinquents, and neglected and dependent children are all disproportionately high for Mexican-American areas.[7] And most studies of groups who are either poor[8] or in the process of acculturating[9] show a high incidence of mental illness; many Mexican-Americans are both poor and acculturating.

Also relevant is the fact that Mexican-American family structure makes it less likely that family members will seek outside help. Mexican-American families are often close and interdependent. They are expected to provide mutual support in crises and not to seek outside help. Taking problems to someone who is not a family member constitutes loss of face for the whole family. Furthermore, it is said that these families tolerate a greater degree of deviant behavior and therefore make psychotherapeutic help less necessary.

Utilization of Curanderas

Perhaps the major reason for the underutilization of Anglo psychotherapists by Mexican-Americans is that they have their own informal mental health system of *curanderas* and other indigenous therapists. Such healers run a broad range and include the *señora* who is an expert in home remedies; the *adivina,* who just diagnoses the illness but doesn't treat it;[10] the *albolaria,* who relies mostly on herbs for treatment;[11] the *médica,* who also relies on herbs;[12] and the *mágica,* who combines herbs with spiritualism.[13] Herbalists alone may form a separate category of curers in some areas.

Similarly, spiritualists may be looked upon as a separate category, and are also called mediums. Some people distinguish spiritists from spiritualists, the second being thought of as much more religious.[14] Spiritualists often have diplomas from schools in Mexico (they may be obtained by correspondence courses), converse with spirits of the dead, and use trances; they usually charge higher fees than *curanderas.*

All of these healers may either be "general practitioners," treating the whole range of human ills, or they may be "specialists." The latter may specialize either in a specific disorder (e.g., *susto,* a Mexican-American disease category to be discussed below) or in specific technique (e.g., holy water). It should also be stressed that there is great geographical diversity in how these healers are conceptualized and named. A *curandera* in San Jose may correspond to a *señora* in San Antonio, a *médica* in New Mexico, an *albolaria* in parts of Mexico, and a *parchera* in parts of Guatemala.

The *curandera* is the best-known indigenous therapist among Mexican-Americans. The majority are female; male *curanderos* are not uncommon, however, and in some areas may even outnumber *curanderas. Curanderas* come to their profession by apprenticing themselves to a relative or friend who is one, and many claim that they were instructed to do so by divine inspiration.

The major characteristic of a *curandero* is religiosity. As described by Dr. Ari Kiev in his excellent book on these healers: "His knowledge, intuition, humility, and interest in people may be important, but his religious demeanor, untrammeled by the authority of the Church, is his paramount virtue."[15] Most of them do not charge a direct fee, but expect a small offering or gift. The insistence on not charging a fee is so strong in some that one *curandero* said that God would punish him by removing his power to heal if he did charge a fee.[16] In a study of sixteen *curanderas* in

San Antonio, only one was found to charge a fee, and the researchers concluded: "The curers themselves play down the matter of fees and insist that financial considerations are not to be confused with what is essentially a spiritual vocation. Our study indicated that a committed, humanitarian generosity is the primary component that motivates the curers in their practice."[17]

The *curandera* works at her profession only part time, and sees patients either in her own house or in theirs. The setting invariably includes religious objects. Usually the patient is accompanied by his or her whole family. Diagnosis of the illness is made by the history, symptoms, and retrospectively by the response to treatment. The patient's complete recent history of interpersonal relations is inventoried in search of etiological factors. Occasionally *curanderas* simply take the patient's pulse and announce a diagnosis.[18]

The techniques of treatment used by *curanderas* are many, but there are a few things they do *not* do. They do not become possessed, nor exorcise spirits, nor prophesy, nor communicate directly with a guardian spirit. They also do not do witchcraft. Because Anglos often confuse *curanderas* with witches, many *curanderas* refuse to treat cases of people who believe they have been bewitched.

The techniques they do use include the following: massage, cupping, "cleansing" rituals (using herbs and eggs), herb remedies (now being replaced by vitamins and antibiotics), magic potions, religious vows and promises (such as votive candles or a visit to a shrine), prayers, holy water, rules and advice (e.g., about diet), confession, and reassurance. Some *curanderas* tend to specialize in one healing technique alone, as was the case with the most famous *curandero* of all, Don Pedrito Jaramillo, who used holy water for everything.[19] One enterprising *curandero* even used a stethoscope for curing, though not for diagnosis.[20]

The family of the client is present throughout the curing session and members become intimately involved. They may be specifically told how to help the client, or to make votive offerings. This enables the *curandera* to make extensive use of family and social manipulation if she wishes. "Thus treatment is not merely the result of the doctor-patient relationship but is instead a form of social reintegration through socially recognized methods."[21]

In Santa Clara County, *curanderas* continue to exist and provide a mental health resource for Mexican-Americans. How important a resource they provide is not clear. Most Mexican-Americans vehemently deny their existence because they associate *curanderas* with being superstitious and backward. *Curanderas,* for their part, are loath to discuss their practice with an Anglo because of a deep fear (not without reason) of the medical society and the Internal Revenue Service. In East Los Angeles, Edgerton et al. claimed in 1970 that *curanderas* had become unimportant as mental health resources,[22] while in San Antonio in 1977, Alegria et al. reported that *"curanderismo* was found to be alive and well."[23] One *curandera* even displayed a sign that read: "El Hospital Invisible." A study of the utilization of these healers by seventy-five Mexican-American housewives in a southwestern city found that half had been treated by a *señora* and one fifth by a *curandera.*[24]

An example of a *curandero* in Santa Clara County is Mr. R. He is a seventy-five-year-old man who lives with his wife in a modest but well-kept house in San Jose. There is no sign outside. He became a healer at age ten in Mexico, and came to the United States at age twenty-two. He sees five to ten clients a day for a wide variety of reasons, including physical illness, mental illness, social and domestic problems, and divining the future. He also claims to be able to influence the release of prisoners and pick winning numbers in Reno. His fee is whatever a client wants to give. His techniques include suggestion and practical advice (obtained from his contacts with the spirits), as well as occasional herb medicines from Mexico.

Because Mr. R. would not discuss his practice directly with me, I sent a research assistant to him as a client. This woman, brought up in South America, speaks fluent Spanish. She feigned depression and anxiety, due ostensibly to domestic problems. On the first visit he listened to her history, went through a ritual of alternately feeling her pulse and a crucifix, told her to return with a picture of her husband, and promised to commune with the spirits about her problem three evenings hence. On the second visit he told her whom her husband was having an affair with (which was not true), asked whether she wished to keep her husband or divorce him, and went through another ritual, using "holy water" and a crucifix on her hand. On the third visit he claimed that he had "cured" her husband's purported philanderings and offered specific advice on how to act at home to alleviate her domestic problems.

I interviewed two clients who sought help from Mr. R. The pattern of treatment was similar. Both told about other friends who had been treated by him. One woman wanted a divorce from an alcoholic husband who was beating her. Each time the woman suggested divorce, the husband threatened to kill her if she persisted. Mr. R. told the woman to get the divorce, and that his spirits would protect her. Another woman was said to have come to him with domestic problems. Mr. R. told her to go home and she would find her husband in bed with a neighbor. She did and found exactly that. Returning, she demanded of Mr. R. what he was going to do next. He countered by asking what *she* was going to do. She filed for divorce.

There is another group of people who often call themselves *curanderas* but who are not mental health resources. These are fortune-tellers. One of them, a women who advertises herself as a *curandera* on her business card and offers "advice on love, health, and business," speaks practically no Spanish. All of them that I had contact with had starting fees of ten to twenty dollars, and were most concerned with extracting as much money as possible from their clients. They should not be confused with true *curanderas*.

Another type of psychotherapist used by Mexican-Americans is what I call the mental health ombudsman. These people are at least as important mental health resources in Santa Clara County as *curanderas* are, though I am not aware of descriptions of them elsewhere. They are the community leaders to whom people turn with problems. In some cases these individuals overlap the political leadership as well. Their role is similar to the all-understanding ward bosses of the past, who were politically important but who also served as a listener, adviser, legal counsel, social worker, and referee for individual and domestic problems of all kinds.

In East San Jose, I identified about twenty such individuals. They are the people named when you ask a Mexican-American the question: "If you had such and such a problem, who would you go to?" All of them are Mexican-Americans themselves. They are of both sexes. Most have regular jobs, and supply mental health services during their off-hours. None of them would consider accepting payment for their services. Many of them are aware that what they are doing is "psychotherapy" in the Anglo frame of reference. Most of them tend to specialize in certain types of problems. They see the entire range of mental health problems except for psychoses.

An example is Mr. J. He is a middle-aged man who is outgoing, warm, positive, sensitive, and energetic. During the day he works as a blue-collar worker. During evenings and weekends he often sees adolescents with drug and/or school problems. He averages three calls a week. Usually they come to his home, but sometimes he makes the visits. He provides support and practical advice in his attempts to solve the person's problem. He often borrows library books on psychology and counseling in an attempt to improve his ability to help people. He has had opportunities to join the Anglo establishment in a "community liaison" capacity but fears that he would lose his credibility within the Mexican-American community if he did.

Another example is Mrs. P. She is a quiet, warm middle-aged woman who gives freely of her own feelings and conveys confidence. She has worked intermittently for several Anglo agencies, and has averaged three calls a week for primarily domestic problems over many years. She usually visits the home. She allowed me to come with her on several calls, including problems such as a mentally retarded girl's reported disruption of a family (she was being scapegoated), a woman with anxiety and obsessive thinking, a woman with multiple sclerosis and mental deterioration, and a couple with severe marital discord.

Mrs. P. describes her technique as listening and ventilation: "I listen mostly. They they often feel better. Sometimes they understand what's going on better just by telling me. I also encourage them to express their feelings. They're scared to. I tell them I know it will be hard at first."

Some of Mrs. P.'s empathy is a product of her own past domestic difficulties. At one point she sought traditional Anglo psychiatric help. Its failure typifies the reason she is a major mental health resource for the Mexican-American community: "I couldn't talk to him. All he ever did was ask me about things way in the past. My problem was in the present. I couldn't talk to him at all."

It should be noted that *not* included as significant psychotherapeutic resources for Mexican-Americans are the community "caretakers" described by Lindemann and Caplan for Anglo middle-class communities—the clergy, teachers, probation officers, police, etc.[25] It was the existence of this group, in fact, that led to community consultation being included as one of the five essential services for community mental health centers. For Mexican-Americans, however, these "caretakers" are identified with the establishment and are to be avoided whenever possible. The only exceptions are a few Catholic priests and a rare teacher or welfare worker. To go to the police with a problem would be accepted as prima facie evidence by Mexican-Americans that the person *must* be psychotic. Thus not only are the formal Anglo psychotherapists rejected by Mexican-Americans but the informal ones as well.

Mental Illness and the Mexican-American Worldview

Having described the psychotherapists that Mexican-Americans do use, what can be said about this preference in the light of the components of psychotherapy? Is the congruence Mexican-American clients have with Mexican-American psychotherapists and lack with Anglo psychotherapists sufficient to explain the underutilization of Anglo mental health services by Mexican-Americans?

Beginning with the worldview of the Mexican-American subculture (and keeping in mind the limitation of generalizations), there are many cultural values and potential areas of conflict that would not be readily apparent to an Anglo psychotherapist but are shared by a Mexican-American therapist and her client. These potential areas of conflict are points of stress, and the more aware of them the therapist is, the more effective she is likely to be. It is useful to review some of these points of stress, bearing in mind the possible difference between how an Anglo and a Mexican-American psychotherapist might perceive the situation.

The first point, often overlooked, is that most Mexican-Americans by definition are culturally deviant in terms of striving for economic advancement. This is the main motivating factor that brings Mexicans to the United States, yet economic advancement of the individual is a cultural value held in low esteem in traditional Mexican culture. The result is that first-generation Mexican-Americans as a group are motivationally estranged from their parent culture, and one would expect conflicts in direct proportion to their acceptance of Mexican cultural values.

The second point of cultural stress is the role of women. Girls are valued primarily for their virtue, and an unmarried girl's honor is equated with that of the family. Young women are expected to get married, and the maternal role is very highly valued. Women are late to mature, often because the grandmother lives with the family and competes in maternal care of the grandchildren. There is a concomitant undervaluation of the sexual and companionship roles of women; sex is prudishly accepted by "nice women" only as an obligation. If a woman enjoys sex she may be suspected of being a prostitute. The net result is a submissive, masochistic woman who feels inferior and unable to live up to the ideals of her culture.[26] She tends toward depressive reactions, and is more acutely and affectively disturbed than her counterpart in Anglo culture.[27] One study, which confirms this association of the status of women with psychiatric symptomatology, suggests that "women whose status approaches that of men in the same community report fewer symptoms."[28]

The expectations of men constitute another major point of cultural stress. Virility is measured primarily by sexual potency (exercised by the double standard), and secondarily by strength, courage, and audacity. There is a belief in the biological superiority of men, and the traditional Mexican family is founded upon absolute authority of the man and absolute self-sacrifice of the woman. The result is an exaggerated ideal of *machismo* or masculinity. Some authors have suggested that this idea may be a logical reaction formation to the oedipal dynamics of Mexican families, with the son strongly attached to the mother, but this remains to be demonstrated.[29] What *is* certain is that "to be labeled 'homosexual' is the ultimate debasement in the sphere of male behavior.''[30]

Out of this cultural stress one would expect men to have problems with authority and submission, sexual potency, and relations with women generally. It might also be anticipated that a man would act out his aggression, and in fact Mexico does have a high reported murder rate.

These problems become worse as men get older. The discrepancy widens between what they feel they should be and what they actually are. "As they grow older they lose their dominant position and the older adults appear disturbed, impulsive, and anxious. They seem to be losing the grip on society that the older women are taking over.''[31]

Viewing the world as hostile and having extremely poor interpersonal relationships are other major points of cultural stress. Life in general is seen as a struggle between good and evil, with health and prosperity maintained only by sustaining the delicate balance between the forces. The saints are on the side of the good, but devils and witches are opposed. An individual views himself as a passive victim of forces in his environment.[32] Projection comes easily.

Interpersonal relationships are seen from this same vantage point. There is a general distrust of extrafamilial social bonds; interpersonal relationships are unstable; there is fear of intimacy and a general lack of social cohesion. Rubel, in describing the Mexican-Americans of San Antonio, says: "The themes of invidious sanction and malevolent intent are incessant in Mexiquito, and the means by which such hostile intentions are believed to be projected are manifold.''[33] Mexican-Americans see themselves as being unable to get along with each other and the main stresses as intragroup. In an interesting thesis, Rubel tries to associate these poor interpersonal relationships with the strong nuclear family, and draws an analogy from the Mexican-Americans to the Ojibwa Indians.

The projection that commonly ensues from this hostile environment and from poor interpersonal relationships is best summarized by one author: "The Latin does not think he missed the bus because he arrived too late. He blames the bus for leaving before he arrived."[34] The corollary of this projection is that personal failures or shortcomings are not easily admitted in Mexican-American culture, not even to trusted friends.

Another aspect of these poor interpersonal relationships is the importance of "correct behavior" and the suppression of emotions. Relationships are characterized by restraint and constriction, and role behaviors clearly marked in the traditional culture. There is a premium on self-control, and great fear of behaving incorrectly. "The Mexican grows up with much fear of his emotions, particularly hostile and sexual ones, and of the things that arouse these emotions."[35] Emotions are guarded against as having a power of their own.

Finally, perhaps the greatest point of cultural stress in Mexican-American culture is the process of acculturation itself. All of the above points must be seen primarily in the light of contrast between traditional Mexican and Anglo cultures. The ambivalence about economic striving is seen in the college graduate who returns to his father's grocery store to work as a clerk. The different and changing Anglo role expectations of both men and women often contrast sharply with traditional Mexican culture, from simple dating patterns to the increasing difficulty unskilled Mexican-American men have in obtaining jobs and maintaining their supreme role as provider for the family. Other cultural values clash when the collectivism of the Mexican-American *barrio* meets the individualism of the city, or when fatalism and resignation meet achievement, progress, and human perfectibility.[36]

Turning to that part of the worldview which involves the causation and classification of disease, it is found that here also Mexican-Americans often differ markedly from Anglos. And therapists trying to cure them may find it a difficult process unless these differences are recognized.

Within traditional Mexican-American culture there are three main causes of illness:

Natural causes—*Empacho,* the symptoms caused by a bolus of food lodged in the intestine, is an example.

Emotional causes—*Susto,* caused by fright; *bilis,* caused by anger; and *envidia,* caused by desire, are examples.

Supernatural causes—These may be caused either by God as punishment or by others. The latter category includes *mal ojo* (the evil eye) and *mal puesto* (witchcraft).

It should be added that Mexican-Americans, in addition to this group of indigenous disease beliefs, accept most Western beliefs concerning the causation of diseases—e.g., bacteria and viruses.

Most mental disorders in Mexican-American culture are conceptualized under the entities of *susto, mal ojo,* and *mal puesto.* Other causes of illness are accepted, such as heredity, preoccupation with sexual activity, sexual frustration, immoral behavior, and overexposure to the sun. The majority of mental disorders are subsumed under the three disease entities, however, and it is for this reason that each deserves more detailed examination. Interestingly, the notion of God's punishment is rarely invoked to explain mental illness; the choice is rather to project the cause onto others.

To avoid confusion, it should be added that there is extensive overlap of symptoms for these disease entities. No one symptom is specific for a given disease. The same disease may have different sets of symptoms and different diseases may have the same symptoms. The ultimate confirmation of the diagnosis is the disease's response to treatment specifically prescribed for that disease entity. This retrospective method of diagnosis could be profitably used by mental health workers with Mexican-Americans.

Susto, known as the "fright disease," is usually the result of a traumatic experience. The source of fright may be natural (e.g., an accident) or supernatural (e.g., a ghost). The latter category is often called *espanto.* Groups of individuals may develop symptoms at one time,[37] and it is more common in children. The result of the fright is that the soul is lost from the body. Rubel contends that *susto* occurs most commonly "as a consequence of an episode in which an individual is unable to meet the expectations of his own society for a social role in which he or she has been socialized."[38]

The symptoms of *susto* include fatigue, restlessness, decreased appetite, decreased interest, weakness, lack of interest in appearance or surroundings, somatic complaints, withdrawal, and sadness. In short, *susto* corresponds loosely to the clinical entities of anxiety and depression. The treatment for *susto* include prayers, votive offerings, herbs, and "sweeping" the patient with a branch by folk healers to draw the soul back.

Bilis and *envidia,* caused by anger and envy, are less common entities used to explain psychiatric symptoms. With *bilis,* the belief is that strong anger causes an overflow of yellow bile and produces diarrhea and vomiting.[39] It is clear that there exists a ready-made framework associating emotions and psychiatric illness in Mexican-American culture, and that this framework could be used to help explain symptoms in therapy.

Mal ojo, the evil eye, is commonly used to explain psychiatric symptoms. It is caused when a person with "strong vision" looks admiringly or enviously at another. "Any kind of special attention paid one individual by another"[40] may cause it. Its causation is usually assumed to be inadvertent and the person is not held consciously responsible; implicit, however, is responsibility for unconscious desires. Here is another ready-made framework with which Mexican-Americans can accept and understand the unconscious. It is also another example of projecting the cause of illness onto others.

Clinically, *mal ojo* occurs more often in the younger age groups. Headaches, crying, irritability, and restlessness are common symptoms, often accompanied by fever, diarrhea, or vomiting. It is usually of rapid onset and short duration. Psychiatrically, it would appear to correspond with transient situational, neurotic, and personality disorders. Traditional treatments include prayers and "sweeping," or "cleansing" the patient with a raw egg. Another approach to treatment is to try and locate the person who inadvertently caused it (usually within the preceeding twenty-four hours); if this person simply touches the afflicted, the illness will be cured.

Mal puesto, witchcraft, is the most common explanation for all severe psychiatric illnesses. It occurs when a hex is willfully put on somebody by a witch, a healer specializing in witchcraft, or a person who knows the intricacies of witchcraft. The witch or the healer may have been hired to do the job. The hex may be administered by torturing effigy figures of the individual, by magically putting foreign objects into the victim's stomach, by turning

into an animal and attacking the person (nagualism), or by sprin-
kling magic potions on the victim or around his or her house.[41]

The major motives for *mal puesto* are envy, jealousy (especially
sexual), and vengeance. The envy is most commonly "envy of the
prosperous individual who indulges in conspicuous consumption
to the discomfort of his less fortunate neighbors."[42] Belief in *mal
puesto* is common in rural and uneducated Mexican-Americans,
but its belief among all groups should not be underestimated. In a
culture where projection is used easily, and where personal in-
tercession by saints (and other forces of good) are common, it is
only a short step toward blaming personalized forces of evil when
things go wrong.

Clinically, *mal puesto* is suspected whenever deviancy or severe psychiatric symptoms occur. Amnesia, hallucinations, ideas
of persecution, hysterical symptoms, and mania are all suggestive.
Chronicity is a hallmark. *Miedo* is its early or milder form—"the
victim is so frightened that he imagines seeing frightful things
that do not exist and cannot be observed by normal people"[43]—
and *demencia* is its full-blown form.

All chronic deviants from Mexican-American society may be
considered as suffering from *mal puesto.* Schizophrenics, epilep-
tics, those with organic brain disorders, psychopaths, and alcoholics may all qualify. Diagnosis is made by looking for the major
motives a person might have for causing it (e.g., unrequited love)
and identifying the witch. Treatment is removal of the hex either
by countermagic or by destroying the magical paraphernalia used
for the hex (e.g., the doll image).

It is apparent that *mal puesto* is a major mechanism for explain-
ing deviancy and projecting the blame for it onto others. It
strengthens the nuclear family "as a social device by means of
which members of one household perceive others outside it as
attempting to influence and sanction their behavior."[44] And it
functions as a "leveling mechanism," like gossip and ridicule, to
enforce adherence to prescribed behavior. "Those most likely to
be victims are those who, by abnormal physical, social, or psychological behavior, deviate from accepted Mexican-American
norms."[45]

These are the major disease entities under which Mexican-

Americans conceptualize psychiatric illnesses. There are several others of lesser importance. For instance, *mal aire,* an imbalance between hot and cold, may be due to relationships or emotions that are not in balance. *Empacho,* intestinal blockage by a bolus of food, may be caused by "permitting another individual to override one's personal autonomy."[46] And *caida de mollera,* the belief that the infant's fontanel is too low, is thought to be caused by neglect by the mother, a serious charge in a culture that values the maternal role so highly.

Some of the social implications and meanings of these diseases have been mentioned above, but it would be useful briefly to tie them together. First, these illnesses frequently enable the client to avoid the precipitating crisis—e.g., a student who is afflicted by *susto* on the way to take an important examination. If the illness begins after the crisis, it may provide relief from guilt or social disapproval—for example, *mal ojo* or *mal puesto,* caused by others, may be invoked to explain the abnormal behavior. This affords an excellent rationale for otherwise unsanctioned social behavior. At a very practical level, these illnesses focus attention on the individual and let society know that something is wrong; this is often the first step toward help.

Perhaps the most important function of these Mexican-American disease entities is to reemphasize Mexican-American values and customs. As such they are a resistance to culture change. They give you a way to "prove" that you are still Mexican, for Anglos never get these diseases. A Mexican-American who has serious cultural conflicts may resolve them by being diagnosed with these illnesses.[47] "Mexican folk medicine thus plays a dual role, for it is designed to maintain the continuity of society as a functioning whole as well as to reintegrate individuals into society."[48]

It is frequently assumed by Anglos who know about the Mexican-American disease system that belief in it is confined to braceros recently arrived from Mexico. Two studies have shown that this is not the case. A study of seventy-five Mexican-American housewives (two thirds of whom had been born in the United States) asked about belief in five common indigenous diseases (*susto, empacho, caida de mollera, mal puesto,* and *mal ojo*). The results were that 97 percent knew of all five diseases, and that 95 percent knew of instances of one of the illnesses in themselves, a family member, or a friend.[49] Another study, of 250 Tucson Mexican-American families, confirmed the high prevalence of belief. For *susto*, for instance, 139 expressed strong belief, fifty-seven were doubtful, and fifty-four had no belief.[50]

In an attempt to confirm these differences in disease classification, I administered a questionnaire to three groups of people: ten psychiatric residents at Stanford University; ten anthropology graduate students at Stanford University; twenty students at a high school in San Jose. Of these, seven were black, seven Mexican-American, and six Anglos.

Directions for the questionnaire were given verbally and were also printed on top of the page as follows:

I am trying to understand how people think about being well and being sick. You can help me by taking the 10 words which are listed below in alphabetical order and dividing them up. Divide them into at least 2 but no more than 5 boxes. A box can contain as few as one word. Divide them in whatever way seems most logical to you. There is no right or wrong way to divide them—just the way that makes the most sense to you.

For example: might be divided as follows:

fast	blue	cold	slow
blue	red	hot	fast
cold	yellow		
hot			
red			
slow			
yellow			

Here are 10 words to divide:

compulsive	neurotic
crazy	normal
depressed	religious
frightened	tired
hears voices	withdrawn

The subjects were told not to put their names on the paper; I divided the papers into groups as I collected them.

In spite of methodological shortcomings of the study, the results suggested differences in categorization of symptoms between the different cultures. For instance, the words "crazy" and "hears voices" were associated by 90 percent of the psychiatric residents, 60 percent of the graduate students, 48 percent of the non-Mexican-American high school students, and only 16 percent (one out of seven) of the Mexican-American students. Such a difference may indicate greater religious belief among Mexican-American students (although only one out of seven made the association between "hears voices" and "religious") and/or it may reflect greater tolerance for hearing voices in the Mexican-American community. In either case, it is clear that an Anglo psychiatrist and a Mexican-American student share less of a frame of reference than the psychiatrist does with a graduate student (a common source of "good" psychiatric patients).

Another example to illustrate this was the association of "frightened" with some combination of "crazy" and "hears voices" by 86 percent of the Mexican-Americans but only 20 percent of psychiatrists and no graduate students. This may well reflect the pervasive cultural belief among Mexican-Americans in *susto*, the syndrome thought to be caused by a severe fright.

Anecdotal material reinforces such evidence. During a home visit to an anxious, depressed Mexican-American housewife, I attempted to explore the origin of her symptoms within the context of her obvious domestic difficulties. Toward the end of the interview I offered her a mild tranquilizer to alleviate her anxiety. She nodded politely, but I knew I had not gotten through. I then went back into the symptoms and discovered that she was convinced they were the result of *susto*. I told her that the tranquilizer was especially good for *susto*, and she brightened up and smiled. Obviously my medicine could not help her until I understood what was really wrong with her.[51]

There is one other important aspect of the Mexican-American worldview in addition to points of stress, concepts of causation, and the system of disease classification. This is the existence of caste. An Anglo psychotherapist, from a Mexican-American point of view, is a member of a different caste. Although the concept of caste overlaps the distinctions of both class and culture, it differs

in implying a more rigid segmentalization of society, with heredi-
tary positions of dominance and submission. These positions implicitly are part of the divine order and dictate such things as
social intercourse and occupation as well as the use of mental
health facilities. Caste goes beyond income level and value systems; it is the Order of Things.

Just as surely as the blacks in our society have been treated as a
lower caste, so have the Mexican-Americans. They receive re-
minders of their place every day. An illustration is the remarks of
a juvenile court judge in Santa Clara County at the trial of a
sixteen-year-old Mexican-American boy accused of incest:

> The County will have to take care of you. You are no particular
> good to anybody. We ought to send you out of the country—send
> you back to Mexico. You belong in prison for the rest of your life for
> doing things of this kind. You ought to commit suicide. That's what
> I think of people of this kind. You are lower than animals and
> haven't the right to live in organized society—just miserable,
> lousy, rotten people.
>
> There is nothing we can do for you. You expect the county to
> take care of you. Maybe Hitler was right. The animals in our society
> probably ought to be destroyed because they have no right to live
> among human beings. If you refuse to act like a human being, then
> you don't belong among the society of human beings.[52]

These remarks are unusual only in that they received publicity.
Until recently, Mexican-Americans have been used to hearing
them. After all, this is the Order of Things.

Inevitably the psychotherapists and mental health facilities provided by the Anglo caste become associated with perpet-
uating this order. A widely circulated story in the local
Mexican-American community concerns the fate of three
Mexican-American county employees who went to Washington
for the Poor Peoples' March. Upon their return they were ordered by their superiors to have psychiatric examinations. It is
also common for the Welfare Department to order psychiatric
examinations to get recipients classified as psychiatrically dis-
abled and thus off the general welfare roles. If they refuse, their
check is withheld. Little wonder that for Mexican-Americans the

psychiatry of the Anglos is looked upon as just one more way to degrade them.[53]

Other Components of Therapy

Indigenous therapists among Mexican-Americans differ from their Anglo counterparts in many other important ways. In terms of personal qualities, *curanderas* are self-selected, but they must have a predominantly religious motive in order to be effective. The denigration of fee collection among true *curanderas* ensures that individuals interested primarily in personal income are unlikely to select this vocation. Beyond having a solid religious base, the personality types of Mexican-American indigenous therapists appear to be diverse. An active and authoritarian manner is common[54] and there is less value placed on being warm and empathetic.

Similarly, both the client's expectations and his emerging sense of mastery are intimately tied to the religious nature of the healing process. The *curanderas* studied by one psychiatrist in San Antonio varied from an illiterate man to the son of a physician; all were alike, however, in being considered very religious.[55] Since healing is a gift of God, Mexican-Americans wondered how a man can hope to heal anyone if he denies or has no relationship to the source of the cure. It is clear that "the validity of a *curandero's* claims rest in large part on the extent of his basic devoutness and piety."[56]

Finally, the techniques of therapy used by Mexican-American therapists show a different emphasis than those used by Anglo therapists. The predominant techniques are suggestion, confession, family therapy, and environmental manipulation. These are in accord with such goals in therapy as symptom removal and improved interpersonal relationships (especially those within the family). The use of religion with the techniques also helps achieve the goal of a change in attitude; the client is encouraged to accept God's suffering and to believe that it has a purpose. These techniques and goals are consistent with values in the Mexican-American culture, and should be contrasted with those of Anglo psychotherapists, who are more inclined to strive toward insight, improved personal efficiency, and improved social efficiency.

Co-optation or Cooperation?

Given what is known about *curanderas* and other indigenous therapists in the Mexican-American community, what should be the stance of Anglo mental health services regarding their utilization? Should they be ignored, co-opted, or cooperated with?

Most mental health systems have simply ignored them, often unaware that the *curanderas* are providing alternative services for people with problems just down the street from the community mental health center. Those opposed to their use cite instances of disreputable *curanderas* fleecing gullible clients of their life savings, or diagnosing a case of tuberculosis as *susto*. Oscar Lewis, for one, has said that *"curanderos . . .* are prejudicial to the health of the people and are a definite impediment to the realization of national health programs."[57]

Alegria and his colleagues in San Antonio oppose the incorporation of *curanderas* into the official mental health system on other grounds: "The entire framework of *curanderismo* appears fragile. The healers are sensitive, shy, and careful about their work. *Curanderismo* is based on a very human interaction between individuals. Furthermore we see little evidence to support the notion that the *curanderas* and their patients would be accorded the respect . . . due them as professionals."[58] Instead of incorporation, Alegria et al. suggest working with the *curanderas* to educate them on when to refer their clients to existing health and mental health services.

The close ties of *curanderas* to the Catholic Church might also be an impediment to incorporation into the official mental health structure. Religiosity and faith are central to this healing system. This of course is no different from the fusion of medicine and religion in the Navaho healing ceremonies (Chapter 10), yet Navaho medicine men have been given grants by the U.S. Public Health Service and allowed to practice openly in many Indian Health Service government hospitals. There is a fundamental difference between the religion of traditional Navahos, centering on the Great Spirit and nature, and the religion of the *curanderas*, Catholicism, which seems more threatening when juxtaposed with medicine. Western medicine has only fully separated from its religious origins by a few generations and likes to think of itself as fully objective and scientific. We are willing to allow chaplains and priests into our houses of healing as long as they remain in their religious roles, but we would be uncomfortable with practitioners of established religions who claim to be fusing their religion with healing. This was illustrated at the San Ysidro Community Mental Health Center in California when a decision was made to put two *curanderas* on the consultative staff as medical specialists; staff raised great opposition until the job title was changed to "religious specialist."

Other professionals have advocated *curanderas* on the mental health team on a formal basis. In Cuba, for example, *curanderas* were given a two-month training course and then "given positions as educators and assistants to auxiliary personnel working in the health centers."[59] At a conference on mental health planning in 1972 sponsored by the National Institute of Mental Health, one of the official recommendations was to "incorporate the community methods of curing mental illness, such as *curanderas*, spiritualists, and *santerismo* [a Puerto Rican healing system] in community mental health centers serving the Spanish speaking."[60]

Even when indigenous Mexican-American therapists such as *curanderas* are not incorporated into the system, most professionals agree that increased awareness of Mexican-American beliefs about illness will make Anglo therapists and physicians more effective when caring for that segment of the population. This was aptly demonstrated when two professionals at a community mental health center in Denver were faced with twelve Mexican-American patients who believed they had been bewitched, and who had symptoms of anxiety and depression. A psychiatrist selected an antidepressant with bright colors on the capsule, then told the women that it was a new medicine "made from the herbs used by the *curanderas* of Northern Mexico." Within six weeks all twelve women "appeared greatly improved."[61] Not surprisingly, three other patients, who had psychosis, did not respond to this treatment.

Whatever the formal relationship, the most important attitude of mental health professionals toward indigenous healing systems is one of tolerance. This is illustrated by a village in Mexico where the same vehicle carries sick people to a nearby hospital and a nearby *curandera*, dropping some at each stop,[62] and by a *curandera* in the United States who herself terminated an interview with a researcher by saying: "I have to go take a nap now. My doctor says I need plenty of rest, and I don't want to disobey his orders."[63]

Chapter 9

Espiritistas Among Puerto Rican–Americans

Puerto Rican–Americans, comprising a large immigrant group in the northeastern United States, come from an island settled by Spaniards and imported African slaves. Like Mexican-Americans, they vary considerably in their origin, length of time on the mainland, and socioeconomic status. The group of Puerto Rican–Americans discussed in this chapter live in poor circumstances in the South Bronx, in neighborhoods that look like Dresden following British and American air raids; burned-out tenements and abandoned cars line the streets, and junkies vie with cockroaches for preeminence in the buildings.

The dominant psychotherapeutic system among Puerto Ricans in these neighborhoods is *espiritismo*,[1] a healing system that originated in France in the nineteenth century, then spread to Spain and eventually to the Caribbean islands. The main codifier of this belief system was Leon H. Rivail, a Frenchman whose writings, under the name Allan Kardec, are highly valued by followers of *espiritismo*. Briefly, Rivail/Kardec taught that many problems in life are caused by *causas*, wandering spirits of deceased persons, which may cause pain, disease, unhappiness, anxiety, and interpersonal problems. All of us have *facultades*, the ability to communicate with these spirits, but in only a few persons does this ability become developed so the person becomes an *espiritista*

155

(also called a medium). People who are troubled by *causas* consult *espiritistas* either privately (a *consulta*) or in a group meeting (a *reuniones*), usually held on a regularly scheduled basis in storefronts called *centros*. The therapy session consists of the *espiritista*'s attempting to educate and influence the wayward *causa* so that it will no longer cause problems and the person will be well.

Although the theoretical underpinnings of this healing system are relatively straightforward, in practice it becomes much more complex. Much of the theory of *espiritismo* is intricately bound up with Catholic theology, despite the fact that Catholicism officially disclaims it and says it is a sin for a person to consult an *espiritista*. The Pentecostal Church is also prominent among Puerto Rican–Americans, and its theology, too, has been incorporated into *espiritismo*. Moreover, *santería*, an Afro-American religious-healing cult, which originated among the Yoruba in Nigeria and is prominent in Cuba, has merged with traditional *espiritismo* among some groups. Add to this an infusion of African and Latin American witchcraft (*brujería*), and the product is a syncretic healing system that may involve Catholic saints, Yoruba divinities, Hindu gods, and historical figures from many traditions.

Who Uses Espiritistas *and Why*

Studies of Puerto Ricans living in New York have found that at least one third have visited *espiritistas*.[2] Among those using outpatient mental health services, the percentage who have used *espiritistas* approached 75 percent in one study[3] and 50 percent in another.[4] In 1973, Dr. Pedro Ruiz, at that time chief of psychiatric services at Lincoln Hospital in the South Bronx, estimated that there were twenty thousand *espiritistas* in New York City.[5]

The types of problems that take Puerto Rican clients to an *espiritista* are virtually identical to those that take Anglo clients to a psychiatrist, psychologist, or social worker. Dr. Vivian Garrison, who did an extensive study of *espiritistas* and lived in one's home for several months, analyzed the presenting problems of fifty Puerto Rican clients. The most common complaints were marital problems, other family problems, anger, depression, and an interest in self-understanding ("learning about oneself," "trying to find my own value").

Garrison also attempted to ascertain when Puerto Ricans use *espiritistas* and when they use doctors, and concluded that *espiritistas* are used for interpersonal and intrapersonal problems, doctors are used for symptoms that appear to be organic in origin, and often both *espiritistas* and doctors are consulted when the complaints are psychosomatic—e.g., headache, nervousness. She concluded: "The spiritists recognize as their domain to treat almost the same range of thoughts, feelings and behaviors as do the mental health professions. In general, they view the same things as disorder that would be considered psychiatric disorder in the clinic and they attempt to bring about change in these."[6] Garrison then had her interview material (e.g., notes and tapes) rated by a psychiatrist to establish a final diagnosis. The fifty Puerto Rican clients were rated as follows:

19 neurosis
12 personality disorder
 2 adjustment reaction of adolescence
 2 marital maladjustment
 4 alcoholism
 3 schizophrenia
 5 diagnosis unclear
 3 no mental disorder

The Goals of Therapy

Many of the problems brought to an *espiritista* for treatment would seem very familiar to Anglo mental health professionals. Here, for example, is a case described by Dr. Alan Harwood, another anthropologist who did an extensive study of *espiritismo* in the South Bronx:

> Miguel is a man of about 45, the father of four children. He and the eldest child, a woman of about 20, have had a very stormy relationship ever since she entered puberty. His constant concern

about her whereabouts led to persistent fights that continue even now, two years after her marriage and absence from his home. About a year ago father and daughter had a violent argument, after which she swore never to see him again.

After the argument Miguel began waking frequently at night and claiming to hear strange breathing. At his wife's insistence he consulted a spiritist who told him that the breathing he heard was either the spirit of his paternal grandmother or a spirit sent by her. Miguel's father had been very attached to his mother and in fact had left his wife when she was pregnant with Miguel to live with her. The older woman also succeeded in getting Miguel away from his mother and raised him herself. Miguel's mother reportedly tried taking him back with her several times, but he would always return to his grandmother. The medium claimed that the grandmother had performed sorcery on the boy to keep him near her, and it was her continued influence that came between Miguel and his own daughter. At the time the daughter was also having problems with her young son, which was attributed to his ancestor's sorcery as well.

To break this "chain," Miguel or the daughter would have to go to a medium and have the grandmother's hold on them removed. Only then, according to the medium, could the relationship between them be worked out. The only other solution would be for both to carry special protection against the grandmother's spirit their whole lives. When I heard about this case, Miguel's wife was trying to get him to the medium to have the grandmother's influence removed.[7]

In such a case the *espiritista* could either try to strengthen the protective spirits of Miguel and/or his daughter, or could attempt to weaken or reeducate the wayward *causa* of the grandmother, which was thought to be causing the trouble. The identification of protective spirits is one of the most common methods used by *espiritistas* to help clients; such spirits may come from among the client's ancestors or they may come from totally unrelated sources. An example of the latter is provided by Harwood from the experiences of Stanley Fisch, who was at the time a medical student at Albert Einstein College of Medicine in New York and was studying *espiritismo*. In one session in a *centro*, an *espiritista* whom Fisch had got to know summoned some protective spirits to help him with his future career. The *espiritista* became possessed, then asked Fisch to stand in front of her:

> She took my hands and began, "I am the spirit of a famous Spanish doctor, and I want to help you. You have shown much faith in spiritual things, and you want to help people with their spiritual problems. I am F—— de O—— of Spain. I died in 1897. I was a good doctor. You will be a doctor for children. When you need help, call me, and I will help you. Remember all the things you have learned here, and you will be a great doctor." Then she paused and rubbed my shoulders and arms and banged on the rim of the bowl. She made a few passes and then spoke again; "I am M—— S—— of Spain. I will also help you. When you need help, just call me, and I will come. You will be a great doctor, famous for medical and spiritual things. But remember, I am only for you. You must not tell anyone about me." Then she recovered.[8]

Harwood noted that the goals of therapy in *espiritismo* are remarkably similar to the goals of Anglo psychotherapy. In *espiritismo*, the client's unwanted social behavior or feelings are caused by bad spirits, of which the client is usually unaware; in psychodynamic psychotherapy, the unwanted behavior or feelings are caused by early childhood experiences of which the client is unaware, and in behavioral therapy it is learned behavior from the past that is being generalized to the present and causing the difficulty. The goal in all these therapies is to make the client aware of the origin of his or her problems and then strengthen the person (by spirits, reeducation, or new learning) in order to make him or her stronger and immune to the bad behavioral influences.

The Components of Therapy

The shared worldview between *espiritista* and client makes possible the identification of the offending agent—the specific *causa*. The fact that somebody knows what is wrong affords considerable relief to the worried client, and the naming process itself thus becomes therapeutic.

In terms of how a person becomes an *espiritista*, it is usually by self-selection and often runs in families. In the majority of cases it occurs in women, although men are capable of developing their powers as well. Often they have been confronted with a crisis or an unusual experience in their own life that convinces them they are destined for the role. The following is an example:

> Juana began by telling me that her power to take on spirits was inherited. Her grandmother had been a great medium. She first knew that her destiny was to have such power in the course of a dream in which she was seated at a White Table with her grandmother. Suddenly a spirit moved in from behind her "from outer space." She woke up making the motions used to induce possession.
>
> Since that dream, spirits have kept coming to Juana and visiting her, although her real dedication to development came later, about 13 years ago. At that time she was applying for a job and was having pictures taken for the application when she suddenly "blacked out" and didn't know where she was. She later went to a medium who told her that this occurrence was a sign that she should not take the job and should instead develop her faculties.[9]

Harwood, after studying many *espiritistas*, was impressed by the empathy and other therapeutic personality characteristics in those whom he got to know. Most *espiritistas* do not charge a fee, but the client leaves a donation depending upon ability to pay.

Given the emphasis on communicating with spirits of the dead, it might be expected that schizophrenic individuals who often hear voices might be attracted to *espiritismo*. Garrison found that only three of the fifty clients she studied were diagnosable as schizophrenic, and according to her, "there is some question of the extent to which spiritists actually treat severe psychiatric disorder."[10] She also noted that Puerto Rican patients in mental hospitals frequently speak of themselves as having *facultades* and being in touch with spirits, but she did not find anyone with schizophrenia actually practicing as an *espiritista* in the *centros*.

The healing session is structured in such a way as to increase the client's expectations and produce emotional arousal. It is common practice for the *espiritista* to tell what is wrong before the client has offered any history. The following account is by a young Puerto Rican man (Carmelo) who went to an *espiritista* for the first time:

> When I came in, M told me to sit down in a chair next to her table. She asked me if I believe in the spirits. I told her I wasn't sure. Before the medium began the consultation, she took a long drag on a cigar that was lying in an ashtray on her table. She then put my hand over a pitcher of water and put her two hands on top of mine. Then she bent her forehead over her hands and kept her eyes closed for a while. Finally the medium raised her head and blinked her eyes.

MEDIUM: Sometimes you are unhappy.

CARMELO: Yes.

M: Sometimes you find it hard to sleep and get up and walk around.

C: Yes.

M: Sometimes you are nervous.

C: Yes.

M: Sometimes you have headaches and the back of your neck hurts.

C: Yes.

M: Sometimes your eyes burn.

C: No.

M: Sometimes you walk the streets because of nerves.

C: Yes.

M: Sometimes you walk in the street and feel something or someone behind you.

C: Yes.

M: You have a girl.

C: No, I am married.

M: You are not happy with your wife.

C: Yes.

M: You come home and argue with your wife.

C: Yes.

M: You haven't been married long.

C: That's right.

M: She isn't the same person you knew before. Sometimes you go home, and she doesn't seem herself.

C: Yes.

M: Sometimes you go home, you fight, and you walk out.

C: Sometimes.

M: She is jealous. She gives you jealous nonsense.

C: Yes. . . .

After probing several other social relationships of the client and suggesting the identity of one of his protectors, the medium summed up the situation as follows:

M: Let's see, you are unhappy. I can see that. You are sorry now that you married. You have a spirit wife from another existence. She is clinging to you and won't let you live in peace with your wife. We must help you get rid of this spirit. You must come to our session this Saturday, but first you must do what I tell you.[11]

Carmelo was told to bring his wife with him for the next session.

The group setting of the *reuniones,* with the person to be healed surrounded by family, neighbors, and others from the Puerto Rican–American community, also functions to increase expectations and emotional arousal. Once treated, many individuals return to attend the *reuniones* on a regular basis; therefore many of the audience at a healing session are people who themselves have already been healed.

In terms of mastery and learning, the acquisition of one's own protective spirits would inevitably produce a greater confidence in one's ability to cope with adversity. It is necessary to remember to pray to the spirits and make the proper offerings, but if that is done, then the spirits should be available to help when they are needed.

Much advice giving goes on during healing sessions with *espiritistas*, both in private consultations and in public *reuniones*. Because the healer often knows the client or has heard gossip about him or her, the advice may be targeted on highly specific behaviors. The following is an example given by Harwood of a public healing session:

Moving from one member of the audience to another, the medium stopped in front of two members of the *centro*, a mother of about 37 and her daughter, about 16. The daughter was known to the membership as a troublemaker—quick to take offence and frequently involved in arguments.

MEDIUM: You'd like to be a boy, wouldn't you?

GIRL: No.

MEDIUM: You make love to the boys instead of them doing it to you. Don't look at me like that, or I'll tell your mother what happened. You know what happened. (To the mother) You are the man and the woman in your house. [She is separated from her husband.] Your children make you suffer a lot. You give them everything and don't get anything back from them. Why don't you go to a movie or a dance? You have to entertain yourself, have fun. Go out to a movie or dance![12]

On other occasions, the *espiritista* may advise clients how to dress, how to behave in social situations, how to raise their children, or to seek medical care for physical complaints. Some of the advice comes directly from the *espiritista* herself, while at other times the advice is from one of the *espiritista*'s protective spirits, speaking through her.

Techniques of Therapy

Confession is one of the most important therapeutic techniques used in *espiritismo*. The fact that the confession is often elicited by spirits (who are presumed to know everything) speaking through the mouth of the *espiritista,* and often occurs in public *reuniones,* makes it all the more effective. Abreaction often accompanies confession, as when the wayward *causa* is identified as that of a lover or spouse who is now dead but toward whom the client feels much guilt. All of us would like to be able to atone for past misdeeds and expiate our guilt, and this possibility is built into *espiritismo.*

Suggestion is used liberally and is one of the most visible aspects of the healing sessions. The client is advised to pay homage to his or her protective spirits, and this may be done through candles, statues, incense, or pictures of specific saints. An important step toward changing one's behavior is to rid the house or apartment of the offending *causas,* and to accomplish this a special housecleaning, cigar smoke, and containers of water may be prescribed by the *espiritista.* Other symbolic objects (e.g., incense, black coffee) may be used to help attract protective spirits to replace those that are departing. Most of the objects needed for *espiritismo* healing are available for sale in *botánicas,*[13] small shops that function as folk pharmacies; the number of such *botánicas* on the streets of the South Bronx testifies to the prevalence of *espiritismo* beliefs and practices.

Altered states of consciousness are also integral to *espiritismo,* especially in communicating with the spirits, and the ability to enter an altered state of consciousness at will is regarded as a hallmark of an effective healer. While the spirits are possessing the healer, the client can pursue a dialogue with them, questioning them about why they are causing problems and ascertaining what actions or behavior is required to induce them to leave the client alone. Occasionally the client will also enter an altered state of consciousness during the healing session, but this is less common.

Group healing techniques are integral to *espiritismo.* The client is usually accompanied to the *centro* by family members and/or friends and they often become involved in the healing process. They provide information regarding the client's history and behavior, and may also be given specific tasks to do by the *espiritista* to help the person get well. Many clients who are helped by *espiritismo* return to the *centro* regularly; watching other people going through the same healing process that they underwent reinforces their belief in the efficacy of their protective spirits. Such *reuniones*, then, serve a group therapy function for the spectators as well as the participants.

Espiritismo *in the Mental Health System*

Mental health professionals who work with Puerto Rican–Americans in New York City are usually aware that the alternative *espiritismo* healing system is in competition with them. It is relatively common for clients to utilize both systems simultaneously in order to maximize their chances of improvement; unless asked, such individuals will not usually tell the mental health professional about their sessions with the *espiritista*.

In the early 1970s, Lincoln Community Mental Health Center in the South Bronx, whose mental health services were under the direction of Dr. Pedro Ruiz, began an informal collaboration with *espiritistas* in the neighborhood.[14] Mental health professionals were encouraged to identify *espiritistas* and visit their *centros*. *Espiritistas* were brought to the mental health center and conducted healing sessions so that the professionals could observe. Both were encouraged to exchange views. According to Ruiz, "discussions of symptoms and treatment goals took place in regularly scheduled workshops and seminars where there [was] a free exchange of views by practitioners from both systems."[15] From these exchanges a system of informal collaboration emerged, which resulted in joint treatment such as the following case described by Ruiz:

> The patient in question, treated during early 1977, was a 26 year old male who was born in Puerto Rico and had lived in mainland United States since the age of 17. His father had committed suicide in 1974 while hospitalized in a state mental hospital in Puerto Rico. The patient married a Puerto Rican woman who had previously migrated from the island, and had two children. While both the patient and his wife were Catholics, the wife was also a devout follower of Spiritism.
>
> For seven years the patient had worked successfully as manager of a laundry store in the South Bronx section of New York City where they lived. Late in 1976 he began to suffer from skin lesions,

characterized by blisters which became ulcers and later scars. Appearing first on his wrists, these later spread to his forearms and legs. As sometimes occurs among Hispanics, he resisted seeking medical help, and it was not until the lesions began to appear on his neck that he decided to seek medical help at a nearby municipal hospital in Manhattan. He feared that the lesions might spread to his face, affecting his appearance and thus threatening his "masculine image."

When first seen at the hospital he had great difficulty in communicating with the attending physician as his English was poor and the doctor spoke no Spanish. He was given a prescription for a skin ointment which he used for two weeks without any improvement in his condition. Quite disappointed, he returned to the hospital seeking further help. On his second visit he saw a different physician but, as this doctor did not speak Spanish either, communication problems continued. A scrub biopsy and blood samples were taken and he was told to return a week later for the results. On his return he was told that he might have "lupus" and was asked to sign a special permission form authorizing the hospital to give him a new medication which was being tested there. On this occasion he was quite frightened when he left the hospital and was extremely concerned about his physical condition and about the well being of his family if he were to die. He was afraid that he had cancer and decided not to return to the hospital. Needless to say, he did not take either of the medications given to him. A few weeks later his overall personality and functioning began to deteriorate. He felt quite depressed, lost his appetite and sexual desire, began to lose weight, and had difficulties in falling asleep. For the first time in seven years he began to have difficulties in keeping up with his work because he felt tired in the morning and stayed in bed later. He also had difficulties in concentrating at work as he was continually worried about his condition. His self-esteem, pride, and dignity rapidly diminished. He began to think that the best solution to his problems was to commit suicide as his father had done.

At this point his wife, who was quite worried, decided to seek spiritual help at the Spiritist Center. During the spiritual consultation she was told by the medium that her husband was suffering from a "causa" and that she should bring him to the center for proper spiritual care. She discussed the matter with her husband who, being quite desperate, agreed to go with her to see the medium. This was the first time he had visited a spiritist center. On consultation he was told that he suffered from both a spiritual and a material (physical) "causa." The spiritual "causa" had been inflicted upon him by a woman friend who was trying to destroy his marriage because she was in love with him. Furthermore he was told that on a special occasion he had eaten a "preparation" prepared by a "santero" to influence him. He was told that his spiritual problem was probably complicating his physical condition. It was recommended that he participate in a special ceremony at the Spiritist Center for the purpose of liberating himself from his bad influence (despojo) and that he visit the "Centro" regularly to pray.

Fortunately the "Centro" in question was one of the few with which we have developed a liaison through our program at the Lincoln Hospital Community Mental Health Center. The medium thus discussed the case with the nonprofessional mental health worker assigned by the Mental Health Center to the Spiritual Center. After this discussion we proceeded, at the request of the medium and with the patient's permission, to provide a mental health evaluation of the patient. At this time we determined that he was suffering from a nonpsychotic "depressive reaction" and that he was in need of further examination regarding the diagnoses of his skin condition. As regards his "depression," we decided not to intervene as the patient had developed excellent rapport with the medium and was, rightly so, distrustful of medical professionals in general. We told the medium that we would be available to him if he should need our help, particularly regarding the patient's suicidal thoughts. We also told him that we would like, eventually, to take the patient to the hospital in order to further study his skin condition. The medium, as a Hispanic, had no problems in communicating with the patient or in understanding him from a cultural point of view. With hope, support, and reassurance, the "depression" slowly began to lift and a few weeks later the patient agreed to come to the hospital. This time a Hispanic physician attended him and determined that he was suffering from an allergic reaction secondary to a new detergent that had been introduced at the laundry where he worked. After application of proper measures the skin lesions disappeared and, by the spring of 1977, the patient had totally recovered from both his mental and physical difficulties. He continues to visit the Spiritual Center with his wife and has become a devout follower of Spiritism.[16]

Both anthropologists quoted above who studied *espiritismo* also made attempts to foster collaboration between the *espiritistas* and health and mental health professionals. In Garrison's experience, "all of the nine spiritist *centro* presidents I interviewed formally were open to such collaboration. The health and mental health professionals with whom I discussed it have been much more reluctant."[17] Harwood instituted a model program in a neighborhood health center (Neighborhood Medical Care Demonstration) in the Bronx, in which he educated the health professionals on how to work most effectively with Puerto Rican patients—e.g., prescribe medicine with directions that are consistent with the Puerto Rican hot-cold theory of disease.[18]

Ruiz and his colleagues at Lincoln Community Mental Health Center had originally hoped to move from an informal to a more formal collaboration between *espiritistas* and mental health professionals. In 1976, he wrote: "The next step may be to mount a formal training for folk healers that would acquaint them with the medical aspects of psychiatric health and illness and perhaps lead to credentialed status on our mental health teams as assistant therapists."[19]

For a variety of reasons, this formal collaboration never came about. One strong reason was the opposition of the Catholic Church, which believes that *espiritismo* is the work of the devil; collaboration would thus have engendered strong opposition. Mental health professionals, with a few exceptions, have also not been enthusiastic. They are already regarded by many of their medical colleagues as fringe members of the healing professions, and collaboration with those professing to communicate with spirits would not enhance their standing. Further, over the last decade, more Puerto Rican mental health professionals have been trained, thus making available to clients in the mental health centers therapists who share a worldview and a language with Puerto Rican clients.

Despite these impediments to collaboration, informal referrals of clients between mental health professionals and indigenous therapists continues to take place in the growing Hispanic communities in the United States: Not just among Mexican-Americans or Puerto Rican–Americans, but also among Cubans, Salvadorans, and other Latinos migrating northward. Such collaboration is likely to continue and should be encouraged, for it improves the services available to a segment of the population that is not otherwise being served.

Chapter 10

Medicine Men Among Native Americans

If one wants to appreciate why Anglo psychotherapists are ineffectual for Navaho Indians who have problems of living, it is only necessary to drive west from Albuquerque on Interstate 40. Shortly before arriving at the Gallup Indian Medical Center, the central medical and psychiatric facility for the region, one passes Fort Wingate, where on September 22, 1861, United States soldiers shot and bayoneted Navaho women and children in a dispute over who had won a horse race.

Crossing the Arizona state line and turning north, one comes to Window Rock, site of the Navaho Area Mental Health Office. Just down the road is Fort Defiance, from which in 1864 several thousand Navahos began their Long Walk into forced exile in New Mexico so that their land could be turned over to ranchers and miners. When the Navahos were allowed to return, several years later, and reclaim the poorer parts of their land, one fourth of them had died of disease or starvation.

Continuing northward, one comes to Chinle, with a small Indian Health Service Hospital. It stands at the western end of the Canyon de Chelly, the last stronghold of the Navahos who resisted being forced off their land until Colonel Kit Carson hunted them out like dogs, destroying all their homes and food supplies and cutting down an orchard of five thousand peach trees for good measure. Such treatment from Anglos is deeply etched into the Navaho history and psyche, and affects how they see themselves and who can be trusted. Perhaps most disconcerting, given this history, is Dee Brown's historical assessment in *Bury My Heart at Wounded Knee:* "Bad as it was, the Navahos would come to know that they were the least unfortunate of all the western Indians."[1]

Given a century of starvation, struggle, deceit, and disease as white men pursued their "manifest destiny," it is no surprise that Native Americans today have little faith in government services. This is especially true for mental health services, where trust between client and therapist is an essential part of the therapeutic process. The lack of trust in government services is yet another reason why Native Americans in recent years have increasingly moved toward setting up their own mental health services, often utilizing their indigenous therapists (medicine men) in the process.

The Navaho school for medicine men is a good example of this trend. Located at Rough Rock, Arizona, in the heart of the Navaho reservation, it was conceived by the Navahos in the late 1960s as they realized that the older medicine men were dying off and new ones were not being trained. The school does not instruct the Navaho herbalists who dispense medicinal plants, nor the diagnosticians who use hand trembling or star gazing to ascertain the cause of a person's illness, but only the most important Navaho indigenous therapist, the medicine man.

To obtain funding for the school, the Navahos first applied to the federal Office of Economic Opportunity, which turned them down. A special mental health training program in the National Institute of Mental Health was more receptive, and in 1969 the Navaho school was funded. Understanding of the program at the Washington level was limited, however, as is illustrated by an official project summary that stated: "This program provides mental health manpower for that proportion of the Navaho Nation still nonlingual and unable to benefit from Anglo forms of therapy."[2] Whether the writer equated non-English-speaking with being "nonlingual," or thought that large numbers of Navaho were mutes, is not entirely clear. NIMH at the time was supporting training programs for psychiatrists, psychologists, social workers, and psychiatric nurses, the therapists of Anglo culture, so in fact the support of training for Navaho therapists was logical and consistent.

The purpose of the training program was to teach apprentice medicine men (and one woman) the exhaustive and intricate Navaho healing ceremonies, using experienced medicine men as teachers. These ceremonies, of which there are over forty, take from two to nine days to perform. Dr. Robert L. Bergman, a government psychiatrist who was very supportive of the training program and who assisted by teaching the apprentice medicine men Anglo medicine as well, likened a medicine man conducting a five-day ceremony to a minister conducting "a 60 hour service consisting of reciting the entire Bible from memory while playing the organ and making the stained-glass windows of the church."[3]

Most mental health professionals who have observed Navaho healing ceremonies have been deeply impressed by their power and efficacy. The ceremonies combine ritual with poetry, song, dance, drama, and painting in a religious-artistic-psychiatric amalgam more akin to healing sessions in Bali than to anything found in Western culture. Dr. Alexander H. Leighton, a highly respected psychiatrist who once studied the Navaho, summarized a typical ceremony as conducted by a medicine man (also known as a Singer):

> The patient and others who wish to join in the treatment undress outside. Four pokers are laid on the ground, radiating from the fire toward the cardinal points of the compass, the homes of the gods. The pokers are made of carefully selected lightning-struck pinyon and cedar and represent men who chase evil away.
>
> The patient and the other participants enter the hogan and sit around the fire at specified spots. The heat grows intense. At the fire is a pot which contains an emetic composed of buckthorne, limberpine, bearberry, wild currant, juniper, and Colorado blue spruce. Each person gets a portion of it and washes himself from the feet up, then drinks and vomits. The Singer takes a brush made of wing and tail feathers from an eagle and an owl feather that fell out while the bird was flying. He brushes the patient, the others present, and then the whole hut, making motions that sweep evil toward the door. The ends of the pokers are warmed and applied to the patient's body by the Singer. Then the others apply them to

themselves, rubbing the warm wood on any part that hurts. The patient and the other participants walk around the fire sunwise, stepping over the pokers. Evil cannot cross the pokers and thus they leave evil behind. The live coals represent lightning. Songs and prayers accompany each stage of the ritual. The heat is continuously very intense and all sweat profusely.

At the end, the door blanket is lifted with one of the pokers and the patient steps out, followed by the others. After fire, ashes, and vomitus have been disposed of, all return and the Singer, using the eagle feathers, sprinkles participants and hut with a fragrant lotion made of mint, horsemint, windodor, and penny-royal, kept in an abalone shell. Glowing coals are placed before each participant and on these is sprinkled a fumigant made of a plant root, sulphur, corn meal, down from chickadee, titmouse, woodpecker, bluebird, and yellow warbler. These have been previously ground together by a virgin while the Singer sang songs. Every one breathes the fumes and rubs them into his body. After this the coals are thrown out the smoke hole, taking evil with them. [4]

Ceremonies such as this continue for up to nine days, and involve the family and friends of the person being healed. The therapist shares a worldview with the client and knows that the cause of the problem is disharmony between the client and the universe (including other men, nature, and the gods). The medicine man shares Navaho values with the client—the primary importance of family and clan, the desirability of family members' dependence on each other, the superiority of group over individual decisions, and the low status accorded the accumulation of wealth beyond a basic needs level. The medicine man is also familiar with the interpersonal problems that arise when Navaho extended families are forced to live close together in a single-room hogan throughout a long and cold winter. Client and medicine man share a common system for categorizing certain symptoms and diseases, such as "moth craziness," in which the person has uncontrolled paroxysms of erratic and aggressive behavior (and thus may jump into a fire like a moth), or "ghost sickness," in which the person experiences confusion, panic, or extreme anxiety.

The Navaho healing ceremony "constitutes a symbolic reenactment of something which went wrong in the past and which is now being set right."[5] The medicine man and his client view the individual as a totality with nature and the universe. Rather than a dualism of body and soul, a Navaho healer sees "personality as a totality . . . a part of a family, clan and terrain . . . inseparable from the ecology of his clan and tribe. Medicine is not only dedicated to restore the health and harmony of the individual, but to restore family and clan ecology, and any segments which have become disharmonious with nature."[6] Such an approach to healing is now labeled by Western medicine as holistic.

The personality characteristics of most Navaho medicine men are therapeutic, according to a psychiatrist who interviewed fifteen of them. "These men seem to me . . . to be for the most part stable, dependable persons. They are cultural leaders, often quite fatherly and kind, but also shrewd and careful."[7] The medicine man functions as priest, community leader, and artist as well as healer, so deviants are not likely to be tolerated by the Navaho community in that role. Training is arduous and involves considerable sacrifice. According to D. F. Sandner, for example, one medicine man took "three solid years to learn the Night Chant from his instructor whom he supported during that time and also gave gifts of livestock."[8] The apprentice is considered ready to practice as a medicine man when he can carry out the entire healing ceremony without a mistake. Ultimately it is the Navaho community, and not just the teacher, that accredits the apprentice medicine man: "The community has the final power for that, because the Indian community will not simply accept certification by the teacher. A medicine man is fully accepted after several years of public scrutiny, not only of his practice but of his life as well."[9]

Preparations for a Navaho healing ceremony are expensive and may cost the family the equivalent of several months' income. This induces great expectations in the person being healed, for "the Navaho, like ourselves, are prone to develop strong faith in anything that has cost them time, money and thought and are very loath to have it said that the show was after all a failure."[10] Emotional arousal is also facilitated by the prestige and authority of the medicine man, who is "the object of respect and sometimes fear . . . the medicine man is likely to generate ambivalent feelings."[11]

The ceremony itself acts as a powerful stimulant to increase the client's expectations. Drama, poetry, song, and music are all included, and the ceremony becomes an aesthetic pageant of Navaho history and cultural identity. The authority of the medicine man derives directly from the Navaho gods, who are an integral part of the healing ceremony, and "in the height of the ceremonial the patient himself becomes one of the Holy Beings, puts his feet in their moccasins, and breathes in the strength of the sun."[12] Added to this is the pressure on the person from participating family and friends, many of whom have contributed to the preparations. Given these accumulated expectations, it is little wonder that Navaho healing ceremonies are very efficacious and have a high rate of cure.

Finally, there is the sense of mastery the Navaho client derives from the ceremony. At one point the medicine man makes a sand painting that addresses the client's needs. Such paintings are very elaborate and may take several hours to complete. As soon as the sand painting is finished the client sits on it, thereby transferring the power of the painting (and the gods) directly into his body. The painting is then destroyed, but the client now has powers with which to overcome adversity.

In addition to the more mystical aspects of mastery, mundane learning and advice giving is also part of the healing ceremony. As described by Alexander and Dorothea Leighton,

> a good deal of informal chat goes on between the Singer and the patient and the other members of the family. Since the Singer is usually an intellectual type, often knowing the habits and tendencies of his clientele in the same manner as did the old country doctor, it is very probable that he often does what the country doctor did—gives good sound practical advice based on his knowledge of his people. It is to be suspected that quite a few personal and interpersonal problems get a boost nearer adjustment at the time of a ceremonial.[13]

The techniques used by Navaho medicine men vary from ceremony to ceremony, according to the needs of individual clients.

As mentioned in Chapter 6, the techniques are consistent with Navaho cultural values. Pharmacological preparations are often included, such as the emetic used in the ceremony described earlier. Physical therapies such as a sweat bath or the sauna-like atmosphere of the healing ceremony are quite common. Confession is almost always included, with the subject of the healing confessing to taboos broken or cultural roles unfulfilled. When a healing ceremony fails, it is often said to be because the subject did not confess fully.

Suggestion is the main psychological technique used in Navaho healing, just as it is in healing ceremonies in most of the world. Evil is swept out the door and thrown out the smoke hole with the embers from the dying fire, leaving the client clean and well. The medicine man proclaims over and over that the person is getting well, and this idea is repeated in songs, poems, and prayers, hour after hour throughout the length of the ceremony:

> Today you must make me well. All the things that have harmed me will leave.
> I will walk with a cool body after they have left me.
> Inside of me today all will be well, all fever will have come out of me, and go away from me, and leave my head cool!
> I will hear today, I will see today, I will be in my right mind today!
> Today I will walk out, today everything evil will leave me, I will be as I was before, I will have a cool breeze over my body, I will walk with a light body.[14]

Altered states of consciousness are not a prominent part of Navaho healing, though the rhythmic chanting and the rattle used by the medicine man undoubtedly bring about such states to some degree in suggestible participants. Peyote is associated with Navahos by many people, but its use is confined to purely religious ceremonies and it is scorned by most medicine men.

Psychoanalytic techniques, on the other hand, are prominently used by Navahos and partially explain the fascination these healing ceremonies have held for American anthropologists and psychiatrists. The client is encouraged to recall dreams, which are then interpreted by the medicine man in the group setting. Great importance is placed on the unconscious by Navaho medicine men, as Dr. Robert Bergman discovered when he went to interview Mr. Largewhiskers, a well-known healer. Asked to become a consultant to the Navaho medicine men training school, Mr. Largewhiskers agreed but told Dr. Bergman that Navaho ideas of illness probably would not be comprehensible to the Anglo doctor. As Bergman related it, Mr. Largewhiskers patiently explained: "I don't know what you learned from books, but the most important thing I learned from my grandfathers was there is a part of the mind that we don't really know about and that it is that part that is most important in whether we become sick or remain well."[15] Bergman also found that Navaho medicine men interpreted a person's errors (e.g., slips of the tongue) psychodynamically.[16]

Since healing ceremonies last several days, there is inevitably much interaction between the client and the group of family members and close friends who participate. This takes place under the eyes of the medicine man, whose task it is to put interpersonal relationships back into harmony with nature. The Navaho healing ceremony is therefore a form of group therapy, and individual healing (as in individual psychotherapy) is virtually unknown. All Navaho therapy is group therapy, which is consistent with the supreme importance Navaho culture places on the ability of the individual to exist within the group setting.

Active medicine men have remained an important symbol of Navaho culture on the reservation. There is a formal organization of medicine men, which applied to the U.S. Department of Health and Human Services to be designated as eligible for third-party payments for Medicaid and Medicare patients; their application stalled, however, over questions of quality assurance and the Navaho's reluctance to furnish the government with written details of the healing ceremony.

Physicians working within the Indian Health Service in Navaho areas have learned to refer appropriate cases to medicine men, and medicine men in turn often refer cases to the physicians. Dr. Bergman relates the history of a Navaho Vietnam War veteran with extreme anxiety whom he referred for a healing ceremony called the Enemy Way.[17] In another instance, a young Navaho woman presented herself at an Indian Health Service hospital "in a prolonged and apparently intractable hysterical convulsive state"; using hypnosis, the physician ascertained that the woman "had panicked over a serious violation of a traditional Navaho taboo" and referred her to a medicine man, "who provided definitive treatment."[18] Even when medicine men are not needed, it is useful for health professionals who have Navaho patients to understand their culture so as to make Anglo healing arts more effective. Alexander Leighton gives a good example of why this is so:

> If an Indian is told to take digitalis every day he will probably munch a few tablets and then forget about them. If he is told that this green medicine comes from the leaves of the foxglove, that his body must never be without it any more than his mind without a good song, and that he must take it every morning of his life when the first brightness of the day is in the east, one stands a much better chance of having the instructions carried out.[19]

Other Native American Tribes

Although the Navaho medicine man training school is the best-known of such programs, other tribes have moved toward making their mental health services more relevant to their cultural needs. A good example is the Papago Indian psychology services set up in the early 1970s by Native Americans in consultation with the University of Arizona Department of Psychology in Tucson.[20] Papago Indians were recruited and trained as mental health workers. The training consisted of "interview skills and clinical evaluation . . . once those skills were in hand, training moved to techniques of supportive treatment, marital and family counseling, and individual counseling." These mental health workers were then used as primary therapists for Native Americans referred for counseling and were given ongoing access to supervision and consultation. In addition, Papago medicine men were consulted "about cases which involve traditional Papago beliefs" and the medicine men were "considered as professional consultants and paid a professional fee."

According to a psychologist involved in setting up the program, there are many aspects of Papago culture that make tribal therapists more effective than their Anglo counterparts for Papago clients. Age and social status elicit great respect among the Papago, "and respect within the Papago culture is often expressed by silence." Eye contact is to be avoided even among friends, and those who insist on eye contact may be regarded as rude or angry. Psychotherapy tends to be crisis oriented, and may consist of a single session lasting several hours rather than scheduled meetings each week. A Papago expects a therapist or healer to be very active in the healing session, and to make suggestions freely rather than passively wait for the client to decide the next steps.

Confrontation, on the other hand, is assiduously avoided by Papagos, and "the therapist who confronts a Papago client in a manner that causes intense anxiety will lose the client." Even an opening question such as "What brings you here" may be interpreted by a Papago as confrontational before therapist and client have had an opportunity to exchange amenities and get to know each other. As with the Navahos, group therapies have been found to be especially effective within the Papago cultural framework. Most commonly seen by the Papago mental health workers were clients who had problems with their spouse or children, or with other persons, or who suffered from alcohol abuse, depression, and suicidal thoughts.

Most Native American tribes have an abundance of individuals with these problems. According to Dr. Robert Bergman, "there are men and women in every Indian community who have years of experience talking with people about personal problems."[21] The logical thing, of course, is to connect the individuals in need with the personnel resources available in a formalized therapy system. The use of indigenous therapists ensures that the local variants of human problems—for example, *windigo* among the Ojibwa, *hiwa-itck* among the Mohave, and *wacinko* among the Sioux—will be understood for what they are and treated appropriately in the framework of the culture.

Within the past decade, more Anglo mental health services have begun to appreciate the unique skills and effectiveness of Native American indigenous therapists. In Portland, the University of Oregon Health Sciences Center advertised for a medicine man to come on staff.[22] In Seattle, the Indian Health Service clinic employed an apprentice medicine man.[23] In Michigan, the Chippewa Indians sought permission to use federal money to hire a medicine man for its alcoholism treatment program.[24] And across the border in Ontario, the provincial government approved the hiring of an Ojibwa medicine man for a rural mental health program for Indians.[25]

The hiring of such individuals as therapists is solidly based on theoretical foundations such as are described in Part I of this book, but also on observation by those who have seen them work. N. K. Opler testified to the efficacy of Ute Indian healers,[26] and M. E. Opler was similarly impressed by Apache medicine men.[27] Anthropologist S. H. Posinsky studied a Yoruk Indian woman healer and described his findings as follows: "Her psychotherapeutic skills are revealed not only in her treatment of psychosis, neurosis and psychosomatic ailments, but also in her voluntary decision to limit child therapy only to behavioral disorders."[28]

Eskimo Shamans

At the International Symposium on Circumpolar Health in 1974, scientists from ten countries agreed that the changing culture of Eskimos had been socially and emotionally disastrous for them. It was said that "the social and behavioral disorders of Alaskan Eskimos have been accompanied by a virtual epidemic of suicides . . . the homicide rate has doubled . . . domestic disturbances and child abuse had risen . . . these problems were related to pervasive abuse of alcohol." Conference participants also agreed that "efforts to meet the mental health crisis among the 25,000 Eskimos in Alaska with modern psychiatric methods have failed because of the cultural gap between Eskimos and whites." There was one hopeful note, however: "There is promise of success in treating Eskimo mental disturbances by indigenous techniques, including the use of native healers or shamans, the specialists said."[29]

The Eskimo shaman was thought to be long since dead, replaced by the pharmacy of the Indian Health Service and set adrift on an ice floe like an aging and useless Eskimo. Once a community leader and stabilizing influence, the shaman lost power early in the twentieth century when white whalers came and broke the sacred taboos, and missionaries came and offered medicines more powerful than those the shaman had to offer. By 1955, in remote Eskimo villages such as Gambell on St. Lawrence Island, it was still possible to find an occasional shaman in practice, but no young people were being trained to replace the older ones as they died.[30]

Reviving the concept of shamans may seem like a radical idea, but given the magnitude of Eskimo social problems, a radical solution is demanded. Probably nowhere in the United States has a traditional culture been disrupted so massively in so short a time as when the airplane, commercial fishing, snowmobiles, television, and oil exploration suddenly descended upon remote villages that had undergone little change in centuries. The change culminated in 1971, when, through the Alaska Native Claims Settlement Act, corporations were set up under which Eskimos whose early life skills emphasized stalking a walrus or harpooning a whale were suddenly expected to manage millions of dollars in financial assets like an Ivy League–trained veteran of Wall Street. A remarkable number of Eskimos have successfully made the transition, but it has often been at the cost of massive interpersonal and intrapersonal problems. Mental health services set up under the Indian Health Service have been ineffective and irrelevant, as might be expected, given the lack of a shared worldview, the nontherapeutic personality characteristics of many therapists, and the inability of the government mental health services to raise client expectations or bring about a sense of mastery.

Traditional Eskimo culture had five principal theories to explain deviant behavior[31]—theories that could be used today with only minor modifications:

> *Breach of taboo:* Traditionally, Eskimos believed that mental illness could be produced if a person broke one of the many sacred taboos, most of which concern the hunting of sea mammals. For instance, one should never allow dogs to chew on the bones of the whale. The illness caused by this breach could be translated into more modern terms as the result of guilt for

having done something one should not do. Abreaction and public confession would be just as therapeutic now as they were in the past.

Soul loss: The theory that illness was caused by one's soul wandering off (or being sneezed or frightened "out") was very prevalent. The soul could then be captured and held by evil spirits. Translated into psychiatric terms, the evil spirits could be unconscious conflicts that hold the soul; release would come when these conflicts were resolved.

Object intrusion: The idea that a physical object had intruded to cause disease would have to be refuted, but it is a short step toward seeing the "object" as an undesirable or unpermissible thought—e.g., a compulsion to steal. This thought could then be extruded or expelled by the shaman-therapist.

Sorcery: The idea of sorcery and witchcraft would have to be modified considerably. First of all, there would no longer be any evil shamans; all shaman-therapists would be regarded as benevolent. Therapeutically, however, it might well be possible to use some of the "homework" assigned by traditional shamans to counteract sorcery to correspond with the "homework" of behavioral therapy to treat analagous problems of mental illness.

Spirit intrusion: This is the most common Eskimo explanation of psychosis. It could be modified as necessary to a chemical basis —e.g., the "spirit" would be thought of as some metabolic intruder in the nervous system.

The personality characteristics of shamans in the past were generally thought to be therapeutic. Jane Murphy, one of the only people to do a study of this question, concluded that the best shamans were stable, intelligent, and empathetic. "The full-fledged shaman," she wrote, "who is capable of dealing with the crises of illness and death and of offering psychological support to the individuals taken into his spiritual custody displays qualities that can hardly be separated from those of leadership, responsibility, and power."[32] Modern-day shaman–mental health workers could be selected on the basis of such personality characteristics.

The idea of therapy and counseling on a one-to-one basis is foreign to Eskimo culture. According to one expert, "Eskimos would regard the seclusiveness of the relationship as impolite, boorish. They have no concept of going to another person for help, and it is considered childish to ask questions."[33] Rather the expectation of Eskimos is that problems should be worked out in a group setting. Traditionally, this was done in the *karigi,* the community meeting place for Eskimos during the long, dark months. It is there that the shaman effected many of his cures, while a large group watched. Especially important group activities were the Messenger Feast and the Spring Whaling Ceremony.

When trapping replaced sea-mammal hunting in the 1920s, the *karigi* began to lose its importance. Instead of living together during the winter, the Eskimos began living alone in distant cabins. Some of the functions of the *karigi* were slowly lost to the church, school, store, and movie theater, and by 1960 it was difficult to find a functioning *karigi* remaining (two at Point Hope were being used as clubhouses).

The *karigi* provided a setting for group therapy, and was a highly integrative structure in the society.[34] In terms of mental health needs for Eskimo society, it would be desirable to have such a structure today, and there is no reason why a modern-day *karigi* could not be built as part of newly developing villages— e.g., around government and oil installations. It might include the functions of clubhouse and gymnasium, but would also give the shaman-therapist a place to meet with groups from the community. For instance, he or she might meet with groups of mothers to discuss traditional Eskimo child-rearing practices that lead to friendliness and cooperation, and the advantages of these practices over some Western methods. The shaman-therapist might also meet with groups of alcoholics or juvenile delinquents, even in a public meeting, as might have been done in traditional Eskimo society. Another group in need of counseling services are Eskimo students sent to boarding schools often hundreds of miles from home for higher education; depression, alcohol abuse, and anomie among this group have been very high.

The reactivation of elements found in the traditional culture as a hypothetical model for Eskimo mental health services does not mean that the services are designed to be technologically retrogressive—indeed, such a system would be progressive by Western standards. What it means is that the mental health services would be those of Eskimos, not those of psychiatrists from another culture. If created and run by Eskimos themselves, such services would promote dignity, a commodity in short supply in subcultures. The promotion of dignity is itself a step toward a better self-image and thus better mental health. The goal is for an Eskimo to be proud that he or she is an Eskimo; such pride does not come from designer jeans alone.

Perhaps the best summary of psychotherapy services for Native Americans is provided by Drs. Wolfgang Jilek and Norman Todd, physicians who worked for many years with Canadian Indians in the Fraser River Valley in British Columbia. In an article entitled "Witchdoctors Succeed Where Doctors Fail," they wrote:

> The conclusion to be drawn is that many Indian patients are likely to benefit more from involvement in native therapeutic activities than from exclusive contact with Western resources. The persistence or revival of indigenous healing should be looked upon as an asset in the total health care for the native population. Here in the Fraser Valley a two-pronged approach is made in health care delivery to Indian patients. This aims at combining Western treatment with indigenous procedures in close cooperation with native therapists.[35]

Chapter 11

Witchdoctors in the Third World

The utilization of indigenous healers in the health and mental health systems of developing countries has become a subject of considerable interest in recent years. In 1977, the World Health Organization convened a meeting on the Promotion and Development of Traditional Medicine, and in 1979 the First World Congress of Folk Medicine was held in Peru. The University of Arizona School of Medicine began tours to Africa for American physicians interested in traditional medicine, while *Lancet,* the world's most influential medical journal, editorialized in 1980:

Traditional practitioners constitute a very large corps of people who identify themselves, and are identified by the population, as health workers. Already living on the spot they can, the argument runs, with some retraining and technical support, make a useful contribution to health care in existing circumstances. . . . Traditional medical practitioners are culturally integrated with the population; they talk to people and are trusted. Even where modern health care is available the people may still prefer to consult their traditional practitioners for certain troubles. This decision may be quite reasonable, because systems of traditional medicine often have a holistic approach to illness, in which the patient is seen in relation to the environment, ecological and social.[1]

Part of the appeal of traditional medicine to Western observers is undoubtedly its holistic approach of viewing the patient (in medicine) or client (in psychotherapy) as more than simply a sum of organ systems and neurophysiological hydraulics. The traditional healer is renowned for treating the whole person and paying more attention to family and social relationships as they may influence or be influenced by the person's malady. As described by Dr. Thomas A. Lambo in talking of African medicine: "The concepts of health and disease can be regarded as constituting a continuous transition with almost imperceptible gradations. In these and related cultures, the determinants of health and disease are conceptualized holistically. Psychotherapy . . . is an indispensable phase of a variety of institutionalized processes to promote human well-being."[2] Because the healer plays a variety of roles in the community, he or she is able to address many different aspects of the problems of living brought by the client. As one observer describes it: "Your rural witchdoctor is, in addition to medicine man, something of a social and probation worker, teacher, priest and JP [justice of the peace]. He may tackle the problem, of which his patient's symptoms are only a part, with an across-the-board approach impossible to the fragmented social, penal, and medical services in the West."[3]

Regardless of what one believes about the desirability of promoting or not promoting the use of indigenous therapists in third world cultures, the fact remains that such therapists are today the only psychotherapeutic (and often medical) resource for the majority of the world's population. In Latin America, *curanderas* and other healers form the backbone of rural health care; Dobkin, for example, estimated that 10 percent of men in northern Peru are healers on a part-time basis.[4] Throughout the Arab world, sheikhs and *marabouts*, usually thought of as Islamic religious leaders, are the primary first source for care of health and personal problems for most people. In Africa, it has been estimated that there is one traditional *mganga* for every 350 residents of Dar es Salaam, the capital of Tanzania, and the number is higher in rural areas.[5] In

Nigeria, it is said, "eighty percent of the rural population are ill-provided with doctors, nurses, midwives and other paramedical health workers. . . . The traditional healers are the only available source of health care."[6]

In Indonesia, over three quarters of the people who come to general hospitals for care have already consulted traditional healers;[7] in Singapore and Thailand, the figure is 90 percent.[8] Malaysia has ten practicing *bomohs* for every Western-trained physician; even in the elite psychiatric unit at the University Medical College, over half the patients have already consulted a *bomoh*.[9] In South Korea, there are estimated to be 100,000 shamans, one shaman for every 314 people.[10] In southern Indian villages, a survey identified a traditional healer for every 391 people;[11] another study in the same area estimated that "the indigenous medical systems generate primary medical care services nearly eight times the volume of patient-visits offered by the organized government health system of the area."[12]

There is every reason to suspect that traditional healers are highly effective in treating clients who come to them with problems of living. The healers share the worldview of the client and are able to put a name on what is wrong; they often have therapeutic personality characteristics; their reputation is usually sufficient to raise the client's expectations; and they utilize techniques that generate emotional arousal and give the client a sense of mastery.

It is the techniques of their therapy that are most difficult for us to accept. How can witchdoctors, relying primarily on such techniques as suggestion and hypnosis, achieve as good results as Western therapists, who use techniques that are so much more "sophisticated"? First, as we have seen, therapists elsewhere use on occasion the same sophisticated techniques as Western therapists. Second and more important, we consistently underestimate the power of techniques like suggestion and hypnosis. Their low status in Western therapy blinds us to their real strengths. Yet the basic components of psychotherapy operate in all cultures and lead to a remarkably high level of effectiveness in healers everywhere.

A Kali Therapist

Given what is now known about psychotherapy and its effective components, it would seem reasonable for mental health professionals in third world countries to establish collaborative working relationships with indigenous healers. This in fact has been done in a number of places, and the reports are encouraging.

An example of such a collaboration took place in the early 1960s in Guyana, a South American country with half a million people of Indian and African descent. The only psychiatrist in the country, who ran the mental hospital, became friends with a Kali healer who resided in a temple near the hospital and was being studied by an anthropologist. The psychiatrist, the healer, and the anthropologist began meeting and from such meetings a collaboration developed in which some psychiatric patients were treated jointly. Kali therapy is a semireligious type of healing based on Hindu beliefs and similar to what in Western culture would be called reality therapy. The client—having prepared by several days' abstentions (e.g., from meat, alcohol, sex), by obtaining clean clothes, and by preparing special foods with new cooking utensils—is taken to the healing temple on several successive Sundays. The healer then takes a history that especially utilizes dreams, makes a diagnosis, and tells the client what he or she must do to get well.

Over time, the psychiatrist and the Kali healer began making referrals to each other. The psychiatrist taught the healer to look for certain signs and symptoms that suggested organic disorder or psychosis and to refer such individuals for assessment. In exchange, the psychiatrist referred to the Kali healer any individuals who presented symptoms such as depression, anxiety, or hysteria. An example was a seventeen-year-old girl who had attacks in which "she would scream, curse and then stiffen up and be temporarily withdrawn and unresponsive for a few minutes." Treatment with benzodiazepine tranquilizers and sedatives were of no value, and a diagnostic trial on anticonvulsant medication made the girl's symptoms worse. Finally, referral to the Kali healer produced a dramatic and lasting remission of symptoms. According to the psychiatrist, "many cases of this nature have been referred to the Kali healer for treatment and generally have shown remarkable improvement."[13]

On cases that the Kali healer referred to the psychiatrist, the two would often take the history together. When the person was hospitalized, the healer would visit regularly to get follow-up, and in preparation for discharge the healer would be invited to a joint discharge conference. Over time, the psychiatrist, the healer, and the anthropologist developed criteria for the kinds of clients who did best when referred for Kali therapy; included were those who were not psychotic and were able to define the goals of therapy, those from more rural areas, those whose families were willing to participate in the treatment, and those whose worldview most closely approximated a Hindu belief and value system.

Collaboration in Africa

Probably the best-known collaboration between a Western-trained psychiatrist and the local indigenous therapists was that set up in 1954 by Dr. T. A. Lambo, a Nigerian psychiatrist trained in England, who subsequently became a deputy director of the World Health Organization. The enterprise's "guiding premise was to make use of the therapeutic practices that already existed in the indigenous culture and to recognize the power of the group in healing."[14] A system of therapeutic villages was set up near a mental hospital and patients were placed in the villages after a short stay in the hospital. Traditional Nigerian healers were utilized both in the hospital and in the villages "to supervise and direct the social and group activities of our patients."[15] The healers also participated in therapeutic sessions, "sometimes through a simple ceremony at a village shrine, sometimes in elaborate forms of ritual sacrifice, sometimes by interpreting the spiritual and magical causes of their dreams and illnesses."[16] According to Lambo: "We assessed the work of these healers and found their results in certain areas were better than ours. They understood the philosophy of the people and were especially adept at handling the African's dreams."[17] Lambo also pointed to the reason for the healers' effectiveness: "Just as New Yorkers have faith in their psychoanalysts, and pilgrims have faith in their priests, the Yoruba have faith in the Nganga [healers] and faith, as we are learning, is half the battle toward cure."[18]

Another view of Nigerian healers is provided by psychiatrist Raymond Prince. After studying forty-six of them, Prince concluded that "Western psychiatric techniques are not in my opinion demonstrably superior to many indigenous Yoruba practices."[19] He observed many quacks as well as highly skilled therapists, and judged that the therapeutic results obtained by the latter are about equal to those obtained in Western psychiatric clinics and hospitals. Prince even occasionally referred refractory cases he had treated to the native healers.[20] Even the federal minister of health in Nigeria has utilized native therapists for disturbed government employees. According to him, "many of these patients returned within a few weeks to see me, apparently completely cured and ready to fit themselves into society."[21]

Another psychiatrist in Africa who set up a successful system for collaborating with indigenous therapists was French-trained Henri Collomb in Senegal. At the mental hospital he ran for many years in Dakar, native healers were welcomed and included in the daily community meetings.

Ghana is another West African nation that is rich with native therapists. A psychologist in Accra did a careful study of five native therapists. Visiting each one every ten days for a period of six months, he analyzed 302 of their cases, and concluded that these therapists were often very effective.[22] Another field study, of twenty-three healers, in Ghana produced a similar conclusion.[23] Also in Ghana, Margaret J. Field, a physician and an anthropologist, did an extensive study of healing shrines and the therapists who run them. Her book documents 146 case histories, including patients with depression, anxiety, obsessive-compulsive neurosis, involutional psychosis, and schizophrenia, to show the therapeutic effectiveness of these healers.[24]

In East Africa, the most productive working relationship between psychiatrists and traditional healers took place in the Sudan. There, according to psychiatric observers,

two outstanding psychiatrists set a new pattern of treatment. Dr.

Tigani El Mahi, who was both an Arabic scholar and a London-trained specialist, set out to enlist the co-operation of the Mollahs or Moslem priests to whom the simple citizen first turns for help, especially in cases of mental derangement. He showed that he respected their knowledge of the Koran and their spiritual authority, and this encouraged them in turn to acknowledge his "foreign" skills. In time, Dr. Tigani and his able successor, Dr. Taha Baasher, established a working relationship with numerous Mollahs both in Khartoum and in distant towns and villages, whereby the Mollahs learned how to recognise cases of schizophrenia and epilepsy, which could not be cured by spiritual means alone, and they would refer such cases to the psychiatrists' clinic. The psychiatrists, in turn, recognised that shared religious belief, and participation in sacred rituals, could be of great value to sufferers from neurosis and also to their own psychotic patients, following their discharge from hospital or outpatient clinic treatment.[25]

Also in the Sudan, a World Health Organization report claimed, "traditional medicine is so successful . . . that it is extensively used in the control of neuroses and alcoholism, and as such possesses a potential for research on the treatment and rehabilitation of neurotic reactions, alcoholism and drug dependence."[26]

In Tanzania in the 1970s, a government grant was used to study the techniques and medicines used by the traditional *mganga*. Dr. Wolfgang Jilek, a psychiatrist, reported: "His counselling and curing is psychoprophylactic and psychotherapeutic activity of high relevance to the mental health of his society."[27] Another mental health professional experienced with *mgangas* found that:

Tanzanians seem to find that the highly personalized and warm style . . . is more comforting than the detachment of the western clinician. Moreover, the conceptual superstructure is related to a world view which is shared by both therapist and patient. Perhaps most important, the fundamental anxieties experienced by the afflicted Tanzanian patient seem infinitely better addressed within the traditional scheme of causation. What is most striking about the present day medicine man is that he is not in competition with the psychiatrist. In spite of long-term negative publicity, East Africans continue to find value in the way he supplements western treatment.[28]

There have been other attempts to integrate indigenous therapists into mental health services. In Australia, for example, five aborigines were recruited and trained for three months as "behavioral health workers" to provide psychological and counseling services to disturbed aborigines. The training program included "basic interviewing and relationship skills, case identification, . . . crisis intervention, family counselling, and alcoholism counselling," and was set up on the same model used to train Papago Indian therapists in the United States (see Chapter 10). Trainees were selected who were "warm responsive people capable of comfortably relating to a variety of individuals."[29]

Increasingly, mental health professionals in these countries are realizing the importance of recognizing, if not working with, their indigenous counterparts. For a professional from a third world country who has been trained in Western systems of psychotherapy, however, collaboration with a *mganga* may threaten professional identity or expose the person to ridicule from colleagues. In such instances a passive tolerance of the indigenous healing system may be reasonable, given the cultural realities. The following account by a psychiatrist is an example of this and is more typical of the situation in most third world countries today than is active collaboration:

A young Goan woman appeared to be suffering from the manic phase of a manic-depressive illness. Her entire family of middle-class shopkeepers was anxious and concerned. The prescription of chlorpromazine was followed by notable improvement within 3 days, although the patient was not entirely symptom free. When I visited her home at this time, however, the family atmosphere was strained. Her brother, a retail store manager, after much hesitation finally asked me if his sister would really get better with medicine and some counseling from me alone; he wondered if I would object if he called in a witch doctor to rid her of the evil spirits which might be present. I explained that they were free to call in whoever they thought might help. My only request was that regardless of whoever treated her, she should continue with my medicine; if she got better, they were free to give credit to whoever they thought had cured her.[30]

Official Sanction for Witchdoctors

India and Sri Lanka are countries in which traditional medicine
and its practitioners have been integrated into the existing framework of government health services. According to the World
Health Organization, in India in 1978 there were 108 colleges of
indigenous medicine, over 500,000 practitioners, "and a statutory National Central Council [that] directs their activities, controls standards of training, education and practice, and awards
recognition status which is necessary for employment in the public health services."[31] The major systems of indigenous healing
are Ayurveda, Unani, Siddha, and Yoga. Ayurveda, for example,
has been used since the first century A.D., when, according to
Gunnar Myrdal:

> ayurvedic medicine had developed into a system that in some re-
> spects resembled and in others surpassed that of Hippocrates and
> Galen. Its most accomplished practitioners, usually resident at the
> royal courts, were learned in such basic subjects as anatomy, in-
> cluding dissection and physiology, pathology, and therapeutics.
> Pharmacology was relatively well developed.[32]

The Indian system of traditional healing that probably has been
used most widely for psychological problems has been Yoga. Dr.
N. S. Vahia, a respected psychiatrist at a medical school in Bom-
bay, studied Yoga techniques for many years in an attempt to
determine their scientific validity and possible therapeutic utility.
These techniques, consisting of exercises and meditation to bring
about mind control over the body, were employed by Vahia and
his associates on thirty psychiatric patients. Biochemical and
electrophysiological studies were performed in conjunction with
the treatment. Vahia concluded that the techniques were indeed
effective, especially for psychoneurotic and psychosomatic
disorders.[33]

Western practitioners turned a skeptical eye on such experiments for many years because of doubts that the mind was capable of controlling the autonomic nervous system. In addition, the effects of such therapeutic systems are often difficult to measure scientifically, and in Western culture if something cannot be measured then it has no credible scientific status. In the 1960s, however, experiments showed that rats could be taught to voluntarily control autonomic nervous responses such as blood pressure and pulse rate. When rewarded for increased blood pressure, the rats responded by raising it still further; conversely, they were successfully taught to decrease it as well. The author of this report, in commenting on the extension of these findings to people, added: "I believe that in this respect they are as smart as rats."[34] Since then, meditative techniques to control both physiological and mental functioning has become fashionable in Western psychotherapy and forms the basis for many of the newer brands, such as Transcendental Meditation.

In Sri Lanka, there has also been an integration of traditional therapies into the official health and mental health structure. According to the World Health Organization:

> ten thousand practitioners are already registered and 6000 more are being considered for registration. The therapeutic scope of the practice is wide and includes preventive, curative, and specialized aspects. Most of the traditional systems follow the classical pattern of taking a history, determining the etiological factor complex, making a diagnosis, providing appropriate treatment, following up progress, and offering the appropriate rehabilitative measures.[35]

But it is China that is held up as the model country where traditional and Western systems of healing have been integrated most fully; the World Health Organization calls it "the shining example of the potential which lies in integration for the promotion and development of systems of traditional medicine." Traditional healers are trained in medical schools and are taught basic medical sciences. Most large hospitals have a department of traditional Chinese medicine, appoint traditional healers on staff, and maintain an herb garden so that ancient Chinese remedies will be available. The integration is said to be so successful that "in modern China the dividing line between traditional medicine and Western medicine has become blurred."[36]

The ultimate sanction of traditional systems of healing and indigenous therapists came in 1977, when the World Health Organization convened a meeting and subsequently published a report with recommendations. WHO praised traditional medicine for its holistic approach, and also recognized that because they were so widely available, the use of indigenous therapists was the only way WHO could achieve its stated goal of "total health care coverage of the world population using acceptable, safe, and economically feasible methods by the year 2000." WHO went on to recommend that "all the possible resources at its command [should] continue to promote and develop traditional medicine. . . . National governments should favor the policy of integrating traditional medicine into their general comprehensive health care system." Education and training programs were urged for traditional healers, with efforts made "to assure [them] that they will be the promoters and dispensers of the new health care system in their own cultural setting."[37] The witchdoctor had indeed come of age in terms of both official recognition and sanction.

PART III

TOWARD THE FUTURE
OF PSYCHOTHERAPY

Chapter 12

The Efficacy of Psychotherapy: On Making a Horse-and-Canary Pie

There is an old Spanish recipe for making horse-and-canary pie: Take one horse, add one canary, mix thoroughly, and bake.[1] This also turns out to be the recipe for successful psychotherapy, with the horse represented by the basic components of psychotherapy and the canary represented by specific techniques of the various schools or brands. It is not to say that the canary adds nothing to the pie—to a highly discerning palate it may make the difference between a mediocre and a really tasty pie. Rather what this recipe implies is that for most clients it is fatuous to spend long hours arguing about what specific type of canary would go best in the pie.

Arguments about the efficacy of psychotherapy began in earnest in 1952 when H. J. Eysenck published his classic paper reviewing nineteen studies of psychotherapy; the inescapable conclusion, said Eysenck, was that psychotherapy does not work.[2] Since that time, critics and researchers have slung scientific arrows back and forth supporting and criticizing, condoning and condemning, discussing the findings and often injecting ad hominem innuendo to further liven the debate. In 1983, over thirty years after his initial paper, Eysenck was still able to write:

The effectiveness of psychotherapy has always been the specter at the wedding feast, where thousands of psychiatrists, psychoanalysts, clinical psychologists, social workers, and others celebrate the happy event and pay no heed to the need of evidence for the premature crystallization of their spurious orthodoxies. The need to do so, emphasized by experimentalists and other critical spirits, has also threatened to upset the happy union.[3]

To a Martian psychotherapist, viewing the battle from on high, it must all look a little silly. The very existence of thousands of Western psychotherapists, many with full waiting rooms, is rather solid evidence that they are successfully doing something for their clients. Intelligent people will not voluntarily give up an hour a day or an hour a week, at a sizable fee, if they are not getting anything in return. Indeed, if psychotherapy did not "work," it would have died off long since, with the dinosaur and the dodo bird, not only in Western culture but in all cultures. Saying that psychotherapy does not work is like saying that prostitution does not work; those enjoying the benefits of these personal transactions will continue doing so, regardless of what the experts and researchers have to say.

Why, then, all this confusion? How could there be a spectacular increase in the business of psychotherapy during the same three decades when academics were arguing fiercely over whether psychotherapy works or not? The answer is that psychotherapy *does* work and that its effectiveness is primarily due to the four basic components—a shared worldview, personal qualities of the therapist, client expectations, and an emerging sense of mastery. Studies of psychotherapy that included these components have consistently shown that psychotherapy is effective. On the other hand, when researchers have ignored these basic components and attempted to show that one specific set of techniques is superior to another set of techniques, the outcome has been consistently negative and the researchers have concluded, erroneously, that psychotherapy does not work.

The error can be seen in Eysenck's original review, in which he included as "controls" people who had been hospitalized but received no formal psychotherapy. Yet the very act of hospitalization activated the basic components of psychotherapy: a name was put on the person's malady; personal interactions with hospital personnel took place, some of which were therapeutic; the person's expectations were raised; and he or she became convinced that mastery and cure were possible. Other studies in the 1950s utilized as "controls" people applying for psychotherapy who were given a single interview and then placed on a waiting list; those on the waiting list did equally well as those in ongoing psychotherapy because all the effective ingredients of psychotherapy had been activated.[4]

Over the past three decades, almost five hundred studies of psychotherapy have been undertaken, and Eysenck's error in neglecting the basic components of psychotherapy has become increasingly apparent. One of the better of these studies was that by psychiatrist Bruce Sloane and his colleagues at Temple University in Philadelphia.[5] They compared the outcome in eighty-nine "outpatients with anxiety neurosis or personality disorder," of whom twenty-nine were given behavior therapy for four months, thirty were given psychoanalytically oriented psychotherapy for four months, and thirty were given an initial assessment interview and psychological testing, and then placed on a waiting list, with telephone calls every few weeks to ask them how they were getting along. At the end of four months, all three groups had significant reduction in their symptoms, with those who had received behavior therapy or psychoanalytically oriented psychotherapy slightly more improved. At follow-up testing at the end of one year and two years, however, there were no differences among the three groups in terms of reduced symptoms, work adjustment, or social adjustment; each group had improved. Reflecting on the results of the study, Sloane noted: "The minimal contact afforded the control group proved to be surprisingly helpful to them. Seventy-seven percent were considered by the independent assessor on a global judgment to be improved or recovered."[6]

Another respected set of psychotherapy researchers who have arrived at similar conclusions are the Johns Hopkins University group under Dr. Jerome Frank. In 1978, Frank and his colleagues reported a follow-up of individuals who had been given individual psychotherapy for one hour per week, group therapy for one and one half hours per week, or "minimal contact" of half an hour every two weeks, for a period of six months. In assessing the results of follow-up five, ten, and twenty years later, "the improvement noted at follow-up was independent of the therapy procedure employed, whether individual therapy, group therapy, or minimal contact therapy. . . . One explanation which may be offered is that effective ingredients common to all therapies initiate changes in patients' behaviors. These changes then enable the patients to interact with their environments in such a way as to lead to progressive improvement."[7]

Psychotherapy as a Caucus Race

Research efforts on psychotherapy continue, but it is the astute observations of Lewis Carroll that seem best to summarize the results. After reviewing a broad array of psychotherapy studies and comparing those utilizing individual versus group therapy, time-limited versus time-unlimited therapy, behavior therapy versus individual psychotherapy, and client-centered versus other traditional psychotherapies, Dr. Lestor Luborsky and his colleagues concluded that all entrants in the psychotherapy race had tied. "Everyone has won and must have prizes," Luborsky noted, quoting the Dodo bird from *Alice in Wonderland*.[8]

Specifically, Luborsky et al. found two things:

1. Most comparative studies of different forms of psychotherapy found insignificant differences in proportions of patients who improved by the end of psychotherapy. It is both because of this and because all psychotherapies produce a high percentage of benefit (see conclusion 2) that we can reach a "Dodo bird verdict"—it is usually true that "everybody has won and all must have prizes."

2. The controlled comparative studies indicate that a high percentage of patients who go through any of these psychotherapies gain from them.[9]

Since people who enter psychotherapy do so to feel better, and since most of them do feel better after psychotherapy, then "everyone has won." It should be remembered that the Dodo was handing out prizes for the caucus race, a race in which everyone was "placed along the course here and there . . . [and] began running when they liked and left off when they liked, so it was not easy to know when the race was over." The Dodo had devised the race as a way for everyone to dry off, for they had been swimming in a pool of Alice's tears; after a half hour of running, everyone *was* dry and so indeed everyone *had* won.

A more sophisticated version of the "Dodo bird verdict" was published by Smith, Glass, and Miller in 1980. Using a statistical technique called meta-analysis, they did an exhaustive review of 475 controlled studies of psychotherapy. After sifting through the mountain of data, they concluded that

> psychotherapy is beneficial, consistently so and in many different ways. Its benefits are on a par with other expensive and ambitious interventions, such as schooling and medicine. The benefits of psychotherapy are not permanent, but then little is. . . . Different types of psychotherapy (verbal or behavioral; psychodynamic, client-centered, or systematic desensitization) do not produce different types or degrees of benefit. . . . No school of psychotherapy has a franchise on therapeutic efficacy. Indeed, no school of psychotherapy can claim that research proves its effects on a particular problem or type of client are superior. . . . We did not expect that the demonstrable benefits of quite different types of psychotherapy would be so little different. It is the most startling and intriguing finding we came across. . . . Apparently, little that the therapist controls bears any strong relationship to the effects of psychotherapy. The method of psychotherapy counts for little; nor do such gross features of the therapy as its length, whether it is administered in groups or alone, or the training and experience of the therapist. . . . Those elements that unite different types of psychotherapy may prove to be far more influential than those specific elements that distinguish them.[10]

Psychotherapy was found to be effective because in these studies no effort was made to distinguish the effects of the basic components of psychotherapy from the effects of the techniques or type of therapy. The bottom line was that the psychotherapies were effective, whatever the reason. Everyone had indeed won.

Since 1980 there has been a variety of technical criticisms of the Smith et al. work (e.g., meta-analysis is statistically flawed, the clients in the 475 studies ranged from college students to traditional psychiatric patients to felons and thus were too diverse to allow any conclusions to be drawn) but no serious challenge to it.[11] Probably the most significant development was a reanalysis of thirty-two of the studies, in which the basic components of psychotherapy (which the authors called the "placebo effect") were compared with the techniques of therapy.[12] As might be predicted from past studies along this line, the basic components were found to be the more important ingredient.

Harmful Effects of Psychotherapy

In recent years, as evidence has accumulated that psychotherapy is effective because of the basic components, it has also become clear that on occasion psychotherapy may be harmful. This is logical, for if psychotherapy really did not work at all, then there could be no possible harmful effects from it. Conversely, the fact that psychotherapy may be harmful can be used as additional evidence that it does work.

How often psychotherapy has an adverse outcome on the client is not certain. In a survey of the literature up until 1975, Dr. Allen E. Bergin reviewed twelve studies involving almost one thousand individuals and concluded that psychotherapy per se is harmful in one out of twenty individuals.[13] Some types of psychotherapy may have a higher adverse reaction rate than this. For example, in a careful study of 170 Stanford University undergraduates who entered encounter groups, it was found that sixteen of them "got markedly worse—a negative change that lasted more than six months and was directly attributable to the group experience. A similar number showed milder negative change."[14]

The types of harmful effects suffered by individuals in psychotherapy vary widely. Most obvious is the male therapist who exploits a female client sexually, a phenomenon that occasionally comes to light (usually as litigation) among therapists of all types and levels of training. Probably more common, but difficult to document, are the therapists who exploit their clients emotionally, as when a male therapist makes demands on a female client to disclose more of her sexual and/or emotional life than she is ready to reveal. Encouragement to get in touch with one's feelings is a valid objective, but at some point the line gets crossed between the benefit of the client and the voyeuristic or sadistic needs of the therapist.

Another adverse effect of psychotherapy may be the significant deterioration of clients who, beneath their problems of living, really have a brain disease like schizophrenia or bipolar disorder. Such people are referred to in the psychotherapy trade as "borderlines," and under the stress of psychotherapy they may rapidly slide downhill into psychosis. As mentioned in Chapter 1, psychotherapy (except the supportive variety) is contraindicated for people with brain diseases. Most experienced therapists have learned by trial and error not to accept such individuals for psychotherapy, but inexperienced therapists not infrequently begin psychotherapy with them before realizing that the person is becoming sicker.

Even individuals who do not have a brain disease may become agitated, anxious, and severely depressed by psychotherapy. As one book on the subject notes:

> Significant change in these therapies is often predicated upon an intense emotionally-charged experience the patient is required to undergo. It is clear, of course, that any massive assault on a person's defenses, as occurs in weekend encounter groups, marathon groups, primal therapy, Erhard seminars training, and others, heightens the potential for uncontrolled arousal of powerful affects and the possibility of decompensation or other negative effects.[15]

Most experienced psychotherapists have had or known of clients who have committed suicide while in therapy. Obviously some of these suicides would have taken place anyway, but others may have been directly precipitated by the therapy.

There are other adverse effects of psychotherapy, which occur more commonly with insight-oriented therapies as found in the United States. One is a syndrome described by Dr. Judd Marmor, a psychoanalyst, as the "utilization of a psychotherapeutic experience to rationalize feelings of smugness, superiority over others, or utilizing 'insights' to aggressively comment on other people's behavior."[16] This may be viewed as an excess growth of the feeling of mastery, but it can lead to an individual who is socially obnoxious. It is found among clients and, occasionally, among therapists as well. A variant of this is the fully "analyzed" client or therapist whose insight becomes a rationalization for self-serving behavior. I have been personally impressed by how often this occurs among people who have undergone psychoanalysis, although it is difficult to ascertain how often such personality characteristics were there prior to their psychoanalysis. As I was once told in the heat of argument by a psychiatric nurse whose destructive interpersonal relationships were legendary, "You think I'm bad now—you should have seen me *before* my analysis!"

Another undesirable effect of psychotherapies of all types is that they may become an end in themselves. This may occur in insight-oriented therapies, where the client may have an "endless and interminable therapeutic experience and fail to change while verbalizing insights and formulas of living."[17] It can also occur in other therapies, as seen in the "therapy junkies" who migrate from one type of therapy to another, looking for the ultimate insight or therapeutic experience.

Researchers who have studied the harmful effects of psychotherapy are unanimous in believing that such effects occur more often with certain therapist personality types. As described by observers of the therapists who produced the most harmful effects in the Stanford encounter group study, "the most damaging leaders used an intrusive, aggressive approach, frequently challenging and confronting the group members. These leaders tended to be impatient and authoritarian, and usually insisted on immediate self-disclosure, emotional expression, and attitude change."[18]

It is of course true that therapists in all cultures can produce harmful as well as helpful effects—the witchdoctor may be equally exploitive as the psychiatrist. The fact that such harmful effects may occur is further evidence that psychotherapy is indeed efficacious. The harmful effects also have implications for the selection, training, and licensing of psychotherapists, as will be discussed in Chapter 13. Witchdoctors, because of their unique techniques, may bring about certain harmful effects of psychotherapy not seen in Western culture. An example is the case of Okeke Okezi, a Nigerian witchdoctor who gave a client a powerful charm to ward off evil. Mr. Okezi said that the charm was so strong that it could protect against bullets as well as evil, and to prove his point he discharged his shotgun at the client. At postmortem, it was agreed that the client had not been helped by the therapy and Mr. Okezi was sentenced to death for murder.[19]

Efficacy of Untrained Therapists

By the standards of Western psychotherapy, most of the indigenous therapists described in Chapters 8 to 11 are untrained in techniques of therapy. And yet anecdotal reports suggest that many of them are effective psychotherapists and produce therapeutic change in their clients. Insofar as they do this without training in specific techniques, it implies that such training is not the crucial ingredient in psychotherapy. Rather these indigenous therapists are utilizing the same basic components of psychotherapy as do psychotherapists everywhere—a shared worldview, therapeutic personal qualities, client expectations, and a sense of mastery. The efficacy of untrained therapists is yet another piece of evidence that psychotherapy does work.

In the last two decades in the United States there has been a series of projects using untrained or minimally trained psychotherapists. Some of these have arisen out of the need to provide psychotherapy and counseling services for burgeoning mental health services (e.g., community mental health centers, suicide prevention services, military bases), while others have been planned and supported as grants by the National Institute of Mental Health, often under the rubric "paraprofessionals" or "new careers training." Analyzing the effectiveness of such individuals may shed further light on what is necessary for psychotherapy to work.

One of the earliest of these projects was Rioch's attempt in the 1960s to train housewives to do psychotherapy. The women were carefully selected, trained over two years, and extensively evaluated. They were very favorably rated as psychotherapists both by outside professionals who listened to tapes and by their supervisors on the job. Rioch concluded: "the experiment demonstrated that a college degree is not a necessary prerequisite for training as a Mental Health Counselor."[20] In another project, an army psychiatrist at Fort Devens, Massachusetts, found the solution to his overwhelming caseload by using medical technicians as psychotherapists. He gave them six weeks of on-the-job training, then called them "social work consultants" and let them go to work. With good supervision, they performed individual and group therapy, did consultations for the dispensary physicians, and even acted as the primary therapist for attempted suicides. The psychiatrist reports the results as very favorable.[21]

A particularly interesting study, using college students as group therapists, was done by Poser. He assessed the results of the students against those obtained by professional psychiatrists and psychiatric social workers; the students got better results than the professionals.[22] Other programs have successfully used college students to do "affiliative therapy" and "companionship therapy" with preadolescent and adolescent disturbed boys.[23]

Medical students with no formal training in psychotherapy have also been used as therapists. Because such students are functioning in a medical setting and wearing white coats, they engender all the powerful expectations usually reserved for individuals associated with the medical center. One study using them as individual psychotherapists with psychiatric outpatients reported that 82 percent of the patients felt improved as a result of the contacts.[24] A study of 128 psychoneurotic outpatients and medical student therapists reported a 72 percent improvement after short-term psychotherapy.[25]

As word spread about the favorable results of these early projects, and as money became available from the National Institute of Mental Health to fund them, they continued to grow. By 1979, Dr. Joseph Durlak evaluated forty-two such projects, more than half of them begun after 1970, in which the psychotherapeutic effectiveness of paraprofessionals was compared with that of mental health professionals (experienced psychiatrists, psychologists, and social workers). The projects included academic counseling and psychotherapy for college students as well as individual psychotherapy, group psychotherapy, and crisis intervention for adults with various psychological problems. The training of the paraprofessionals varied from none up to fifteen hours.

The outcome of Durlak's review was described by the author as follows:

> Overall, outcome results in comparative studies have favored para-professionals. . . . There were no significant differences among helpers in 28 investigations, but paraprofessionals were significantly more effective than professionals in 12 studies. . . . In only one study were professionals significantly more effective than all paraprofessionals with whom they were compared. . . . The provocative conclusion from these comparative investigations is that professionals do not possess demonstrably superior therapeutic skills, compared with paraprofessionals. Moreover, professional mental health education, training, and experience are not necessary prerequisites for an effective helping person.[26]

It was yet one more piece of evidence for the efficacy of psychotherapy, and for the source of that effectiveness being basic components of psychotherapy rather than specific techniques acquired through training.

Current Status of Psychotherapy Research

It seems well established that psychotherapy is effective, and that its effectiveness arises from the basic components of psychotherapy rather than from specific techniques. Even the Commission on Psychotherapies of the American Psychiatric Association, the bastion of protectionism for psychiatrists, acknowledged as much in a 1982 report that stated: "psychotherapy appears efficacious more often than not, but the conditions under which it works are not well understood."[27]

It is not that the specific techniques of therapy are without value; the canary remains part of the horse-and-canary pie. But the horse provides the overwhelming amount of flavor and sustenance. As noted by Strupp several years ago: "We are approaching a fuller realization that the similarities of all forms of psychotherapy are probably far more important than the differences vaunted by a host of 'schools' and that these common elements are shared with all psychological processes by which human beings are influenced to modify their feelings, attitudes, beliefs, values, and behavior."[28] Elsewhere Strupp noted that "the modern psychotherapist . . . relies to a large extent on the same psychological mechanisms used by the faith healer, shaman, physician, priest, and others, and the results, as reflected by the evidence of therapeutic outcomes, appear to be substantially similar."[29]

With such unanimity of evidence to date, it seems unlikely that additional studies of psychotherapy will dislodge this general conclusion. Rather what are needed are research attempts to more accurately describe the effective basic components—what conditions are necessary for a shared worldview, what personality characteristics are most therapeutic for what kinds of clients in which cultures, how can client expectations best be maximized and how can a sense of mastery be enhanced.

The largest psychotherapy research project currently in progress is a $3.4 million study sponsored by the National Institute of Mental Health to compare various techniques of psychotherapy for depression—a traditional psychodynamic technique ("interpersonal psychotherapy") versus "cognitive behavioral therapy" versus the use of tricyclic antidepressant pharmacotherapy.[30] A total of 239 depressed clients were randomly divided among the three modes of therapy; a fourth group was treated with a placebo drug "plus about half an hour per week of 'supportive discussion,' but not psychotherapy, with a psychiatrist." The depressed clients were people whose depression apparently arose from interpersonal or intrapersonal problems; patients with recurrent, apparently chemically based depression or those with manic-depressive disorders were not included.

On the basis of the common ingredients of psychotherapy, it would be expected that the three "treatment" groups, as well as the "placebo" group, would all improve. In May 1986, the initial results of the study were announced with much fanfare (front page coverage in the *New York Times*): clients treated by "interpersonal psychotherapy" or "cognitive behavioral therapy" or tricyclic antidepressants all improved equally (between 50 and 60 percent improved), while those treated with placebos improved 29 percent.[31] Since the first three groups had much more intensive treatment (which raised expectations and a sense of mastery, and provided more exposure to the personality characteristics of the therapist) it is not surprising that they improved more. A follow-up is in progress to determine how each of the groups does over the next two years and whether there are any long-term differences.

Dr. Morris Parloff, for many years the chief of psychotherapy research at NIMH and one of the originators of the psychotherapy of depression study, contributed perhaps the last word on efforts to prove that techniques of psychotherapy are uniquely effective. After reviewing the large number of studies on techniques of psychotherapy, he paraphrased the proverbial farmer and declared: "The best I can say after years of sniffing about in the morass of outcome research literature is that in my optimistic moods I am confident that there's a pony in there somewhere."[32] In fact, if the basic components of psychotherapy are taken into consideration, the creature is found to be a full-grown horse.

Chapter 13

The Implications of Comparing Witchdoctors and Psychiatrists

The observation that witchdoctors and psychiatrists are cultural variations of the same person should not be relegated to the realm of Believe It or Not, or placed on a platter of hors d'oeuvres at a cocktail party. It should be held, studied, criticized, polished, and used in the conceptualization and delivery of mental health services. This chapter examines the general implications of what we know about psychotherapy—who should do it, how they should be trained, whether they should be licensed and accredited, and who should pay them.

The first implication is that psychotherapy is most likely to be effective when therapist and client share a worldview. Ideally the therapist should share the client's worldview by virtue of sharing a culture—i.e., by having been brought up in the same culture. This is not to rule out the possibility of a therapist's learning another worldview and thus becoming an effective therapist in another culture. But it is an arduous process to learn another culture's values, points of stress, theories of causation, and system of disease classification. While possible, it clearly is a second choice to utilizing therapists who are indigenous to the culture concerned.

Also implied by this relativistic approach is the admonition that one culture has no right to impose its concepts of causation or its system of classification upon another. The only exception is when there are relevant data that are scientifically proved (as opposed to being just empirically validated) and could be helpful to the other culture. An example of this would be the scientifically proved relationship between the metabolic abnormality of the disease phenylketonuria and subsequent mental retardation in the child. It is known that a certain kind of diet, if begun early enough in the child's life, will minimize or obviate the retardation. Western cultures have an obligation to share this kind of data with other cultures and encourage them to use it. It does not, by contrast, have the obligation to impose the concept that sexual deviancy is caused by a traumatic childhood experience. Such a concept may be true, may be false, or may be culture bound, but in any case rests upon data that is on exactly the same scientific plane as the idea that sexual deviancy is caused by a lost soul or a broken taboo.

Since a shared language is a first step toward a shared worldview, the use of the client's first language is mandatory if the therapist hopes to be effective. This importance should be reflected in recruitment and selection of psychotherapists everywhere. The utilization of translators in an established program of psychotherapy is always a last choice, and should never be used if there is an alternative.[1]

Another implication of a shared worldview is the necessity for community control of psychotherapy services. In order for these services to be relevant, they must be organized by those who have a worldview similar to that of the prospective clients. This is especially true for services aimed at subcultures in the United States, but it applies equally to the many subcultures in developing countries that will have to be planned for. In other words, Anglo services should not be imposed on Mexican-Americans any more than Yoruba services should be imposed on Hausas in Nigeria. The Mexican-Americans and the Hausas should conceptualize their own services.

It can be validly argued that efforts of one culture to impose its services on another culture are antithetical to mental health. It is psychiatric imperialism. The dominant culture disparages and discredits the beliefs and techniques of the other, effectively rendering them useless yet offering nothing to take their place. The beliefs and techniques of the dominant culture fail to take root in the new soil, composed as it is of elements of a different world-view. Mental health services are suspended in midair; anxiety is inevitable, and the culture as a whole suffers.

Training of Whom?

There are profound implications to the fact that the personality characteristics of the therapist are an important component in determining psychotherapy outcome. In Western cultures, psychotherapists in the past were selected on the basis of personal interest (self-selection) and on their academic achievement (successfully passing courses given in schools of medicine, psychology, social work, or nursing). Whether or not that individual possessed therapeutic personality characteristics (e.g., genuineness, empathy, warmth) was not part of the selection criteria. Since most individuals who became psychotherapists migrated into that role secondarily after having gone into medicine, psychology, social work, or nursing, their selection for those schools may have taken into account personality characteristics but *not* necessarily those characteristics thought to be important for psychotherapists. The consequence of this traditional method of selecting therapists in Western cultures is an assortment of personality types doing psychotherapy, some of whom are well suited for the role and others of whom are gross misfits despite their academic training.

In the last decade, as psychotherapies have mushroomed, the selection process has become more chaotic. Currently *anyone* can call himself or herself a psychotherapist—there is no legal restriction on who may use the term—and the ranks have been joined by ex-ministers, history majors who cannot decide what to do after college, encyclopedia salesmen, drug company detail persons, retired businesspersons, and other assorted individuals without any specialized training. The only requirement for calling oneself a psychotherapist is the desire to do so. There is not now, nor has there ever been, a separate profession of psychotherapy, despite suggestions by many people over the years that there should be. Clearly, if we take seriously what is known about psychotherapy, there should be a separate profession, and individuals would be selected into it, with personality characteristics being of paramount importance.

How can personality characteristics be incorporated into the selection process? It can be done by having candidates take psychological tests, though these should not be relied upon exclusively. Probably more important is to have candidates for training programs interviewed by a series of lay persons who rate the candidates on a scale of would-you-want-to-go-to-this-person-if-you-had-problems. Selection interviews are usually done by the faculty of the training programs but such interviews are of limited utility; faculty are interested in qualities such as academic potential, research abilities, and personal compatibility with academic types. Lay persons, on the other hand, are much more likely to focus on the crucial qualities of genuineness, empathy, and warmth.

Presumably there are in Western society several pools of potentially valuable psychotherapists that could be tapped if selection procedures were revised. One such group is middle-aged women who have raised families and gained experience in life's problems; as mentioned in Chapter 12, Rioch and her associates showed that there are many mature, empathetic potential therapists among this group. Other groups that might yield good therapists include those, such as military medics or psychiatric hospital aides, who have gone into human service professions and found that they really enjoy helping people sort out life's problems.

Finally, there is a large potential source of psychotherapists among the bartenders, barbers, hairdressers, pharmacists, industrial foremen, probation officers, and housemothers of Western culture.[2] These are often empathetic, insightful people who have therapeutic personal qualities, are able to name what is wrong, and innately use techniques of therapy skillfully. With a little training and social sanction, they could also raise patient expectations to get well. When I made the suggestion in print previously that such individuals could be used as psychotherapists,[3] I received many confirmatory letters in reply, one of which read as follows:

I am one of those who without a degree or any conscious effort seem to attract the troubled, the lonely, the drinker, the ex-convict, the handicapped, and others. . . . I term the disease the "you know" symptom. People who only want someone to listen, and consequently emphasize every sentence with a "you know."

There are many people in Western culture with the "you know" syndrome. It is time that we utilized our knowledge and provided them with therapists.

Training for What?

The first thing a properly trained psychotherapist should know anywhere in the world is which clients are likely to benefit from their services and which should be referred for medical services. As basic as this sounds, it is *not* part of the training for most psychotherapists anywhere; even highly trained therapists in Western culture, such as psychologists with doctoral degrees or psychiatrists, often are not skilled in sorting out clients who may be helped from those who are not likely to be helped.

The type of clients most likely to be helped by psychotherapy, according to Dr. Morris Parloff, are those with anxiety, fears and phobias, compulsions, sexual dysfunctions, reactions to life crises, and problems of living "such as vocational and marital adjustments."[4] Some individuals with depression can also be helped, whereas others have primarily a biological basis for the depression and should be referred to a physician for pharmacotherapy. Others who can be helped are clients looking for improvement in the quality of their life—the life-enhancement seekers who form a majority of those attracted to the newer therapies.

Psychotherapists all over the world have learned by trial and error that they are not effective with people who have brain disorders or diseases such as schizophrenia, and in fact some of these individuals may be made worse by psychotherapy. It is remarkable how constant this observation is in every culture; for example, the psychiatrist doing a follow-up of individuals treated by a shaman in South Korea noted that "temporary symptom relief was obtained with the four psychoneurotic cases. . . . Of the eight schizophrenics, six deteriorated following the ceremonies."[5] Moreover, in tropical countries, patients presenting with signs and symptoms that may appear superficially like schizophrenia in fact may have a variety of other brain diseases, which are treatable; in one study in a Nigerian health center where thirteen patients presented with "psychosis," investigation revealed that five of them had typhoid fever, three had encephalitis, two had cerebral malaria, and only three had schizophrenia or bipolar disorder.[6] In all cultures, then, individuals who have symptoms of psychosis either overt or suspected should be referred to medical facilities for treatment.

Psychiatrists have commonly used this screening function as a justification for why psychotherapists should be medically trained (i.e., should be psychiatrists). This is fallacious, because psychotherapists can be trained easily to look for signs and symptoms indicating brain disease and then refer those individuals for medical evaluation. For example, there are simple pencil-and-paper tests (e.g., Draw-a-Clock, Write-a-Sentence) that can be used. The training necessary for a psychotherapist is summarized in a valuable book by Dr. Robert Taylor called *Mind or Body: Distinguishing Psychological from Organic Disorders* (New York: McGraw-Hill, 1982).

There are other elements to the training of psychotherapists. Some researchers have claimed that therapeutic personality qualities such as empathy and warmth can be enhanced through training, but this has not been unequivocally established. Training in diagnostic systems is important so the therapist can correctly name what is wrong. Such training also provides the therapist with the background and sanction (e.g., a certificate or diploma) needed to raise the expectations of clients; in addition, the training raises the therapist's own expectations, thereby making him or her more effective.

Many psychotherapists around the world would argue that training as a therapist should include learning about oneself. Although there is no scientific data to settle this question one way or the other, common sense would suggest that it is true. The more therapists understand their own psychological workings, the more skilled they should be in using their personality characteristics therapeutically and the less likely they should be to exploit the client.

Training can also be used to teach a psychotherapist new techniques that may increase his or her effectiveness. For example, the use of calcium gluconate or nicotinic acid to induce tingling sensations in the client can produce a marked increase in emotional arousal and client expectations. Or take the example of the general practitioner in rural South Carolina who, when removing a hex from a patient who has had roots "worked" on him, gives the patient methylene blue (a dye that turns the urine blue) in pill form, with the following instructions: "I give them these pills and say that one of three things will happen. I tell them that if in the next 24 hours the color of their urine remains unchanged, they are to come back and we'll try again. If it turns red, I tell them they're doomed, that no one can help. But if it turns blue, I tell them the root is off and they'll never have to worry again."[7]

Licensing and Accreditation

A psychiatrist who did a recent survey of psychotherapists in the United States came to the following conclusion: "More and more people with less and less training are now designating themselves as therapists. How is the public, how are third-party payers, how are psychotherapists themselves to distinguish who is able and who is not, who has been adequately trained and who has not?"[8]

It is a valid question and may be asked in many parts of the world. In New York and San Francisco, a variety of people with widely varying abilities and training are declaring themselves psychotherapists, but in Accra and Singapore and Bangalore there are also large numbers of individuals, some of them patently fraudulent, claiming healer status. For charlatans in all cultures, the roles of psychotherapist and healer offer an easy life, for in all cultures there are gullible people seeking relief from their personal problems. If psychotherapy were not effective, then there would be no need for concern; psychotherapists would be like fortune-tellers providing an innocuous pastime for dreamers and believers, and let the buyer beware. But psychotherapy is effective, as was shown in Chapter 12, and has the potential to do both good and harm.

Concern about the competency and ethical conduct of psychotherapists in the United States has increased in recent years. In New York State in the 1970s, the attorney general conducted a six-month investigation into the practices of "unlicensed mental health therapists" and found "widespread quackery, sexual misconduct, and the deception of clients through the use of phony academic credentials and titles." Investigators found adorning the walls of these psychotherapists' offices degrees such as one from the London Institute for Applied Research, purchased for twenty-five dollars from an advertisement in a Diners Club magazine. There was also reported to be "a pattern among male therapists and young female patients whereby the therapist informs the patient that in order for her to work out her problems she should engage in sexual activities with him. . . . Ironically they were still being charged for it."[9] On the other side of the world, in Papua New Guinea, members of parliament were "debating a proposal to license witchdoctors who can prove their skill at sorcery. Calling for consumer protection, Parliament member Gideon Apeng warned that unscrupulous practitioners could exploit the people by taking money for imperfect sorcery."[10]

Attempts to conceptualize regulatory schemes for psychotherapy, such as licensing and accreditation, are complicated by the variety of individuals who are doing it. In the United States, it is being done by family physicians, psychiatrists, psychologists, social workers, nurses, clergy, counselors of various kinds, and many people with no training whatsoever. In other cultures it is no less complicated; for example, among the Yoruba in Nigeria there are seven separate categories of traditional healers.[11]

It seems evident that steps need to be taken to protect consumers from incompetent and fraudulent psychotherapists in all cultures. No psychotherapist should be allowed to practice without having met minimal standards of competence and character, and a system of licensure should be required so that consumers could know who was accredited to practice. The World Health Organization recognized this in the report "The Promotion and Development of Traditional Medicine," in which it recommended "encouraging traditional medicine practitioners to form clubs or societies as a means of checking harmful practices, eliminating quacks and charlatans, assuring continuous informal education, cultural loyalty, and the conservation of a high level of professional ethics and practice."[12] Licensure of traditional healers has taken place in some countries (e.g., China, India, Sri Lanka, Kenya), and in others official associations have formed, such as the Mganga Association in Tanzania, which claims over thirty thousand members.

In the United States, licensure of health and human service professionals has traditionally been a state function. All states require licensure of physicians and nurses (but just to practice medicine; there is no additional licensure required to call oneself a psychiatrist or nurse therapist or to practice psychotherapy). And increasing numbers of states are beginning to license psychologists, social workers, and marriage and family counselors, but attempts to deal with the issues of psychotherapy and psychotherapists at the state level have been sparse. In the state of Washington, for example, a bill was considered "which would define an ethical code for counselors and psychotherapists and which would include penalties for infractions."[13]

At a national level, the most vigorous efforts to date to deal with the psychotherapy problem were made by Senators Spark Matsunaga and Daniel Inouye, who in 1980 introduced into the Senate a bill that would have created a National Commission on Mental Health Therapies, with the authority and funds "to propose research . . . to validate mental health services for which the safety, efficacy and appropriateness are still in doubt."[14] Only those therapies approved by the commission would qualify for reimbursement under federal mental health services—e.g., Medicare, Medicaid. Although widely discussed, the proposal died quietly, while advocates and opponents argued vigorously whether it was possible to license specific modes of therapies as opposed to licensing therapists.

Since all psychotherapies can be effective because they use the same basic components, it would seem to be a waste of time to do further research to establish this. Under the proposed Senate bill, est, primal therapy, and scream therapy would presumably have been equally as reimbursable under government insurance plans as behavioral therapy or psychoanalytic psychotherapy. The crucial question rather is the character, competency, and ethics of the individuals practicing the therapy—the therapists.

Moving toward a system of licensing and accreditation of psychotherapists would require cooperation among the various disciplines that constitute the psychotherapy pool. They would have to agree, for example, on the designation of psychotherapy as a discrete entity requiring minimal standards of conduct for the protection of clients. The prospect of such cooperation is not bright at present, when the leading disciplines—the psychiatrists, psychologists, and social workers—are engaged in constant warfare against each other as each tries to protect and enlarge its turf. A *Washington Post* article in 1985 headlined "Social Workers Vault into a Leading Role in Psychotherapy: Psychiatrists and Psychologists Defend Territory as Competition Increases."[15] It is, in the words of Dr. Morris Parloff, a continuing dogma eat dogma existence."[16]

Who Pays the Therapist?

Disputes and lack of cooperation among different kinds of psychotherapists in the United States are partly based on disciplinary biases, but at the bottom of much of the animosity is the question of reimbursement. As mentioned in Chapter 1, in 1980 almost two thirds of psychiatrists' fees and over one third of psychologists' fees came from government and medical insurance plans. In England, where the same kind of internecine warfare is taking place among psychotherapists of various professional origins, "one of the major objectives of such debate has been expressed indelicately but bluntly . . . as the determination of whose snout goes into the trough."[17]

Prior to the 1960s in the United States, the question of who paid the therapist was not a question—the client paid. This is still the case in most parts of the world; the *mganga*, *curandero*, and *balian* may be paid in kind (e.g., a goat or a chicken), but they are paid, and the responsibility for payment rests with the client and his or her family.

With the spread of private medical insurance plans (e.g., Blue Cross) and the advent of government medical insurance plans (e.g., Medicaid, Medicare), the burden of payment for psychotherapy in the United States has slowly shifted from the individual to "third-party payers," as they are called. Psychiatrists and psychologists have become increasingly dependent on these sources of income, and in many states social workers are also agitating for equal reimbursement rights. Marriage and family counselors doing psychotherapy in California are eligible for reimbursement by medical insurance, and (as mentioned in Chapter 10) Navaho medicine men have claimed that their psychotherapeutic services should also be reimbursable under Medicare and Medicaid.

Logically the Navaho medicine men are correct: If psychiatrists and psychologists are eligible for reimbursement for their services under medical insurance programs, then everybody doing psychotherapy in the United States should be eligible. The psychotherapists all utilize the same components of psychotherapy for their effectiveness and each type gets about the same results. (Within each type there are some therapists who are more effective and some who are less effective; however, all the evidence to date has failed to show any differences in effectiveness when different types of psychotherapists are compared with each other.) Therefore, if Blue Cross and Medicaid are going to reimburse psychiatrists and psychologists for doing psychotherapy, they should also reimburse social workers, psychiatric nurses, marriage counselors, est trainers, primal scream therapists, *curanderos, espiritistas*, and root doctors, as well as Indian medicine men, Eskimo shamans, Haitian *hungans*, and Bahamian Obeah men among those cultural groups. Reimbursing only psychiatrists and psychologists is discriminatory, implying that psychotherapists for some cultural groups are more important than those for other cultural groups, when in fact the evidence suggests that the psychotherapists are equal.

It does not take a mathematician to realize that if all psychotherapy were equally reimbursable under medical insurance plans in the United States, the plans would soon go bankrupt. Even with restricting reimbursement for psychotherapy to psychiatrists alone there have been accusations that this has increased insurance premiums unduly. As one Blue Cross official said: "With psychotherapy, the problem is that the psychiatrists can't specify the problem, or the likely outcome, and can't give a good description of the method in between, either."[18] Such medical insurance officials are used to dealing with the costs of removing a gall bladder, or treating a patient with chronic rheumatoid arthritis or terminal cancer; trying to reduce a client's interpersonal problems or existential crises to the same formula is impossible.

And that is precisely the problem—psychotherapy is an activity that has nothing to do with medicine. It may decrease unhappiness, increase productivity, and enhance the quality of life for the client, all worthwhile activities to be sure. Indeed, it is much more an educational than a medical activity. And to reimburse psychotherapy out of medical insurance funds is both illogical and unworkable.

Given what is now known about psychotherapy, it would seem reasonable to put restrictions on its utilization when paid for by medical insurance funds. The care of patients who have identifiable brain diseases, such as schizophrenia and bipolar disorder, would of course be covered just as is the care of patients with multiple sclerosis and Alzheimer's disease. There is another group of disorders in which a biological basis has not yet been proven but is strongly suspected; recurrent depressions and anorexia nervosa are examples. Given the weight of scientific information it is probably reasonable to cover psychotherapy in these as well with medical insurance funds.

There is a third group of medical conditions, such as ulcers, asthma, and colitis, which have a biological base but which are aggravated by a patient's personal problems. The management of these conditions has been found to be most effective when both the biological and psychological aspects of the condition are addressed. Thus it is as logical to utilize medical insurance funds to pay for psychotherapy for a person with recurrent asthma as to use them to pay for an office visit to adjust the patient's medication.

Along this same line of reasoning it has been contended by many mental health professionals that psychotherapy, when widely available to persons, ultimately reduces medical costs.[19] The argument claims that many patients using medical services do so because their psychosomatic complaints are really caused by underlying intrapersonal and interpersonal problems. When they receive psychotherapy that helps resolve the underlying problem, it is argued, the individuals have less need to use medical services. It is a persuasive argument. Everyone in the medical profession is aware of how many patients who present themselves for treatment have underlying personal problems, and skilled physicians will often do psychotherapy with such patients in an effort to relieve their symptoms.

The studies done to date showing that psychotherapy ultimately saves money in medical insurance plans have varied widely in methodology and outcome. Moreover, they have mostly been done by psychiatrists and psychologists, who have a vested interest in the outcome, which is somewhat like asking the foxes to do a study on whether chickens are good for their diet. If subsequent objective studies are able to verify that psychotherapy is really cost effective in reducing medical care utilization for certain kinds of medical patients, then it would be expected that medical care organizations would want to hire psychotherapists to help control costs. For example, the prepaid health plan, university hospital, and community hospital would all want to have psychotherapists on their staff to be used in such cases. Since medical care repayment is moving strongly toward reimbursement on the basis of disease (e.g., diagnosis-related groups, or DRGs), then it would be in the best interests of everyone to utilize psychotherapists to get patients well and keep them well. The psychotherapist would be paid by the medical care organization that had been reimbursed for the patient's disease, or by the patient him/herself. Using psychotherapists selectively for certain patients in such a medical scheme is very different from the current situation in which selected psychotherapists (psychiatrists, psychologists) are eligible for reimbursement under medical insurance for virtually any life problem in any individual who is covered by the insurance.

What about the remainder of people who currently obtain psychotherapy services under medical insurance funds? These people use psychotherapy to improve interpersonal and intrapersonal functioning, productivity, the quality of life, or happiness, and even to find meaning in life. These are indeed worthy activities but are educational in nature, not medical. Such psychotherapy should not be covered by medical insurance funds but should be paid for by the client him or herself just as individuals pay for other life-enhancing services they desire. If people want to learn a new language, take a great books seminar, or improve their serve or backswing, they contract with an individual or an organization to obtain the services. Psychotherapy would be exactly the same, with some psychotherapists able to charge more than others because of their skills and reputations just as they do now. As one psychotherapy expert summarized it: "It is an individual's inalienable right to seek therapy, self-enhancement, education, enlightenment, and titillation as long as he or she is willing to pay for it."[20] Or, as columnist and psychiatrist Charles Krauthammer recently summarized it: "After all, if psychotherapy is really an art, it should be supported by the National Endowment, not by Blue Cross."[21]

Chapter 14

Resistance to Indigenous Therapists in Established Systems: The Tarzan Mentality

It is tempting to romanticize indigenous therapists in other cultures and contrast these almost mythical figures with therapists in our own culture. In such a Rousseauan world, the medicine men and *mgangas* are all genuine, warm, empathetic individuals, always available and always effective, willing selflessly to help those in need, for a modest donation. Anyone who has had personal contact with therapists in other cultures will be aware that this view is imaginary.

Equally to be deplored is the tendency to focus exclusively on the shortcomings of therapists in other cultures. There are certainly *espiritistas* and shamans who are incompetent, self-serving, and unethical, just as there are psychiatrists, psychologists, and social workers who have these characteristics. The challenge is to structure our mental health services for people with problems of living in such a way as to minimize the prevalence of these problems and to maximize the availability of competent and caring help within economic realities. To put it another way, just because there are problems, we should not throw out the *babalawo* with the bathwater.

Problems

The greatest problem with psychotherapists all over the world is the mélange of personality types who are attracted to the profession. Many therapists in all cultures have therapeutic personality characteristics and deliver competent and caring services; others, however, migrate to psychotherapy because of their own problems and are ill suited to help others. In no culture, including our own, has this problem been faced. We continue to select psychotherapists for training programs predominantly on the basis of academic achievement, and our professional societies act primarily as guilds to protect the turf and income of its members rather than as regulatory agencies to protect the consumers of services.

In rural areas of the world, word of mouth functions reasonably effectively to warn people of incompetent practitioners. An incompetent *manang* in rural Malaysia and an incompetent psychologist in rural Kansas will be so identified by their neighbors and word of their incompetency will spread along the street at the Saturday market and in the Grand Union. With increasing urbanization and mobility, this regulatory apparatus is lost; word of incompetent or unethical behavior does not spread effectively in urban areas, and therapists can just pack up and move on to another location when their business falters. Even among psychiatrists in the United States, who as part of the medical profession might be expected to be better regulated, there is still virtually no barrier in moving from state to state for those found guilty of flagrantly incompetent or unethical behavior. If this is true for psychiatrists, imagine what the situation is like for the thousands of naturopaths, self-taught hypnotists, scientologists, and encyclopedia salesmen who decide to call themselves psychotherapists and open an office. If this is the best that we have done in our own culture, we can hardly criticize those in other cultures who have failed to regulate the practice of psychotherapy.

Another major problem is ensuring that psychotherapists know enough to refer medical and neurological problems to the medical profession for definitive care. The consequences of a shaman confusing an abscess with ancestral spirits, and a social worker confusing memory deficits due to a brain tumor with the repression of childhood memories, are equally disastrous. Psychotherapists everywhere are usually helpful in solving intrapersonal and interpersonal problems, but when they try to utilize their skills on individuals with schizophrenia and other psychoses, or with neurological or medical problems, the results may be catastrophic.

The solution to the problems both of incompetency and of knowing when to refer clients is accreditation and tighter regulation of psychotherapists. Nobody should be allowed to practice as a psychotherapist without completing a prescribed training program, demonstrating minimal knowledge on an exam (which can be oral for those who are not literate), and being subjected to periodic retesting to ensure that they have kept up in their field. This is as true in Nigeria and Nepal as it is on the Navaho reservation or in New York. Professional associations of therapists could do this if they chose, with government getting involved only if and when the professional associations decline the task. The ultimate outcome would be professional associations of therapists in each culture, and clients who would have some assurance that the practitioners had at least a minimum level of knowledge and skills.

There are other problems in using indigenous therapists. Confidentiality is an issue for all psychotherapists, but becomes of greater magnitude when therapist and clients belong to a small community or social network. The situation in which a psychiatrist in Scarsdale or Sausalito finds that half the people at a cocktail party have been his clients has a counterpart for *balians* in Denpasar or *babalawos* in Ibadan. An associated problem is that indigenous therapists are often so accessible to their clientele that the therapist cannot get away from his or her job. In a project utilizing ten indigenous therapists in a neighborhood in Boston, it was reported that "some patients seek out their therapists on the street between sessions."[1] Proximity of therapists and clients also leads to awkward social interactions, as in the Boston project, where "patients and therapists unavoidably meet each other in the streets, and an uncomfortable interpersonal jitterbug ensues as each tries to determine whether and how to acknowledge the other and who else might notice the encounter and thereby surmise the client's mental patient status."[2] Marriage counselors in small towns are well aware of this problem, as neighbors behind lace curtains across the street regularly broadcast to the town who went up the steps to the office.

Another problem that is inherent in using indigenous therapists in all cultures is what has been called a "shared ethnic scotoma."[3] A scotoma is a blind spot in the visual field, and in this case it refers to cultural blind spots the therapist may share with the client. For example, a young black male with a tendency to project his shortcomings onto others seeks out a black psychologist who shares his worldview. Unfortunately the black psychologist believes that most significant problems of his race are the product of discrimination by white society. The client is reinforced in his tendency to project blame, and is not encouraged to look at his own involvement in causing his problems. There are similar scotomas in all cultures, and it is the inevitable negative side of having client and therapist share a worldview.

Resistances

In addition to problems of incorporating indigenous therapists into established systems for helping people, there are various resistances that act as impediments. Not the least of these is the economic issue wherein broadening the base of accredited and sanctioned psychotherapists will erode the fee schedule of those already in practice. This resistance has been aptly demonstrated in the United States by psychiatrists trying to keep psychologists from being eligible for reimbursement by insurance programs, and by psychiatrists and psychologists together trying to keep out social workers, and by all three trying to keep out family and marriage counselors. It is a phenomenon found in every culture, and best summarized by an old Chinese proverb that translates roughly as "Those who have try to keep."

Closely allied to the economic issue is that of status. In the United States, there seems little doubt that if psychotherapists were selected on the basis of personality characteristics and accredited on their ability to help people, the base of the psychotherapy profession would broaden considerably. If the present exclusive aspects of it were lost—the medicine man and *curandero* being seen as equivalent to the psychologist—there would be a concomitant loss of status for psychologists and other Western psychotherapists. Such a loss of status is not something given up voluntarily; we are willing to grant the less fortunate equal opportunity, as long as they don't have equal opportunity for our job. We want others to have equal dignity as long as it is not drawn out of our account.[4]

Another resistance commonly encountered is the belief—explicit or implicit—that the use of indigenous therapists is merely an interim arrangement until the other culture becomes appropriately "civilized" and able to use Western therapists. Such an attitude can be seen in an article on "Cultural Aspects of Psychotherapy" by two psychoanalysts who stated: "It is our opinion that owing to the scarcity of psychiatrists, psychoanalytically oriented psychotherapy is for the time being hardly feasible in developing countries, that it is probably practical though at present unacceptable, and that its application on a substantial scale depends on an increase in the number of psychiatrists capable of practicing it and, of course, on culture change."[5] The change in the culture would presumably include a change in worldview so members of the culture would share a belief in the critical importance of childhood experiences as antecedents of human behavior. Such ethnocentrism is also evident in many of the programs that have been implemented to use indigenous therapists, such as the Navaho medicine men training program (see Chapter 10), which was justified on the basis that the Navahos were "unable to benefit from Anglo forms of therapy."[6]

The greatest resistance to the use of indigenous therapists involves the concept of magic. Indigenous therapists are closely associated with magical thinking in the minds of many, in contrast with Western psychotherapists, who represent science. Dr. E. L. Margetts, a psychiatrist who worked in Africa for many years, believed strongly that "native healers can do little good in a mental health program. . . . They can have no rational place in the modern technological world and as the educational level of African natives improves and as time affords them cultural wisdom . . . [they] will drift away from the primitive attractions of magic and seek help in science."[7] Lubchansky et al. made a similar point when contrasting Western scientific thought with the spiritualistic beliefs of Puerto Rican healers, which represent "a magical type of thinking that is alien to centuries of Western scientific striving. To a psychiatrist, the concepts of supernaturally caused illness and supernatural cure are not only alien but unprofessional as well. The spiritualist etiology of mental illness is so remote from our own as to be almost unacceptable."[8]

The crux of this resistance resides in our ethnocentrism and can be called the Tarzan mentality. It is our strong underlying belief that we Western psychotherapists practice science in our houses of steel and glass, whereas therapists elsewhere practice magic in their houses of straw and grass. Witchdoctors are assumed to swing through the jungle on vines and live in a simple world where "Me Tarzan, you Jane" suffices to cover most psychological eventualities.

The fallaciousness of this dichotomy has been pointed out. Psychotherapists in our culture and psychotherapists in other cultures practice on the same scientific—or prescientific—plane. We want to believe that the facts are otherwise, so we try to make them such. We don't want to believe that our techniques are not scientific. We look in the mirror and pretend we see a monster that isn't us; once labeled, the monster becomes fearsome, primitive, and a convenient counterpoint for our self-image. Compounding the Tarzan mentality is our Judeo-Christian heritage and the belief that Western culture represents the chosen people. We believe that we are really the end stage of evolution. Not only are we secretly skeptical of Copernicus's claims that the sun doesn't revolve around the earth; we wonder also if it doesn't revolve around Western cultures. All the rest of the world is darkness.

Western psychotherapists are especially sensitive to the issue of magic because other professionals often look down on them as practitioners of exactly that. They want to distance themselves, therefore, from any association with indigenous therapists lest they provide proof of their colleagues' suspicions. This is true when suggestions are made in American hospitals that collaboration with indigenous therapists might be useful, and it occurs in developing countries as well. In Malaysia, for example, when a World Federation of Mental Health workshop suggested collaboration between the university Department of Psychiatry and *bomohs,* "it was pointed out that to do so would only confirm the prejudice against psychiatry as a suspect, unscientific branch of medicine already apparent in the medical school."[9]

In the end, however, these problems and resistances can be overcome. Psychotherapy can emerge as a unified profession, distinct from medicine and proud of its ability to provide help for people in personal crisis. Indigenous therapists can be incorporated into formal psychotherapy programs all over the world and the services will be better for having done so. It will of necessity be an evolutionary and selective process; the psychotherapeutic brew can be distilled, with the supernatant retained and the residue discarded. And this can be done despite the hoary traditions of medicine and psychiatry, their feet firmly planted in the medieval guild system, their voices echoing "You just can't do that!" with each footstep down the hall of innovation.

Chapter 15

Conclusions: Genus—Psychotherapist, Species—Witchdoctor and Psychiatrist

The relationship between clients and psychotherapists, according to one observer, "holds a peculiar fascination. It captures the essence of being human—the effort to gain some degree of understanding and happiness—yet at the same time all rules of normal human relationships are suspended."[1]

This book has attempted to examine that relationship not only in our own culture but in cultures around the world. It postulates that there are four basic components to the process of psychotherapy: a shared worldview, the personal qualities of the therapist, the expectations of the client, and an emerging sense of mastery in the client. Psychotherapists everywhere utilize these same components; the apparent differences between types of psychotherapy within a culture or between cultures are more illusion than substance and are due to differences in techniques used to enhance the basic components. To reduce psychotherapy to a shorthand, one can say that it consists of a magnificent mensch (therapist with therapeutic personal qualities) utilizing an edifice complex (client's expectations and emotional arousal) and invoking the principle of Rumpelstiltskin (naming process arising from a shared worldview) to bring about a Superman syndrome (sense of mastery in the client).

To suggest that therapists in all cultures do basically the same thing—that (to continue the shorthand) psychiatrists and witch-doctors are really the same—may strike some as a radical idea. The implications of the comparison are important, however, in terms of how we organize our psychotherapeutic professions, who become therapists, how they are trained and accredited, and who pays the bills for psychotherapy. If witchdoctors and psychiatrists are indeed the same, then psychotherapists in New York and San Francisco are simply the indigenous therapists of the dominant American culture. Psychiatrists, as it were, are the witchdoctors of Westport. Recognition of this fact should not downgrade psychiatrists; rather it should upgrade witchdoctors.

It should also be noted that everything described in this book regarding psychotherapists and psychotherapies is evolving. These entities are not static, but dynamic and changing, like the cultures that spawn them. Freud's ideas and techniques were as much a product of Victorian Vienna as Perls's ideas and techniques were a product of do-your-own-thing-era San Francisco. In third world cultures, the process of change is also occurring. As urbanization takes place in Zaire, for example, "diagnosis is coming to depend more on dialogue and less on ritual, with the patient taking a more central role in therapy, and the family now acting as assistants rather than as partners."[2] We should expect continued change, so that therapists and therapies twenty years hence may bear little superficial resemblance to what is seen today. The underlying processes will remain, however—individuals seeking better relationships and a better life, therapists offering to help them achieve these.

Given what is known about psychotherapy, what should a person look for who is seeking a psychotherapist? The following seven guidelines are suggestions:

1. Utilize friends and relatives to get the names of psychotherapists who are known and respected. Be less concerned about the person's formal training than with the other issues listed below. Referral lists from professional organizations are of limited value since professional organizations are basically trade unions to protect their own members.

2. If possible, begin with a therapist who shares your worldview. This should include not only culture and language, but values as well. For example, if your Catholicism, Judaism, or Navahoism is a very important part of your identity, then you are likely to do better with a therapist who shares these values.

3. Look for personality characteristics in the therapist that make you feel comfortable. Do you like the therapist? Does he or she seem genuinely interested in you and your problems?

4. Ask yourself why you are going to a therapist. Try to crystallize the questions you are asking and the changes you are seeking. Then go over these with the therapist in the first or second meeting and make a contract; such contracts can be either verbal or written but should include the goals of therapy and the number of times you agree to meet.[3]

5. Clarify with the therapist the fees for psychotherapy. Assess in your own mind whether the cost is commensurate with the goals you hope to achieve. Remember that the psychotherapist also has to make a living.

6. In the words of experts who have studied psychotherapists both good and bad: "Avoid therapists who fail to show common courtesy in human interactions, who are overly zealous, who make extravagant claims, and who in general lack human qualities of warmth, concern, respect, understanding, and kindness. Beware of pompousness, hostility, harshness, lack of seriousness, seductiveness, inappropriate familiarity, and 'phoniness' of all kinds. Above all, make sure the therapist impresses you as a decent human being whom you can trust."[4]

7. If you do not like your therapist or sense that you are being exploited, move on and try another. Remember that psychotherapy is a buyer's market.

In the final analysis, perhaps the most important message in this book is an appeal for open minds. It asks that we put aside our ethnocentrism and look carefully at both witchdoctors and psychiatrists. The world has become too small to accommodate arrogance. The attitude that is needed is well exemplified by a story Dr. Alexander Leighton, one of the senior men in American psychiatry, tells about himself. It occurred when he was interviewing a native healer in Nigeria:

> On one occasion a healer said to me through an interpreter: "This man came here three months ago full of delusions and hallucinations: now he is free of them." I said, "What do these words 'hallucination' and 'delusion' mean, I don't understand?" I asked this question thinking, of course, of the problems of cultural relativity in a culture where practices such as witchcraft, which in the West would be considered delusional, are accepted. The native healer scratched his head and looked a bit puzzled at this question and then he said: "Well, when this man came here he was standing right where you see him now and he thought he was in Abeokuta" (which is about thirty miles away), "he thought I was his uncle and he thought God was speaking to him from the clouds. Now I don't know what you call that in the United States, but here we consider that these are hallucinations and delusions!"[5]

Notes

Preface

1. R. Herink, ed., *The Psychotherapy Handbook: The A to Z Guide to More Than 250 Different Therapies in Use Today* (New York: New American Library, 1980).

2. Congressional Record, August 6, 1980.

3. World Health Organization, "The Promotion and Development of Traditional Medicine" (Geneva: WHO Technical Report Series No. 622, 1978).

4. A. R. Favazza and A. D. Faheem, eds., *Themes in Cultural Psychiatry: An Annotated Bibliography, 1975–1980* (Columbia, Mo.: University of Missouri Press, 1982).

Chapter 1 Introduction: Problems of Living and Psychiatric Imperialism

1. G. L. Klerman, "Psychotherapy and Public Policy: What Does the Future Hold?" in *Psychotherapy Research: Where Are We and Where Should We Go?* ed. J. B. W. Williams and R. L. Spitzer (New York: Guilford Press, 1984), p. 359.

2. C. A. Taube, R. J. Burns, and L. Kessler, "Patients of Psychiatrists and

Psychologists in Office-Based Practice: 1980," *American Psychologist* 39 (1984), 1435–47.

3. Ibid.

4. M. B. Parloff, "Psychotherapy Research Evidence and Reimbursement Decisions: Bambi Meets Godzilla," *American Journal of Psychiatry* 139 (1982), 718–27.

5. See E. F. Torrey, *Surviving Schizophrenia: A Family Manual* (New York: Harper & Row, 1983).

6. G. R. Vandenbos, J. Stapp, and R. R. Kilburg, "Health Service Providers in Psychology," *American Psychologist* 36 (1981), 1395–1418.

7. M. E. Wallace, "Private Practice: A Nationwide Study," *Social Work* 27 (1982), 262–7.

8. Taube et al., op. cit.

9. Ibid.

10. M. B. Parloff, "How Werner Got It," *Psychology Today,* November 1978, 136–47.

11. *Primal Institute Newsletter* 8 (1985).

12. M. L. Gross, *The Psychological Society* (New York: Random House, 1978), p. 49.

13. M. B. Parloff, "Shopping for the Right Therapy," *Saturday Review,* February 21, 1976.

14. Y. Sasaki, "Psychiatric Study of the Shaman in Japan," *Mental Health Research in Asia and the Pacific,* ed. W. Caudill and T. Lin (Honolulu: East-West Center Press, 1969). Another effort at generalization that failed was Loeb's distinction between seers as "noninspirational" medicine men, and shamans, who were supposed to be "inspirational." Loeb hypothesized that seers were older types and that shamans were newer types and confined to "higher cultures." In fact, most cultures have both types. See E. Loeb, "Shaman and Seer," *American Anthropologist* 31 (1929), 61–84.

15. W. Z. Parks, "Paviotso Shamanism," *American Anthropologist* 36 (1934), 98–113.

16. See "Healer Offers Unique Brand of Psychotherapy," *Medical World News,* September 29, 1967, pp. 36–7, and F. Jahoda, "Traditional

Healers and Other Institutions Concerned with Mental Illness in Ghana," *International Journal of Social Psychiatry* 7, no. 4 (1961), 245–68.

17. A. Zempleni, "Traditional Interpretation and Therapy of Mental Disorder Among the Wolof and the Lebou of Senegal," *Transcultural Psychiatric Research* 6 (1969), 69–74.

18. G. P. Murdock, "Tenino Shamanism," *Ethnology* 4 (1965), 165–71.

19. Among the very few general works on therapists are those by J. L. Maddox, *The Medicine Man: A Sociological Study of the Character and Evolution of Shamanism* (New York: Macmillan, 1923); M. Eliade, *Shamanism: Archaic Techniques of Ecstasy*, trans. W. R. Trask (New York: Pantheon, 1964); C. M. Edsman, *Studies in Shamanism* (Stockholm: Almquist and Weksell, 1967); A. Kiev, ed., *Magic, Faith, and Healing* (New York: The Free Press, 1964); and M. Harner, *The Way of the Shaman: A Guide to Power and Healing* (New York: Harper & Row, 1980).

20. Cross-cultural psychiatry is also called transcultural psychiatry, ethnopsychiatry, and psychiatric anthropology. Most of the literature concerns concepts of etiology in various cultures, the incidence of specific diseases or of mental illness in general, how symptoms are related to the culture, culture-bound syndromes, acculturation, child-rearing patterns, and research methodology. There are comparatively few accounts of treatment methods and the therapists themselves.

21. A. Kiev, "Prescientific Psychiatry," in *American Handbook of Psychiatry* III, ed. S. Arieti (New York: Basic Books, 1966).

22. F. C. Redlich and D. X. Freedman, *The Theory and Practice of Psychiatry* (New York: Basic Books, 1966), p. 271.

23. Ibid., p. 272.

24. In an interesting parallel, anthropologist A. I. Hallowell examines "primitive" religion as a rational, empirical system and finds that it is no less empirical than our own. See A. I. Hallowell, "Some Empirical Aspects of Northern Salteaux Religion," *American Anthropologist* 36 (1934), 389–405.

25. K. M. Calestro, "Psychotherapy, Faith Healing and Suggestion," *International Journal of Psychiatry* 10 (1972), 83–113.

26. D. Hill, *Magic and Superstition* (New York: Hamlyn Publishing, 1968).

27. Two good examples of this are E. Berne, "The Cultural Problem:

Psychopathology in Tahiti," *American Journal of Psychiatry* 116 (1960), 1076–81, and W. Bolman, "Cross-Cultural Psychotherapy," *American Journal of Psychiatry* 124, no. 9 (1968), 1237–44.

Chapter 2   A Shared Worldview: The Principle of Rumpelstiltskin

1. C. Lévi-Strauss, *Structural Anthropology* (New York: Basic Books, 1963), p. 193.

2. Ibid., p. 193.

3. G. M. Carstairs, "Medicine and Faith in Rural Rajasthan," in *Health, Culture and Community,* ed. B. D. Paul (New York: Russell Sage Foundation, 1955), p. 120.

4. W. M. Mendel, "The Non-specifics of Psychotherapy," *International Journal of Psychiatry* 5, no. 5 (1968), 400–2.

5. H. Ezriel, "Experimentation Within the Psychoanalytic Session," *British Journal of Philosophy and Science* 7 (1965), 25. Quoted by W. M. Mendel, op. cit.

6. R. Benedict, *Patterns of Culture* (New York: Houghton Mifflin, 1934).

7. P. J. Pelto, "Psychological Anthropology," in *Biennial Review of Anthropology,* ed. B. J. Siegel and A. R. Beals (Stanford, Cal.: Stanford University Press, 1967), pp. 140–208.

8. G. W. Allport and T. F. Pettigrew, "Cultural Influences on the Perception of Movement: The Trapezoidal Illusion Among the Zulus," *Journal of Abnormal Psychology* 55, no. 1 (1957), 104–13; and M. H. Segall, D. T. Campbell, and M. J. Herskovits, *The Influence of Culture on Visual Perception* (Indianapolis: The Bobbs-Merrill Company, 1966).

9. A. K. Romney and R. G. D'Andrade, eds., "Transcultural Studies in Cognition," *American Anthropologist* 66, no. 3 (Special Edition) (1964).

10. B. L. Whorf, "Science and Linguistics," in *Language, Thought and Reality,* ed. J. B. Carroll (Cambridge: The Technology Press of Massachusetts Institute of Technology, 1957).

11. R. W. Brown and E. Lenneberg, "A Study in Language and Cognition," *Journal of Abnormal and Social Psychology* 49 (1954), 454–62.

12. F. Boas, "On Grammatical Categories," in D. Hymes, *Language in Culture and Society* (New York: Harper & Row, 1964).

13. For another example of this, see C. O. Frake, "The Diagnosis of Disease Among the Subanun of Mindanao," *American Anthropologist* 63 (1961), 113–32.

14. H. Conklin, "Hanunoo Color Categories," *Southwest Journal of Anthropology* 11 (Winter 1955), 339–44.

15. Personal communication, R. G. D'Andrade and E. R. Heider, 1969.

16. For a survey of these standards of sexual attractiveness, see C. S. Ford and F. A. Beach, *Patterns of Social Behavior* (New York: Harper, 1951).

17. See J. W. Whiting and I. L. Child, *Child Training and Personality: A Cross-Cultural Study* (New Haven: Yale University Press, 1953).

18. W. Goldschmidt, Foreword to C. Castaneda, *The Teachings of Don Juan: A Yaqui Way of Knowledge* (New York: Ballantine Books, 1969).

19. For a clear analysis of this, see J. Henry, "The Inner Experience of Culture," *Psychiatry* 14 (1951), 87–103.

20. For instance, see R. Prince, "Some Notes on Yoruba Native Doctors and Their Management of Mental Illness," in *First Pan-African Psychiatric Conference*, ed. T. A. Lambo (Ibadan, Nigeria: Government Printer, 1962).

21. M. P. Nisson and K. E. Schmidt, "Land-Dayak Concepts of Mental Illness," *Medical Journal of Malaya* 21, no. 4 (June 1967), 352–7.

22. For a more complete discussion, see S. H. Nelson and E. F. Torrey, "The Religious Functions of Psychiatry," *American Journal of Orthopsychiatry* 43 (1973), 362–7.

23. G. Devereux, *Mohave Ethnopsychiatry and Suicide: The Psychiatric Knowledge and the Psychic Disturbance of an Indian Tribe* (Washington, D.C.: Bureau of American Ethnology Bulletin 175, Smithsonian Institution, 1961).

24. Castaneda, *Teachings of Don Juan*.

25. T. Murase and F. Johnson, "Naikan, Morita and Western Psychotherapy," *Archives of General Psychiatry* 31 (1974), 121–8.

26. W. Caudill and C. Schooler, "Symptom Patterns and Background

Characteristics of Japanese Psychiatric Patients," *Transcultural Psychiatric Research* 5 (October 1968), 133–7.

27. J. S. Neki, "*Sahaja:* An Indian Ideal of Mental Health," *Psychiatry* 38 (1975), 1–10.

28. D. L. Johnson and C. A. Johnson, "Totally Discouraged: A Depressive Syndrome of the Dakota Sioux." *Transcultural Psychiatric Research* 2 (October 1965), 141–3.

29. B. Kaplan and D. Johnson, "The Social Meaning of Navaho Psychopathology and Psychotherapy," in *Magic, Faith and Healing*, ed. A. Kiev (New York: The Free Press, 1964).

30. H. Rin, "A Study of the Aetiology of Koro in Respect to the Chinese Concept of Illness," *International Journal of Social Psychiatry* 11, no. 1 (1965), 7–13.

31. T. Kora, "Morita Therapy," *Transcultural Psychiatric Research* 2 (October 1965), 101–3.

32. See G. Devereux, "Three Technical Problems in Psychotherapy of Plains Indians Patients," *American Journal of Psychotherapy* 5 (1951), 411–23; and G. Devereux, *Reality and Dream: Psychotherapy of a Plains Indian* (New York: International Universities Press, 1950).

33. G. Seward, *Psychotherapy and Culture Conflict* (New York: The Ronald Press, 1956); T. Abel, "Cultural Patterns as They Affect Psychotherapeutic Procedures," *American Journal of Psychotherapy* 10 (1956), 728–40; V. D. Sauna, "Socio-Cultural Aspects of Psychotherapy and Treatment: A Review of the Literature," in *Progress in Clinical Psychology* (New York: Grune and Stratton, 1966); M. M. Bishop and G. Winokur, "Cross-Cultural Psychotherapy," *Journal of Nervous and Mental Disease* 123 (1956), 369–75; and J. A. Bustamente, "Importance of Cultural Patterns in Psychotherapy," *American Journal of Psychotherapy* 11 (1957), 803–12.

34. E. F. Torrey, F. J. Van Rheenen, and H. A. Katchadourian, "Problems of Foreign Students: An Overview," *Journal of the American College Health Association* 19, no. 2 (1970), 83–6.

35. O. Lewis, "The Culture of Poverty," *Scientific American* 215, no. 1 (1966), 19–25.

36. See R. Riessman, J. Cohen, and A. Pearl, eds., *Mental Health of the Poor* (New York: The Free Press, 1964); R. Prince, "Psychotherapy and the Chronically Poor: What Can We Learn from Primitive Psychother-

apy," in *Social Change, Poverty and Mental Health,* ed. J. Finney (Lexington: University of Kentucky Press, 1968); A. B. Hollingshead and F. C. Redlich, *Social Class and Mental Illness* (New York: John Wiley, 1958); R. G. Hunt, "Social Class and Mental Illness: Some Implications for Clinical Theory and Practice," *American Journal of Psychiatry* 116 (June 1960), 1065–69; and Sauna, op. cit.

37. See, for example, H. A. Robinson, F. C. Redlich, and J. K. Myers, "Social Structure and Psychiatric Treatment," *American Journal of Orthopsychiatry* 24, no. 2 (1954), 307–16.

38. K. Davis, "Mental Hygiene and the Class Structure," *Psychiatry* 1 (1938), 55–65.

39. O. R. Gursslin, R. C. Hunt, and J. L. Roach, "Social Class and the Mental Health Movement," in Riessman et al., op. cit., p. 63.

40. Y. Sasaki, "Psychiatric Study of the Shaman in Japan," in *Mental Health Research in Asia and the Pacific* ed. W. Caudill and T. Lin (Honolulu: East-West Center Press, 1969).

41. K. M. Calestro, "Psychotherapy, Faith Healing and Suggestion."

42. M. F. El-Islam, "Arabic Cultural Psychiatry," *Transcultural Psychiatric Research Review* 19 (1982), 5–24.

43. W. S. Tseng and J. F. McDermott, "Psychotherapy: Historical Roots, Universal Elements, and Cultural Variations," *American Journal of Psychiatry* 132 (1975), 378–84.

44. J. P. Hes, "The Changing Social Role of the Yemenite Mori," in Kiev, *Magic,* p. 371.

Chapter 3   Personal Qualities: The Medicinal Mensch

1. F. Kogos, *A Dictionary of Yiddish Slang and Idioms* (New York: Citadel Press, 1966).

2. See K. M. Colby, J. B. Watt, and J. P. Gilbert, "A Computer Method of Psychotherapy: Preliminary Communication," *Journal of Nervous and Mental Disease* 142, no. 2 (1966), 148–52; K. M. Colby, "Computer Simulation of Neurotic Processes," in *Computers in Biomedical Research,* ed. R. W. Stacey and B. Waxman, (New York: Academic Press, 1965); and K. M. Colby, "Computer Simulation of Change in Personal Belief Systems," *Behavioral Science* 12, no. 3 (1967), 248–53.

3. H. F. Harlow, "The Nature of Love," *American Psychologist* 13 (1958), 673–85; and H. F. Harlow, "Primary Affectional Patterns in Primates," *American Journal of Orthopsychiatry* 30 (1960), 676–84.

4. Harlow, "The Nature of Love."

5. For a further analysis, see G. G. Gardner, "The Psychotherapeutic Relationship," *Psychological Bulletin* 61 (1964), 426–37; and especially S. K. Pande, "The Mystique of 'Western' Psychotherapy: An Eastern Interpretation," *Journal of Nervous and Mental Disease* 146, no. 6 (1968), 425–32.

6. T. S. Szasz, *The Ethics of Psychoanalysis* (New York: Basic Books, 1965), presents a clear exposition of the no-responsibility position.

7. G. Jahoda, "Traditional Healers and Other Institutions Concerned with Mental Illness in Ghana," *International Journal of Social Psychiatry* 7, no. 4 (1961), 245–68; and J. Dawson, "Urbanization and Mental Health in a West African Community," in Kiev, *Magic*.

8. P. Singer, E. Araneta, and L. Aarons, "Integration of Indigenous Healing Practices of the Kali Cult with Western Modalities in British Guiana," *Transcultural Psychiatric Research* 4 (April 1967), 65–7.

9. See, for example, J. F. Rock, "Contributions to the Shamanism of the Tibetan-Chinese Borderland," *Anthropos* 54 (1959), 796–818.

10. M. K. Opler, "Dream Analysis in Ute Indian Therapy," in *Culture and Mental Health*, ed. M. K. Opler (New York: Macmillan, 1959).

11. R. Prince, "Indigenous Yoruba Psychiatry," in Kiev, *Magic*.

12. T. A. Lambo, ed., *First Pan-African Psychiatric Conference*.

13. C. Lévi-Strauss, *Structural Anthropology*, p. 170.

14. G. P. Murdock, "Tenino Shamanism," *Ethnology* 4 (1965), 165–71.

15. W. Z. Parks, "Paviotso Shamanism," op. cit., 98–113.

16. C. R. Rogers, "The Necessary and Sufficient Conditions of Therapeutic Personality Change," *Journal of Consulting Psychology* 21 (1957), 95–103.

17. B. J. Betz, "Experiences in Research in Psychotherapy with Schizophrenic Patients," in *Research in Psychotherapy*, ed. H. Strupp and L. Luborsky (Washington, D.C.: American Psychological Association, 1962), pp. 41–60.

18. C. B. Truax and R. R. Carkhuff, *Toward Effective Counseling and*

Psychotherapy: Training and Practice (Chicago: Aldine Publishing Company, 1962). The outpouring was such that during the period from 1961 to 1967, these researchers produced a total of 57 articles.

19. R. R. Carkhuff and C. B. Truax, "Training in Counseling and Psychotherapy: An Evaluation of an Integrated Didactic and Experimental Approach," *Journal of Consulting Psychology* 29 (1965), 333–6.

20. Truax and Carkhuff, op. cit.

21. Ibid.

22. D. N. Aspy, "A Study of Three Facilitative Conditions and Their Relationships to the Achievement of Third Grade Students" (Ph.D. diss., University of Kentucky, 1965), summarized in Truax and Carkhuff, op. cit., p. 116.

23. H. H. Strupp, "The Vanderbilt Psychotherapy Research Project: Past, Present, and Future," in Williams and Spitzer, *Psychotherapy Research*, p. 235.

24. H. H. Strupp and S. W. Hadley, "Specific vs. Nonspecific Factors in Psychotherapy," *Archives of General Psychiatry* 36 (1979), 1125–36.

25. L. Luborsky et al., "Therapist Success and Its Determinants," *Archives of General Psychiatry* 42 (1985), 602–11.

26. M. B. Parloff, I. E. Waskow, and B. E. Wolfe, "Research on Therapist Variables in Relation to Process and Outcome," in *Handbook of Psychotherapy and Behavior Change*, ed. S. L. Garfield and A. E. Bergin (New York: John Wiley, 1978).

27. Op. cit.

28. J. D. Koss, "Ritual Healing and the Reduction of Psychic Stress," presented at the Fifth World Congress of Psychosomatic Medicine, Jerusalem, 1979.

29. P. Lefebvre, review of E. Hoch, "Process in Instant Cure," *Transcultural Psychiatric Research Review* 13 (1981), 130–1.

30. R. R. Holt and L. Luborsky, *Personality Patterns of Psychiatrists* (New York: Basic Books, 1958).

31. A. P. Goldstein, "Domains and Dilemmas," *International Journal of Psychiatry* 7, no. 3 (1969), 128–34.

32. F. Khajani and H. Hekmat, "A Comparative Study of Empathy: The Effects of Psychiatric Training," *Archives of General Psychiatry* 25 (1971), 490–3.

33. Rogers, "Necessary and Sufficient Conditions."

34. R. Prince, "Some Notes on Yoruba Native Doctors and Their Management of Mental Illness," in Lambo, op. cit.

35. E. H. Erikson, *Observations on the Yoruk: Childhood and World Image* (Berkeley: University of California Publications on American Archaeology and Ethnology, 1943), p. 262. Quoted in S. H. Posinsky, "Yoruk Shamanism," *Psychiatric Quarterly* 39 (1965), 227–43.

36. J. M. Murphy, "Psychotherapeutic Aspects of Shamanism on St. Lawrence Island, Alaska," in Kiev, *Magic*, pp. 53–83.

37. Y. Sasaki, "Psychiatric Study of the Shaman in Japan," in Caudill and Lin, *Mental Health Research in Asia and the Pacific*.

38. R. I. Levy, "Tahitian Folk Psychotherapy," *International Mental Health Research Newsletter* 9, no. 4 (1967), 12–15. Abstracted in *Transcultural Psychiatric Research* 6 (April 1969), 51–55.

39. W. S. Tseng, "Psychiatric Study of Shamanism in Taiwan," *Archives of General Psychiatry* 26 (1972), 561–5.

40. M. Eliade, *Shamanism: Archaic Techniques of Ecstasy*, trans. W. R. Trask (New York: Pantheon, 1964).

41. D. Boghen and M. Boghen, "Medical Attitudes, Beliefs and Practices in Martinique," *Transcultural Psychiatric Research* 3 (April 1966), 47–9.

42. See W. G. Jilek, "The Image of the African Medicine-Man," in N. Petrilowitsch, "Contributions to Comparative Psychiatry," *Bibliotheca Psychiatrica et Neurologica* 133 (1967), 165–78, for examples of this.

43. Holt and Luborsky, op. cit.

44. J. F. Greden and J. I. Casariego, "Controversies in Psychiatric Education: A Survey of Residents' Attitudes," *American Journal of Psychiatry* 132 (1975), 270–3.

45. W. Freeman, "Psychiatrists Who Kill Themselves: A Study in Suicide," *American Journal of Psychiatry* 124, no. 6 (1967), 846–7; and P. H. Blachly, H. J. Osterud, and R. Josslin, "Suicide in Professional Groups," *New England Journal of Medicine* 266, no. 23 (1963), 1278–82.

46. W. Bogoras, *The Chukchee* (New York: American Museum of Natural History, 1907).

47. A. L. Kroeber, "Psychosis or Social Sanction," in *The Nature of*

Culture (Chicago: University of Chicago Press, 1952), pp. 310–19. See also G. Devereux, "Dream Learning and Individual Ritual Differences in Mohave Shamanism," *American Anthropologist* 59 (1957), 1036–45; G. Devereux, "Shamans as Neurotics," *American Anthropologist* 63 (1961), 1088–90; and J. Silverman, "Shamans and Acute Schizophrenia," *American Anthropologist* 69, no. 1 (1967), 21–31.

48. L. B. Boyer, "Notes on the Personality Structure of a North American Indian Shaman," *Journal of Hillside Hospital* 10 (January 1961), 14–33.

49. L. B. Boyer, "Remarks on the Personality of Shamans," *Psychoanalytic Study of Society* 2 (1961), 233–54.

50. L. B. Boyer, "Further Remarks Concerning Shamans and Shamanism," *The Israel Annals of Psychiatry and Related Disciplines* 2, no. 2 (1964), 235–57; and L. Boyer et al., "Comparison of the Shamans and Pseudoshamans of the Apaches of the Mescalero Indian Reservation: A Rorschach Study," *Journal of Projective Techniques and Personality Assessment* 28 (1964), 173–80.

51. See Sasaki, op. cit.; M. P. Nisson and K. E. Schmidt, "Land-Dayak Concepts of Mental Illness," *Medical Journal of Malaya* 21, no. 4 (June 1967), 352–7; and Rock, op. cit.

52. For another example of this kind of cultural bias, see S. Fuchs, "Magic Healing Techniques Among the Balahis in Central India," in Kiev, *Magic.*

53. Sasaki, op. cit.

54. Kroeber, op. cit.

55. Murphy, op. cit., also mentions transvestites as occurring among Eskimo Shamans occasionally.

56. Opler, *Culture and Mental Health*, p. 98.

57. T. A. Lambo, "Psychotherapy in Africa," *Psychotherapy and Psychosomatics* 24 (1974), 311–26.

58. S. R. Dean and D. Thong, "Shamanism versus Psychiatry in Bali, 'Isle of the Gods': Some Modern Implications," *American Journal of Psychiatry* 129 (1972), 59–62.

59. C. Kluckholn and D. Leighton, *The Navaho* (Garden City, N.Y.: Anchor Books, 1962), p. 309.

60. Eliade, op. cit.

61. Murdock, op. cit.

62. Eliade, op. cit.

63. Jilek, op. cit.; M. Gelfand, "Psychiatric Disorder as Recognized by the Shona," in Kiev, op. cit.; and R. H. Prince and E. D. Wittkower, "The Care of the Mentally Ill in a Changing Culture (Nigeria)," *American Journal of Psychotherapy* 18, no. 4 (1964), 644–8.

64. J. E. Cawte and M. A. Kidson, "Australian Ethnopsychiatry: The Walbiri Doctor," *Medical Journal of Australia* 2 (1964), 977–83. See also C. H. Berndt, "The Role of Native Doctors in Aboriginal Australia," in Kiev, op. cit.

65. D. Handelman, "The Development of a Washo Shaman," *Ethnology* 6 (1967), 444–64; and J. H. Tenzel, "Shamanism and Concepts of Disease in a Mayan Indian Community," *Psychiatry* 33 (1970), 372–80.

66. J. L. Maddox, *The Medicine Man: A Sociological Study of the Character and Evolution of Shamanism* (New York: Macmillan, 1923), p. 130.

67. Jilek, op. cit.

68. Maddox, op. cit., p. 104.

69. Murphy, op. cit., p. 66.

70. W. LaBarre, "Confession as Cathartic Therapy in American Indian Tribes," in Kiev, *Magic*, p. 39.

Chapter 4   Client Expectations: The Edifice Complex

1. S. Freud, *Collected Papers*, vol. 1, 2d. ed. (London: Hogarth Press, 1940), pp. 249–63.

2. J. D. Frank, *Persuasion and Healing* (Baltimore: Johns Hopkins Press, 1961), p. 60.

3. J. D. Frank, "The Role of Hope in Psychotherapy," *International Journal of Psychiatry* 5, no. 5 (May 1968), 383–412.

4. Some of these are reviewed in A. P. Goldstein, *Therapist-Patient Expectancies in Psychotherapy* (New York: Pergamon Press, 1962).

5. H. H. Kelley, "The Effects of Expectations upon First Impressions of

Persons," *American Psychologist* 4 (1949), 252. Cited in Goldstein, op. cit.

6. C. D. Egbert et al., "Reduction of Postoperative Pain by Encouragement and Instruction of Patients," *New England Journal of Medicine* 270, no. 16 (1964), 825–27. See also I. L. Janis, *Psychological Stress* (New York: John Wiley, 1958).

7. M. D. Altschule, *Origins of Concepts in Human Behavior* (New York: John Wiley, 1977), p. 128, quoting J. Reid.

8. J. D. Frank et al., *Effective Ingredients of Successful Psychotherapy* (New York: Brunner Mazel, 1978), p. 7.

9. A. Weil, *Health and Healing* (Boston: Houghton Mifflin, 1983), p. 227.

10. A. K. Shapiro, "The Placebo Effect in the History of Medical Treatment: Implications for Psychiatry," *American Journal of Psychiatry* 116 (1959), 298–304.

11. D. C. Jarvis, *Folk Medicine: A Vermont Doctor's Guide to Good Health* (New York: Henry Holt, 1958).

12. See for example C. P. Kimball, "Psychologic Responses to Open Heart Surgery," *American Journal of Psychiatry* 126 (1969), 348–59.

13. W. B. Cannon, "Voodoo Death," *American Anthropologist* 44 (1942), 169–81.

14. For a summary of this, see R. Ader, ed., *Psychoneuroimmunology* (New York: Academic Press, 1981).

15. Frank et al., *Effective Ingredients of Successful Psychotherapy*, p. 81.

16. Printed instructions issued to applicants to the Primal Institute, 1985.

17. W. Sargant, *The Mind Possessed: A Physiology of Possession, Mysticism and Faith Healing* (Philadelphia: J. B. Lippincott, 1974).

18. See R. C. Ness and R. M. Wintrob, "Folk Healing: A Description and Synthesis," *American Journal of Psychiatry* 138 (1981), 1477–81.

19. H. A. Wilmer, "Transference to a Medical Center," *California Medicine* 96, no. 3 (1962), 173–80. I have borrowed this term from Wilmer's description of it.

20. Frank et al., op. cit.

21. See, for instance, M. J. Field, *Search for Security: An Ethnopsychiat-*

ric Study of Rural Ghana (Evanston, Ill.: Northwestern University Press, 1960).

22. Goldstein, op. cit.

23. M. Eliade, *Shamanism.* See also A. Kiev, "Primitive Holistic Medicine," *International Journal of Social Psychiatry* 8, no. 1 (1962), 58–61.

24. W. Jilek, "Native Renaissance: The Survival and Revival of Indigenous Therapeutic Ceremonials Among North American Indians," *Transcultural Psychiatric Research Review* 15 (1978), 117–47.

25. W. LaBarre, "Confession as Cathartic Therapy in American Indian Tribes," in Kiev, *Magic.*

26. J. L. Maddox, *The Medicine Man: A Sociological Study of the Character and Evolution of Shamanism* (New York: Macmillan, 1923), p. 91.

27. A. Zempleni, "Traditional Interpretation and Therapy of Mental Disorder Among the Wolof and the Lebou of Senegal," *Transcultural Psychiatric Research* 6 (1969), 69–74, is an example.

28. See W. G. Jilek, "The Image of the African Medicine-Man," in N. Petrilowitsch, "Contributions to Comparative Psychiatry," *Bibliotheca Psychiatrica et Neurologica* 133, no. 6 (1967), 165–178.

29. S. H. Posinsky, "Yoruk Shamanism," *Psychiatric Quarterly* 39 (1965), 227–43.

30. R. Prince, "Some Notes on Yoruba Native Doctors and Their Management of Mental Illness," in Lambo, *First Pan-African Psychiatric Conference.* See also D. D. O. Oyebola, "The Method of Training Traditional Healers and Midwives Among the Yoruba of Nigeria," *Social Science and Medicine* 14A (1980), 31–7.

31. For examples of the last, see Eliade, *Shamanism.*

32. E. Holtved, "Eskimo Shamanism," in Edsman, *Studies in Shamanism,* p. 28.

33. Kiev, *Magic,* p. 15.

34. H. Sigerst, *History of Medicine,* vol. 1 (New York: Oxford University Press, 1951), p. 169.

35. Opler, "Dream Analysis in Ute Indian Therapy," p. 106.

36. Posinsky, op. cit.

37. Maddox, op. cit., p. 104.

38. Prince, op. cit.

39. G. P. Murdock, "Tenino Shamanism," *Ethnology* 4 (1965), 165–71.

40. Ibid.

41. Maddox, op. cit., p. 58.

42. Lambo, *First Pan-African Psychiatric Conference.*

43. P. Pigache, "The Witchdoctor as Psychotherapist—Science or Suggestion?" *World Medicine,* May 16, 1973, 45–7.

44. Advertisement from *Miami Times* reproduced in C. S. Scott, "Health and Healing Practices Among Five Ethnic Groups in Miami, Florida," *Public Health Reports* 89 (1974), 524–32.

45. Quotes are from A. Janov and E. M. Holden, *Primal Man: The New Consciousness* (New York: Thomas Y. Crowell, 1975), pp. 384, 398, 420. For an assessment of Janov's claims, see E. F. Torrey, "The Primal Therapy Trip: Medicine or Religion?" *Psychology Today,* December 1976, pp. 62–8.

46. "Snake Dies After Biting Witch Doctor," *San Francisco Chronicle,* no date.

47. J. M. Murphy, "Psychotherapeutic Aspects of Shamanism on St. Lawrence Island, Alaska," in Kiev, *Magic.*

48. J. F. Rock, "Contributions to the Shamanism of the Tibetan-Chinese Borderland," *Anthropos* 54 (1959), 796–818.

49. Prince, op. cit., and R. Prince, A. Leighton, and R. May, "The Therapeutic Process in Cross-Cultural Perspective: A Symposium," *American Journal of Psychiatry* 124, no. 9 (March 1968), 1171–76.

50. M. Dobkin, "Fortune's Malice," *Journal of American Folklore* 82 (1969), 132–41.

51. W. Wilkins, "Expectancy of Therapeutic Gain: An Empirical and Conceptual Critique," *Journal of Consulting and Clinical Psychology* 40 (1973), 69–77.

52. H. J. Friedman, "Patient-Expectancy and Symptom Reduction," *Archives of General Psychiatry* 8 (1963), 61–7.

53. E. H. Uhlenhuth and D. B. Duncan, "Subjective Change with Medical Student Therapists: Some Determinants of Change in Psychoneurotic Outpatients," *Archives of General Psychiatry* 18 (May 1968), 532–40.

54. L. H. Gliedman et al., "Reduction of Symptoms by Pharmacologically Inert Substances and by Short-Term Psychotherapy," *American Medical Association Archives of Neurology and Psychiatry* 79 (1958), 345–51.

55. J. D. Frank et al., "Immediate and Long-Term Symptomatic Course of Psychiatric Outpatients," *American Journal of Psychiatry* 120 (1963), 429–39. Other studies of placebos are reviewed by Goldstein, op. cit.

56. Frank, *Persuasion and Healing,* op. cit. p. 72.

57. S. Bloch et al., "Patients' Expectations of Therapeutic Improvement and Their Outcomes," *American Journal of Psychiatry* 133 (1976), 1457–60.

58. R. Hoehn-Saric et al., "Arousal and Attitude Change in Neurotic Patients," *Archives of General Psychiatry* 26 (1972), 51–6.

59. J. D. Frank et al., *Effective Ingredients of Successful Psychotherapy,* p. 4.

60. R. H. Prince, "Psychotherapy as the Manipulation of Endogenous Healing Mechanisms: A Transcultural Survey," *Transcultural Psychiatric Research Review* 13 (1976), 115–33.

Chapter 5   Learning and Mastery: The Superman Syndrome

1. Holy Bible, Revised Standard Version, I Samuel 17:37.

2. J. D. Frank et al., *Effective Ingredients of Successful Psychotherapy,* pp. 36–7.

3. J. D. Frank, "Psychotherapy: The Restoration of Morale," *American Journal of Psychotherapy* 131 (1974), 271–4.

4. J. S. Neki, "A Reappraisal of the Guru-Chela Relationship as a Therapeutic Paradigm," *International Mental Health Research Newsletter* 16 (1974), 2–7.

5. R. Rosenthal, "Changes in Some Moral Values Following Psychotherapy," *Journal of Consulting Psychology* 19 (1955), 431–6.

6. H. A. Kim, review of B. Y. Rhi, "Analytical Psychological Study Regarding the Treatment of Spirits of the Dead in Korean Shamanistic Cults," *Transcultural Psychiatric Research Review* 9 (1972), 117–20.

7. See M. Brewer, "We're Gonna Tear You Down and Put You Back Together," *Psychology Today* (August 1975), 35–89.

8. S. Fisher and R. P. Greenberg, *The Scientific Credibility of Freud's Theories and Therapy* (New York: Basic Books, 1977), p. 399.

9. Ibid., pp. 411–2.

10. Ibid., p. 412.

11. Nietzsche, "The Bestowing Virtue" in *Thus Spoke Zarathustra.*

Chapter 6   Techniques of Therapy

1. E. C. Del Pozo, "Empiricism and Magic in Aztec Pharmacology," in *Ethnopharmacologic Search for Psychoactive Drugs*, ed. D. H. Efron, B. Holmstedt, and N. Kline (Washington, D.C.: Public Health Service Publication No. 1645, 1967). This book, and L. Lewis, *Phantastica: Narcotic and Stimulating Drugs* (New York: E. P. Dutton, 1964), give a good overview of what is known in the field of ethnopharmacology. It is disappointingly little.

2. For a review of this literature, see E. F. Torrey, *Surviving Schizophrenia: A Family Manual.*

3. R. H. Prince, "The Use of Rauwolfia for the Treatment of Psychoses by Nigerian Native Doctors," *American Journal of Psychiatry* 118 (1960), 147–9.

4. R. H. Prince and E. D. Wittkower, "The Care of the Mentally Ill in a Changing Culture (Nigeria)," *American Journal of Psychotherapy* 18, no. 4 (1964), 644–8.

5. H. D. Lamson, *Social Pathology in China* (Shanghai: Commercial Press, 1928).

6. Efron, Holmstedt, and Kline, *Ethnopharmacologic Search.*

7. M. Dobkin, "Folk Curing with a Psychedelic Cactus in the North Coast of Peru," *International Journal of Social Psychiatry* 15 (1968), 23–32.

8. R. Prince, "Indigenous Yoruba Psychiatry," in Kiev, *Magic.*

9. E. M. Schimmel, "The Physician as Pathogen," *Journal of Chronic*

Disease 16 (1963), 1–4; and E. M. Schimmel, "The Hazards of Hospitalization," *Annals of Internal Medicine* 60, no. 1 (January 1964), 100–10.

10. A. Leighton and D. Leighton, "Elements of Psychotherapy in Navaho Religion," *Psychiatry* 4 (1941), 515–23.

11. J. Dawson, "Urbanization and Mental Health in a West African Community," in Kiev, *Magic.*

12. D. W. James, "Chinese Medicine," *The Lancet* 1 (1955), 1068–69.

13. J. Cernay, "Psychiatry in China," *Czechoslovenska Psychiatrie* 59, no. 4 (1963), 273–82. Reported in *Transcultural Psychiatric Research* 1 (April 1964), 34–6.

14. V. W. Turner, "An Ndembu Doctor in Practice," in Kiev, *Magic.* See also D. Metzger and G. Williams, "Tenejapa Medicine I: The Curer," *Southwestern Journal of Anthropology* 19 (1963), 216–34.

15. A. Kiev, *Curanderismo: Mexican-American Folk Psychiatry* (New York: The Free Press, 1968).

16. P. Kellaway, "The Part Played by Electric Fish in the Early History of Bioelectricity and Electrotherapy," *Bulletin of the History of Medicine* 20 (1946), 112–37.

17. Ibid.

18. U. Cerletti, "Old and New Information about Electro-Shock," *American Journal of Psychiatry,* 107 (1950), 87–94.

19. A. L. Hessin, "Treatment of the Mentally Ill by San Blas Indian Healers (Panama)," *Transcultural Psychiatric Research* 15 (October 1963), 70.

20. G. Jahoda, "Traditional Healers and Other Institutions Concerned with Mental Illness in Ghana," *International Journal of Social Psychiatry* 7, no. 4 (1961), 245–68.

21. J. G. Kennedy, "Nubian Zar Ceremonies as Psychotherapy," *Human Organization* 26 (1967), 185–94.

22. Hes, "Yemenite Mori"; A. Kiev, "Psychotherapy in Haitian Voodoo," *American Journal of Psychotherapy* 16 (July 1962), 469–76; and W. R. Holland and R. G. Tharp, "Highland Maya Psychotherapy," *American Anthropologist* 66 (February 1964), 41–52.

23. T. Kora, "Morita Therapy," *Transcultural Psychiatric Research* 2 (October 1965), 101–3.

24. W. LaBarre, "Confession as Cathartic Therapy in American Indian Tribes," in Kiev, *Magic.*

25. For this distinction between confession as guilt-sharing, catharsis, and abreaction, I am indebted to Dr. Peggy Golde, Department of Anthropology, Stanford University.

26. W. LaBarre, "Primitive Psychotherapy in Native American Cultures: Peyotism and Confession," *Journal of Abnormal and Social Psychology* 42 (1947), 294–309. See also Castaneda, *Teachings of Don Juan,* p. 152, for a nice illustration of peyote producing an abreaction with the person's father.

27. J. Gillin, "Magical Fright," *Psychiatry* 11 (November 1948), 387–400.

28. Kiev, *Curanderismo,* and A. J. Rubel, "The Epidemiology of a Folk Illness: Susto in Hispanic America," *Ethnology* 3 (1964), 268–83.

29. E. F. Torrey, "The Zar Cult in Ethiopia," *International Journal of Social Psychiatry* 13 (1967), 216–23; Dawson, "Urbanization"; and S. D. Messing, "Group Therapy and Social Status in the Zar Cult in Ethiopia," in Opler, *Culture and Mental Health,* pp. 319–32.

30. J. D. Frank, *Persuasion and Healing.*

31. M. G. Whisson, "Some Aspects of Functional Disorders among the Kenya Luo," in Kiev, *Magic.*

32. Prince, "Indigenous Yoruba Psychiatry."

33. W. M. Hudson, ed., *The Healer of Los Olmos,* Texas Folklore Society Publication no. 24 (Dallas: Southern Methodist University Press, 1951).

34. M. E. Opler, "Some Points of Comparison and Contrast Between the Treatment of Functional Disorders by Apache Shamans and Modern Psychiatric Practice," *American Journal of Psychiatry* 12 (1963), 1371–87.

35. Prince, "Indigenous Yoruba Psychiatry."

36. See V. D. Sauna, "Psychological Intervention in the Arab World," *Transcultural Psychiatric Research Review* 14 (1979), 205–8; N. V. Lateef, "Diverse Capacities of the Marabout," *Transcultural Psychiatric Research Review* 11 (1974), 181–5.

37. T. A. Baasher, "Traditional Psychotherapeutic Practices in the Sudan," *Transcultural Psychiatric Research Review* 4 (October 1967), 158–60.

38. Prince, "Indigenous Yoruba Psychiatry."

39. Holland and Tharp, "Highland Maya Psychotherapy."

40. E. F. Torrey, "A Medical Survey of the Saysay People in the Blue Nile Gorge," *Ethiopian Medical Journal* 4 (July 1966), 4–11.

41. N. W. Winkelman and S. D. Saul, "The Riddle of Suggestion," *American Journal of Psychiatry* 129 (1972), 477–81.

42. H. H. Strupp, "Needed: A Reformulation of the Psychotherapeutic Influence," *International Journal of Psychiatry* 10 (1972), 114–20.

43. The literature on this is voluminous. In terms of a general overview, the best summary is C. T. Tart, ed., *Altered States of Consciousness* (New York: John Wiley, 1967). In terms of application to psychotherapy, the reader should look at the extensive writings of Dr. Raymond Prince, e.g., R. H. Prince, "Psychotherapy as the Manipulation of Indigenous Healing Mechanisms," op. cit.

44. A. Neher, "A Physiological Explanation of Unusual Behavior in Ceremonies Involving Drums," *Human Biology* 34 (1962), 151–60.

45. W. G. Jilek, "Altered States of Consciousness in North American Indian Ceremonials," *Ethos* 10 (1982), 326–43.

46. A. Huxley, *The Devils of Loudon* (London: Chatto and Windus, 1961), p. 369. Quoted from Jilek, ibid.

47. J. L. McCartney, "Neuropsychiatry in China: A Preliminary Observation," *China Medical Journal* 40 (1926), 617–26.

48. J. Hallaji, "Hypnotherapeutic Techniques in a Central Asian Community," *International Journal of Clinical and Experimental Hypnosis.* Reported in *Transcultural Psychiatric Research* 1 (October 1964), 110–11.

49. D. Handelman, "The Development of a Washo Shaman," *Ethnology* 6, no. 4 (1967), 444–64.

50. R. G. D'Andrade, "Anthropological Studies of Dreams," in F. L. K. Hsu, *Psychological Anthropology* (Homewood, Ill.: Dorsey Press, 1961).

51. A. F. C. Wallace, "The Institutionalization of Cathartic and Control Strategies in Iroquois Religious Psychotherapy," in Opler, *Culture.*

52. A. F. C. Wallace, "Dreams and the Wishes of the Soul: A Type of Psychoanalytic Theory Among Seventeenth Century Iroquois," *American Anthropologist* 60 (1958), 234–48.

53. O. Pfister, "Instinctive Psychoanalysis Among the Navahos," *Journal of Nervous and Mental Disease* 76 (1932), 234–54.

54. M. K. Opler, "Dream Analysis in Ute Indian Therapy," in Opler, *Culture.*

55. G. Toffelmier and K. Luomala, "Dreams and Dream Interpretation of the Diegueño Indians of Southern California," *Psychoanalytic Quarterly* 2 (1936), 195–225.

56. O. M. Ozturk, "Folk Treatment of Mental Illness in Turkey," in Kiev, *Magic.*

57. Jahoda, "Traditional Healers."

58. Dawson, "Urbanization."

59. K. Stewart, *Pygmies and Dream Giants* (London: Victor Gollancz Ltd., 1955).

60. E. Sangmuah, "The Healing (Spiritual) Therapy in Ghana," presented at the Second Pan-African Conference on Psychiatry, Dakar, 1968.

61. J. H. Masserman, "The Timeless Therapeutic Trinity," in *Current Psychiatric Therapies*, vol. 7 (New York: Grune and Stratton, 1967), pp. 231–43.

62. H. H. Strupp, "Needed: A Reformulation."

63. See L. Krasner, "Studies of the Conditioning of Verbal Behavior," *Psychological Bulletin* 55 (1958), 148–70; and J. Greenspoon, "The Reinforcing Effect of Two Spoken Sounds on the Frequency of Two Responses," *American Journal of Psychology* 68 (1955), 409–16.

64. Lambo, *First Pan-African Psychiatric Conference.*

65. W. Mischel and F. Mischel, "Psychological Aspects of Spirit Possession," *American Anthropologist* 60 (1958), 249–60; E. Bourguignon, "The Theory of Spirit Possession," in *Context and Meaning in Cultural Anthropology*, ed. M. Spiro (New York: The Free Press, 1965); and especially several excellent chapters in R. Prince, ed., *Trance and Possession States* (Montreal: R. M. Bucke Memorial Society, 1968).

66. D. Akstein, "Terpsichore Trance Therapy: A Form of Group Psychotherapy Based on Ritual Possession," *Transcultural Psychiatric Research* 5 (April 1968), 74–5.

67. Mischel and Mischel, op. cit.

68. R. Prince, A. Leighton, and R. May, "The Therapeutic Process in Cross-Cultural Perspective: A Symposium," *American Journal of Psychiatry* 124, no. 9 (March 1968), 1171–76.

69. E. Douyon, "Trance in Haitian Voodoo," *Transcultural Psychiatric Research* 2 (October 1965), 155–9. See also L. H. Rogler and A. B. Hollingshead, "The Puerto Rican Spiritualist as Psychiatrist," *American Journal of Sociology* 67 (1961), 17–21.

70. J. Dauth, "Malaysia's Bomohs," *World Health*, November 1977, 4–7.

71. M. Gill and M. Brenman, *Hypnosis and Related States: Psychoanalytic Studies of Regression* (New York: International Universities Press, 1961). See also K. Ravenscroft, "Voodoo Possession and Hypnosis," *International Journal of Clinical and Experimental Hypnosis*, 13, no. 3 (1965), 157–82, for an excellent analysis of Haitian voodoo as a form of mass hypnosis.

72. R. Katz, "Empowerment and Synergy: Expanding the Community's Healing Resources," *Prevention in Human Services* 3 (1983/84), 201–26.

73. R. Katz, *Boiling Energy: Community Healing Among the Kalahari Kung* (Cambridge: Harvard University Press, 1982), p. 42.

74. J. Belo, *Trance in Bali* (New York: Columbia University Press, 1960).

75. W. Sargant, "Witch Doctoring, Zar and Voodoo: Their Relation to Modern Psychiatric Treatments," *Transcultural Psychiatric Research* 5 (October 1968), 130–32.

76. J. L. Gibbs, "The Kepelle Moot: A Therapeutic Model for the Informal Settlement of Disputes," *Journal of Africa* 33, no. 1 (1963), 1–11.

77. J. Cawte, *Medicine Is the Law* (Honolulu: University of Hawaii Press, 1974).

78. Whisson, "Aspects of Functional Disorders."

79. Dawson, "Urbanization."

80. Prince, "Indigenous Yoruba Psychiatry."

81. Dawson, "Urbanization."

82. J. R. Fox, "Witchcraft and Clanship in Cochiti Therapy," in Kiev, *Magic*.

83. Turner, "An Ndembu Doctor."

84. B. H. Kramer, "Psychotherapeutic Implications of a Traditional Healing Ceremony: The Malaysian Main Puteri," *Transcultural Psychiatric Research Review* 7 (1970), 149–51.

85. W. E. Mitchell, "The Group and Primitive Therapy," presented at Northeastern Association for Group Psychotherapy, Boston, March 31, 1973.

86. For a good summary of the literature on modal personality and national character, see A. Inkeles and D. J. Levinson, "National Character: The Study of Modal Personality and Sociocultural Systems," in *Handbook of Social Psychology*, ed. G. Lindzey (Cambridge: Addison-Wesley, 1954), pp. 927–1020.

87. A. Kiev, "Primitive Therapy: A Cross-Cultural Study of the Relationship Between Child Training and Therapeutic Practices Related to Illness," in *Psychoanalytic Study of Society*, vol. 1, ed. W. Muensterberger and S. Axelrod (New York: International Universities Press, 1961), pp. 185–217.

88. Even within Western cultures there are different emphases on certain techniques in specific countries which are related to the values of those countries. See V. D. Sauna, "Socio-cultural Aspects of Psychotherapy and Treatment: A Review of the Literature," in *Progress in Clinical Psychology* (New York: Grune and Stratton, 1966); and M. Shepherd, "Comparative Psychiatric Treatment in Different Countries," in D. Richter et al., eds., *Aspects of Psychiatric Research* (London: Oxford University Press, 1962), pp. 110–24. See also S. K. Pande, "The Mystique of 'Western' Psychotherapy: An Eastern Interpretation," *Journal of Nervous and Mental Disease* 146, no. 6 (1968), 425–32, for a cogent analysis of the relationship of Western psychotherapy to deficits in Western cultural values.

89. Prince, "Indigenous Yoruba Psychiatry."

90. B. Kaplan and D. Johnson, "The Social Meaning of Navaho Psychopathology and Psychotherapy," in Kiev, *Magic*, pp. 221–7.

91. S. Nishimaru, "Mental Climate and Eastern Psychotherapy," *Transcultural Psychiatric Research* 2 (April 1965), 24.

92. See Kora, "Morita Therapy." See also W. Caudill, "Observations on the Cultural Context of Japanese Psychiatry," in Opler, *Culture*, and Caudill in I. Galdston, ed., *Man's Image in Medicine and Anthropology* (New York: International Universities Press, 1963).

93. Wallace, "Institutionalization."

94. Another aspect of this temporal dimension is the problem of acculturation. Ideas about treatment techniques change faster in acculturating societies than concepts about causation. The result is a society left with diseases whose cause is known but the treatment for which has been discredited. The stress can be reduced by adapting new treatment techniques to the existing ideas of causation. See Fox, "Witchcraft and Clanship."

Chapter 7 Therapists in Ethiopia, Borneo, and the United States

1. E. F. Torrey, "The Zar Cult in Ethiopia," *International Journal of Social Psychiatry* 13, no. 3 (1967), 216–23.

2. H. M. Workineh, "Teaching of the Ethiopian Orthodox Church on Matters Related to Health and Disease," in *Introduction to Health and Health Education in Ethiopia*, ed. E. F. Torrey (Addis Ababa: Berhanena Selam Press, 1966). This priest was director general of His Imperial Majesty's private cabinet on church affairs.

3. R. Giel, Y Gezahegn, and J. N. Van Luijk, "Faith-Healing and Spirit-Possession in Ghion, Ethiopia," *Transcultural Psychiatric Research* 5 (1968), 64–6.

4. Ibid.

5. Ibid. The other was Dr. Tigani El Mahi, former Mental Health Adviser to the Eastern Mediterranean Regional Office of the World Health Organization.

6. See S. D. Messing, "Group Therapy and Social Status in the Zar Cult in Ethiopia," in Opler, *Culture and Mental Health* pp. 319–32, for a good description of this.

7. Giel, Gezahegn, and Van Luijk, op. cit.

8. D. Freeman, "Shaman and Incubus," *Psychoanalytic Study of Society* 4 (1967), 315–43.

9. K. E. Schmidt, "Folk Psychiatry in Sarawak: A Tentative System of Psychiatry of the Iban," in Kiev, *Magic*.

10. J. Perham, "Manangism in Borneo," *Journal of the Straits Branch of the Royal Asiatic Society* (Singapore, 1887), pp. 87–103.

11. W. Howell and D. J. S. Bailey, *A Sea Dyak Dictionary* (Singapore: American Mission Press, 1900).

12. Perham, op. cit., p. 101.

13. Ibid., and Howell and Bailey, op. cit.

14. M. Eliade, *Shamanism.*

15. During my visit to Sarawak, I unfortunately did not witness a healing ceremony, partly because everybody was busy burning their rice paddies for a new season. The following account is based on a case Digat had recently seen and that he described to me. It corresponds with healing ceremonies described to me by two other *manangs*, with those of Digat that Mr. Beavitt had observed in the past, and with accounts of Iban healing ceremonies in the missionary and anthropological literature dating back seventy-five years. There is remarkably little variation among these accounts.

16. See Freeman, op. cit.

17. For one of the rare ethnographic accounts of these interesting people, see H. Miner, "Body Ritual of the Nacirema," *American Anthropologist* 58 (1956), 503–7.

Chapter 8   Curanderas *Among Mexican-Americans*

1. M. Karno and R. B. Edgerton, "Perception of Mental Illness in a Mexican-American Community," *Archives of General Psychiatry* 20 (1969), 233–8.

2. J. Yamamoto, Q. C. James, and N. Palley, "Cultural Problems in Psychiatric Therapy," *Archives of General Psychiatry* 19 (1968), 45–9.

3. M. Karno, R. N. Ross, and R. A. Caper, "Mental Health Roles of Physicians in a Mexican-American Community," *Community Mental Health Journal* 5, no. 1 (1969), 62–9.

4. M. Karno, personal communication, 1969.

5. E. G. Jaco, "Mental Health of the Spanish-Americans in Texas," in Opler, *Culture and Mental Health*, pp. 467–85.

6. R. Diaz-Guerrero, "Neurosis and the Mexican Family Structure," *American Journal of Psychiatry* 112 (1955), 411–7.

7. Santa Clara County, Ad Hoc Comprehensive Mental Health Planning Committee for Santa Clara County, *Joint Venture in Mental Health 1968* (San Jose, Ca., 1968).

8. See, for example, Hollingshead and Redlich, *Social Class and Mental Illness.*

9. See, for example, L. Tyhurst, "Displacement and Migration," *American Journal of Psychiatry* 108 (1951), 561–8. See also T. S. Langner, "Psychophysiological Symptoms and the Status of Women in Two Mexican Communities," in *Approaches to Cross-Cultural Psychiatry,* ed. J. M. Murphy and A. H. Leighton (Ithaca: Cornell University Press, 1965), pp. 360–92.

10. W. Madsen, *Society and Health in the Lower Rio Grande Valley* (Austin, Tex.: Hogg Foundation for Mental Health, University of Texas, 1961).

11. D. Senter, "Witches and Psychiatrists," *Psychiatry* 10 (1947), 49–56.

12. L. Saunders and J. Samora, "A Medical Care Program in a Colorado County," in *Health, Culture and Community,* ed. B. Paul (New York: Russell Sage Foundation, 1955).

13. O. Lewis, "Medicine and Politics in a Mexican Village," in Paul, op. cit.

14. I. Kelly, *Folk Practices in North Mexico* (Austin, Tex.: University of Texas Press, 1965).

15. Kiev, *Curanderismo.*

16. G. G. Meyer, "Curanderos and Psychiatrists as Professional Healers," presented at Fifth World Congress of Psychiatry, Mexico City, 1971.

17. D. Alegria et al., "El Hospital Invisible: A Study of Curanderismo," *Archives of General Psychiatry* 34 (1977), 1354–57.

18. Holland and Tharp, "Highland Maya Psychotherapy."

19. W. M. Hudson, ed., *The Healer of Los Olmos,* Texas Folklore Society Publication no. 24. (Dallas: Southern Methodist University Press, 1951).

20. W. Madsen, *The Mexican-Americans of South Texas* (New York: Holt, Rinehart and Winston, 1964).

21. Kiev, *Curanderismo.*

22. R. B. Edgerton, M. Karno, and I. Fernandez, "Curanderismo in the Metropolis: The Diminished Role of Folk Psychiatry among Los Angeles Mexican-Americans," *American Journal of Psychotherapy* 24 (1970), 124–34.

23. Alegria et al., op. cit.

24. C. Martinez and H. W. Martin, "Folk Diseases Among Urban Mexican-Americans," *Journal of the American Medical Association* 196 (1966), 161–4.

25. G. Caplan, *Principles of Preventive Psychiatry* (New York: Basic Books, 1964); and E. Lindemann, "The Health Needs of Communities," in *Hospitals, Doctors and the Public Interest* ed. J. H. Knowles (Cambridge: Harvard University Press, 1965).

26. See, for example, Diaz-Guerrero, op. cit.; S. Ramirez and R. Parres, "Some Dynamic Patterns in the Organization of the Mexican Family," *International Journal of Social Psychiatry* 3 (1957), 18–21; and O. Lewis, *Life in a Mexican Village: Tepoztlán Restudied* (Urbana, Ill.: University of Illinois Press, 1951).

27. A. Meadow and D. Stoker, "Symptomatic Behavior of Hospitalized Patients: A Study of Mexican-American and Anglo-American Patients," *Archives of General Psychiatry* 12 (March 1965), 267–77.

28. Langner, op. cit.

29. Ramirez and Parres, op. cit.

30. W. Madsen, "Value Conflicts and Folk Psychotherapy in South Texas," in Kiev, *Magic.*

31. Lewis, *Life in a Mexican Village.*

32. See M. Clark, *Health in the Mexican-American Culture: A Community Study* (Berkeley: University of California Press, 1959); and W. R. Holland, "Mexican-American Medical Beliefs: Science or Magic?" *Arizona Medicine* 20 (May 1963), 89–102.

33. A. J. Rubel, *Across the Tracks: Mexican Americans in a Texas City* (Austin: University of Texas Press, 1966).

34. Madsen, *The Mexican-Americans.*

35. Kiev, *Curanderismo.* See also Lewis, *Life in a Mexican Village.*

36. See F. C. Nall and J. Speilberg, "Social and Cultural Factors in the Responses of Mexican-Americans to Medical Treatment," *Journal of Health and Social Behavior* 8, no. 4 (December 1967), 299–308.

37. Martinez and Martin, op. cit.

38. A. J. Rubel, "The Epidemiology of a Folk Illness: Susto in Hispanic America," *Ethnology* 3 (1964), 268–83.

39. Madsen, *Society and Health.*

40. Rubel, op. cit.

41. Holland, op. cit.

42. Madsen, *Society and Health.*

43. Ibid.

44. Rubel, op. cit.

45. Kiev, *Curanderismo.*

46. Rubel, op. cit.

47. See Madsen, *The Mexican-Americans;* Madsen, "Value Conflicts"; and Clark, op. cit.

48. Kiev, *Curanderismo.*

49. Martinez and Martin, op. cit.

50. Holland, op. cit.

51. Karno and his co-workers in East Los Angeles disagree that cultural factors are as important as I have suggested. As proof they cite their interview data on 444 Mexican-Americans. According to their report, "the core content of the interview was formed by small vignettes describing in everyday language imaginary persons who were depicted as suffering *from what psychiatrists generally consider to be psychiatric disorders*" (italics mine). Thus the very structure of the vignettes is already locked into an Anglo cognitive set, and it is not surprising that their Mexican-American respondents, many brought up in the United States, could respond appropriately within the desired Anglo framework and label the vignettes as depressed, psychotic, etc. The obverse would be to take a group of Americans raised in Mexico, describe a vignette of *susto,*

and they too should be able to correctly label the picture as *susto* even though they didn't necessarily accept it as a disease entity. See Karno and Edgerton, op. cit.

52. *San Jose Mercury*, October 1, 1969.

53. For another example of this, see Yamamoto, James, and Palley, op. cit.

54. See Holland and Tharp, op. cit.

55. Kiev, *Curanderismo*.

56. Ibid.

57. Lewis, *Life in a Mexican Village*, p. 107.

58. Alegria et al., op. cit.

59. V. Navarro, "Health, Health Services and Health Planning in Cuba," *International Journal of Health Services* 2 (1972), 397–431.

60. Proceedings, Mental Health Planning Conference for the Spanish Speaking (Washington, D.C.: National Institute of Mental Health, 1972), p. 75.

61. E. G. Casper and M. J. Philippus, "Fifteen Cases of Embrujada (Bewitched)," *Hospital and Community Psychiatry* 26 (1975), 273–4.

62. Kelly, *Folk Practices*.

63. Martinez and Martin, op. cit.

Chapter 9   Espiritistas *Among Puerto Rican–Americans*

1. The two best background sources are Vivian Garrison, "Doctor, *Espiritista* or Psychiatrist?: Health-Seeking Behavior in a Puerto Rican Neighborhood of New York City," *Medical Anthropology* 1 (1977), 65–180; and Alan Harwood, *Rx: Spiritist as Needed: A Study of a Puerto Rican Community Mental Health Resource* (New York: John Wiley, 1977).

2. I. Lubchansky, G. Egri, and J. Stokes, "Puerto Rican Spiritualists View Mental Illness: The Faith Healer as a Paraprofessional," *American Journal of Psychiatry* 127 (1970), 312–21.

3. Ibid.

4. Santeros, "Botanicas and Mental Health: An Urban View," *Transcultural Psychiatric Research Review* 9 (1972), 176–7.

5. Ibid.

6. Garrison, op. cit.

7. Harwood, op. cit., p. 103.

8. Ibid., p. 108.

9. Ibid., p. 105.

10. Garrison, op. cit., p. 151.

11. Harwood, op. cit., p. 87–8.

12. Ibid., p. 109.

13. A good description of *botánicas* is found in S. Fisch, "Botánicas and Spiritualism in a Metropolis," *Milbank Memorial Fund Quarterly* 46 (1968), 377–88.

14. See P. Ruiz and J. Langrod, "Psychiatry and Folk Healing: A Dichotomy?" *American Journal of Psychiatry* 133 (1976), 95–7; P. Ruiz and J. Langrod, "The Role of Folk Healers in Community Mental Health Services," *Community Mental Health Journal* 12 (1976), 392–8.

15. P. Ruiz, "Folk Healers as Associate Therapists," in *Current Psychiatric Therapies*, ed. J. H. Masserman (New York: Grune and Stratton, 1976).

16. P. Ruiz, "Spiritism, Mental Health, and the Puerto Ricans: An Overview," *Transcultural Psychiatric Research Review* 16 (1979), 37–39.

17. Garrison, op. cit.

18. A. Harwood, "The Hot-Cold Theory of Disease: Implications for Treatment of Puerto Rican Patients," *Journal of the American Medical Association* 216 (1971), 1153–58.

19. Ruiz and Langrod, "Psychiatry and Folk Healing."

Chapter 10   Medicine Men Among Native Americans

1. D. Brown, *Bury My Heart at Wounded Knee* (New York: Bantam, 1972), p. 35. The history of the Navaho is taken from this book.

2. "Innovations in Mental Health Training: Summaries of Experimental and Special Training Projects" (Washington, D.C.: National Institute of Mental Health, 1969, Mimeographed). The school for medicine men is described by R. L. Bergman, "A School for Medicine Men," *American Journal of Psychiatry* 130 (1973), 663–6.

3. R. L. Bergman, "Navaho Medicine and Psychoanalysis," *Human Behavior*, July 1973, 8–15.

4. A. H. Leighton, "Therapeutic Process in Cross-Cultural Perspective," *American Journal of Psychiatry* 124 (1968), 1176–8.

5. Ibid.

6. G. Luce, "The Importance of Psychic Medicine: Training Navaho Medicine Men," in *Mental Health Program Reports*, ed. J. Segal, vol. 5 (Washington: National Institute of Mental Health, 1971).

7. D. F. Sandner, "Navaho Medicine Men—The Psychological Cure," presented at annual meeting of American Psychiatric Association, San Francisco, 1970.

8. Ibid.

9. Bergman, "School for Medicine Men."

10. Leighton and Leighton, op. cit.

11. Luce, op. cit.

12. Leighton and Leighton, op. cit.

13. Ibid.

14. Luce, op. cit.

15. Bergman, "School for Medicine Men."

16. Bergman, "Navaho Medicine."

17. Bergman, "School for Medicine Men."

18. R. L. Bergman, "Paraprofessionals in Indian Mental Health Programs," *Psychiatric Annals* 4 (1974), 76–84.

19. Leighton and Leighton, op. cit.

20. The information in this section is from M. W. Kahn and J. Delk, "Developing a Community Mental Health Clinic on the Papago Indian Reservation," *International Journal of Social Psychiatry* 19 (1973), 299–306; and M. W. Kahn et al., "The Papago Psychology Service: A

Community Mental Health Program on an Indian Reservation," *American Journal of Community Psychology* 3 (1975), 81–97.

21. Bergman, "Paraprofessionals."

22. "Medicine's Week," *American Medical News,* November 24, 1975.

23. J. Hunt, "A Future Medicine Man?" *Seattle Post-Intelligence,* May 22, 1977.

24. "Chippewas Seek Funds to Hire a Medicine Man for Alcoholics," *New York Times,* December 3, 1979.

25. "Canadian Hospital Hires Medicine Man for Indians," *New York Times,* September 9, 1979.

26. M. K. Opler, "Dream Analysis in Ute Indian Therapy."

27. M. E. Opler, "Some Points of Comparison and Contrast Between the Treatment of Functional Disorders by Apache Shamans and Modern Psychiatric Practice," *American Journal of Psychiatry* 92 (1936), 1371–87.

28. S. H. Posinsky, "Yoruk Shamanism," *Psychiatric Quarterly* 39 (1965), 227–43.

29. R. Trumbull, "Eskimo Mental Ills Tied to New Life," *New York Times,* July 15, 1974.

30. J. M. Murphy, "Psychotherapeutic Aspects of Shamanism on St. Lawrence Island, Alaska," in Kiev, *Magic.*

31. J. M. Murphy and A. H. Leighton, "Native Conceptions of Psychiatric Disorders," in *Approaches to Cross Cultural Psychiatry,* ed. J. M. Murphy and A. H. Leighton (Ithaca, N.Y.: Cornell University Press, 1965), pp. 64–107.

32. Murphy, op. cit.

33. Trumbull, op. cit.

34. R. F. Spencer, *The North Alaskan Eskimo: A Study in Ecology and Society* (Washington, D.C.: U.S. Government Printing Office, 1959).

35. W. G. Jilek and N. Todd, "Witchdoctors Succeed Where Doctors Fail," *Canadian Psychiatric Association Journal* 19 (1974), 351–6.

Chapter 11 Witchdoctors in the Third World

1. "Pros and Cons," *Lancet* 1 (1980), 963–4.

2. Lambo, "Psychotherapy in Africa," 1974.

3. Pigache, "Witchdoctor as Psychotherapist."

4. Dobkin, "Folk Curing."

5. H. Rappaport, "The Tenacity of Folk Psychiatry: A Functional Interpretation," *Social Psychiatry* 12 (1977), 127–32.

6. D. D. Oyebola, "Traditional Medicine and Its Practitioners Among the Yoruba of Nigeria: A Classification," *Social Science and Medicine* 14A (1980), 23–9.

7. T. W. Maretzki, "Culture and Psychopathology in Indonesia," *Transcultural Psychiatric Research Review* 18 (1981), 237–56.

8. J. S. Neki, "Psychiatry in South-East Asia," *British Journal of Psychiatry* 123 (1973), 257–69.

9. P. B. R. Kolman, "A Study of Psychiatric Patients at the University of Malaya Medical Centre Who Also Consult Indigenous Healers," *Social Psychiatry* 11 (1976), 127–34.

10. H. Kim, "Folk Psychiatry in Korea," *Transcultural Psychiatric Research Review* 11 (1974), 40–2.

11. G. M. Carstairs and R. L. Kapur, *The Great Universe of Kota* (Berkeley: University of California Press, 1976).

12. C. A. Alexander and M. K. Shivaswamy, "Traditional Healers in a Region of Mysore," *Social Science and Medicine* 5 (1971), 595–601.

13. P. Singer, E. Araneta, and J. Naidoo, "Learning of Psychodynamics, History, Diagnosis, Management, Therapy by a Kali Cult Indigenous Healer in Guyana," presented at International Congress of Anthropological and Ethnological Sciences, Chicago, August 28, 1973. See also P. Singer, E. Araneta, and L. Aarons, "Integration of Indigenous Healing Practices of the Kali Cult with Western Psychiatric Modalities in British Guiana," *Transcultural Psychiatric Research* 4 (1967), 65–7.

14. T. A. Lambo, "Psychotherapy in Africa," *Human Nature* 1 (1978), 32–40.

15. T. A. Lambo, "Patterns of Psychiatric Care in Developing African Countries," in Kiev, *Magic*, pp. 443–54.

16. Lambo, "Psychotherapy in Africa," 1978.

17. "African Sees Gain for Mentally Ill," *New York Times*, March 24, 1968.

18. Lambo, "Psychotherapy in Africa," 1978.

19. R. Prince, "Indigenous Yoruba Psychiatry," in Kiev, *Magic.*

20. Prince, Leighton, and May, "The Therapeutic Process in Cross-Cultural Perspective."

21. Lambo, *First Pan-African Psychiatric Conference.*

22. Jahoda, "Traditional Healers."

23. S. K. Weinberg, "Mental Healing and Social Change in West Africa," *Social Problems* 2, no. 3 (1964), 257–69.

24. M. J. Field, *Search for Security: An Ethnopsychiatric Study of Rural Ghana* (Evanston, Ill.: Northwestern University Press, 1960); and M. J. Field, "Witchcraft as a Primitive Interpretation of Mental Disorder," *Journal of Mental Science* 101 (1955), 826–33.

25. Carstairs and Kapur, op. cit., p. 137.

26. World Health Organization, "The Promotion and Development of Traditional Medicine," WHO Technical Report Series no. 622 (Geneva: WHO, 1978).

27. Jilek, "Image of the African Medicine-Man."

28. Rappaport, op. cit.

29. M. W. Kahn, J. Henry, and J. Cawte, "Mental Health Services by and for Australian Aborigines," *Australian and New Zealand Journal of Psychiatry* 10 (1976), 221–8.

30. W. Otsyula, "Native and Western Healing: The Dilemma of East African Psychiatry," *Journal of Nervous and Mental Disease* 156 (1973), 297–9.

31. World Health Organization, op. cit.

32. G. Myrdal, *Asian Drama,* vol. 3 (New York: Pantheon, 1968), p. 1561.

33. N. S. Vahia, S. L. Vinekar, and D. R. Doongaji, "Some Ancient Indian Concepts in the Treatment of Psychiatric Disorders," *British Journal of Psychiatry* 112, no. 489 (1966), 1089–96.

34. N. E. Miller, "Learning of Visceral and Glandular Responses," *Science* 163, no. 3866 (January 31, 1969), 434–45.

35. World Health Organization, op. cit.

36. Oyebola, op. cit.

37. World Health Organization, op. cit.

Chapter 12   The Efficacy of Psychotherapy: On Making a Horse-and-Canary Pie

1. This recipe is from L. Luborsky, B. Singer, and L. Luborsky, "Comparative Studies of Psychotherapies," *Archives of General Psychiatry* 32 (1975), 995–1008.

2. H. J. Eysenck, "The Effects of Psychotherapy: An Evaluation," *Journal of Consulting Psychology* 16 (1952), 319–24.

3. H. J. Eysenck, "The Effectiveness of Psychotherapy: The Specter at the Feast," *Behavioral and Brain Sciences* 6 (1983), 290.

4. E. E. Leavitt, "The Results of Psychotherapy with Children," *Journal of Consulting Psychology* 21 (1957), 189–96.

5. R. B. Sloane et al., "Short-Term Analytically Oriented Psychotherapy Versus Behavior Therapy," *American Journal of Psychiatry* 132 (1975), 373–7.

6. R. B. Sloane and F. R. Staples, "Psychotherapy Versus Behavior Therapy: Implications for Future Psychotherapy Research," in Williams and Spitzer, *Psychotherapy Research*, p. 210.

7. Frank et al., *Effective Ingredients*, p. 116.

8. L. Carroll, *Alice In Wonderland* (New York: Random House, 1946), p. 28.

9. Luborsky, Singer and Luborsky, op. cit.

10. M. L. Smith, G. V. Glass, and T. I. Miller, *The Benefit of Psychotherapy* (Baltimore: Johns Hopkins University Press, 1980), pp. 183–9.

11. See for example M. Aveline, "What Price Psychiatry Without Psychotherapy?" *Lancet* 2 (1984), 856–8.

12. L. Prioleau, M. Murdock, and N. Brody, "An Analysis of Psychotherapy Versus Placebo Studies," *Behavioral and Brain Sciences* 6 (1983), 275–310.

13. A. E. Bergin, "Psychotherapy Can Be Dangerous," *Psychology Today* (November 1975), 96–104.

14. Ibid.

15. H. H. Strupp, S. W. Hadley, and B. Gomes-Schwartz, *Psychotherapy for Better or Worse* (New York: Jason Aronson, 1977), p. 120.

16. S. W. Hadley and H. H. Strupp, "Contemporary Views of Negative Effects in Psychotherapy," *Archives of General Psychiatry* 33 (1976), 1291–1302.

17. Quoting Salzman, ibid.

18. Bergin, op. cit.

19. "Witchdoctor Condemned When Charm Is Fatal," *New York Times*, August 13, 1972.

20. M. J. Rioch, "Pilot Projects in Training Mental Health Counselors," in *Emergent Approaches to Mental Health Problems*, ed. E. L. Cowen, E. A. Gardner, and M. Zax (New York: Appleton-Century-Crofts, 1967). See also M. J. Rioch, "Changing Concepts in the Training of Therapists," *Journal of Consulting Psychology* 30, no. 4 (1966), 290–2.

21. P. J. Paulbaum, "Apprenticeship Revisited," *Archives of General Psychiatry* 13 (1965), 304–9.

22. E. G. Poser, "The Effect of Therapists' Training on Group Therapeutic Outcome," *Journal of Consulting Psychology* 30, no. 4 (1966), 283–9.

23. G. Goodman, "An Experiment with Companionship Therapy: College Students and Troubled Boys—Assumptions, Selection, and Design," *American Journal of Public Health* 57, no. 10 (October 1967), 1772–77; and J. R. Hilgard and U. S. Moore, "Affiliative Therapy with Young Adolescents," *Journal of the American Academy of Child Psychiatry* 8, no. 4 (1969), 577–605.

24. R. Heine, ed., *The Student Physician as Psychotherapist* (Chicago: The University of Chicago Press, 1962).

25. E. H. Uhlenhuth and D. B. Duncan, "Subjective Change with Medical Student Therapists: Course of Relief in Psychoneurotic Outpatients," *Archives of General Psychiatry* 18 (April 1968), 428–38.

26. J. A. Durlak, "Comparative Effectiveness of Paraprofessional and Professional Helpers," *Psychological Bulletin* 86 (1979), 80–92.

27. Williams and Spitzer, *Psychotherapy Research*, p. 300.

28. Strupp, "Needed: A Reformulation."

29. H. H. Strupp, "On the Technology of Psychotherapy," *Archives of General Psychiatry* 26 (1972), 270–8.

30. G. B. Kolata, "Clinical Trial of Psychotherapies Is Under Way," *Science* 212 (1981), 432–3.

31. P. Boffey, "Psychotherapy Is as Good as Drugs in Curing Depression, Study Finds." *New York Times*, May 14, 1986; S. Squires, "In Depression, Drugs or Talk?" *Washington Post*, May 14, 1986.

32. M. B. Parloff, "Can Psychotherapy Research Guide the Policymaker?" *American Psychologist* 34 (1979), 296–306.

Chapter 13   *The Implications of Comparing Witchdoctors and Psychiatrists*

1. For an example of a program that claims to use translators successfully, see H. Bluestone, R. Bisi, and A. J. Katz, "The Establishment of a Mental Health Service in a Predominantly Spanish-Speaking Neighborhood of New York City," *Behavioral Neuropsychiatry* 1, no. 5 (1969), 12–16.

2. See M. P. Dumont, "Tavern Culture: The Sustenance of Homeless Men," *American Journal of Orthopsychiatry* 37, no. 5 (October 1967), 938–45; J. Shapiro "Dominant Leaders Among Slum Hotel Residents," *American Journal of Orthopsychiatry* 39, no. 4 (July 1969), 644–50; and J. G. Kelly, "The Mental Health Agent in the Urban Community," in *Urban America and the Planning of Mental Health Services, Symposium No. 10* (New York: Group for the Advancement of Psychiatry, 1964), pp. 474–94.

3. E. F. Torrey, "The Case for the Indigenous Therapist," *Archives of General Psychiatry* 20 (1969), 365–73.

4. Parloff, "Psychotherapy Research Evidence."

5. H. Kim, "Review of Shamanist Healing Ceremonies in Korea," *Transcultural Psychiatric Research Review* 10 (1973), 124–5.

6. T. Harding, "Psychosis in a Rural West African Community," *Social Psychiatry* 8 (1973), 198–203.

7. M. Michaelson, "Can a 'Root Doctor' Actually Put a Hex On or Is It All a Great Put-On?" *Today's Health* (March 1972), 39–60.

8. B. D. Beitman, "The Demographics of American Psychotherapists: A Pilot Study," *American Journal of Psychotherapy* 37 (1983), 37–48.

9. I. Peterson, "State Finds Quacks in Mental Therapy," *New York Times*, December 7, 1972.

10. "Guaranteed Sorcery?" *Oakland Tribune*, October 31, 1975.

11. Oyebola, "Traditional Medicine."

12. World Health Organization, op. cit.

13. Beitman, op. cit.

14. Congressional Record, August 6, 1980; see also D. S. Greenberg, "Washington Report," *New England Journal of Medicine* 303 (1980), 539–40.

15. D. Goleman, "Social Workers Vault into a Leading Role in Psychotherapy: Psychiatrists and Psychologists Defend Territory as Competition Increases," *Washington Post*, April 30, 1985.

16. Parloff, "Can Psychotherapy Research."

17. M. Shepherd, "The Statutory Registration of Psychotherapists?" *Bulletin of the Royal College of Psychiatrists* (November 1980), 166–9.

18. P. Hilts, "Psychotherapy Put on Couch by Government," *Washington Post*, September 14, 1980.

19. For a review of this literature, see E. Mumford et al., "A New Look at Evidence About Reduced Cost of Medical Utilization Following Mental Health Treatment," *American Journal of Psychiatry* 141 (1984), 1145–58.

20. Parloff, "Can Psychotherapy Research."

21. C. Krauthammer, "The Twilight of Psychotherapy," *Washington Post*, December 27, 1985.

Chapter 14   Resistance to Indigenous Therapists in Established Systems: The Tarzan Mentality

1. J. F. Borus et al., "Psychotherapy in a Goldfish Bowl," *Archives of General Psychiatry* 36 (1979), 187–90.

2. Ibid.

3. E. T. Shapiro and H. Pinsker, "Shared Ethnic Scotoma," *American Journal of Psychiatry* 130 (1973), 1338–41.

4. One of the few articles to deal with this issue, usually left unstated, is I. N. Berlin, "Resistance to Change in Mental Health Professionals," *American Journal of Orthopsychiatry* 39 (1969), 109–15.

5. E. D. Wittkower and H. Warnes, "Cultural Aspects of Psychotherapy," *American Journal of Psychotherapy*, 28 (1974), 566–73.

6. "Innovations in Mental Health Training: Summaries of Experimental and Special Training Projects" (Washington, D.C.: National Institute of Mental Health, 1969), mimeographed.

7. E. L. Margetts, "Traditional Yoruba Healers in Nigeria," *Man* 102 (1965), 115–18.

8. I. Lubchansky, G. Egri and J. Stokes, "Puerto Rican Spiritualists View Mental Illness: The Faith Healer as a Paraprofessional," *American Journal of Psychiatry* 127 (1970), 312–21.

9. G. M. Carstairs, "Psychiatric Problems in Developing Countries," *British Journal of Psychiatry* 123 (1973), 271–7.

Chapter 15   Conclusions: Genus—Psychotherapist, Species—Witchdoctor and Psychiatrist

1. W. Herbert, "Taking Therapists to Court," *Washington Post Book World*, August 18, 1985.

2. E. Corin and G. Bibeau, "Psychiatric Perspectives in Africa," *Transcultural Psychiatric Research Review* 17 (1980), 205–33.

3. For a model of how to make a contract with a psychotherapist, see S. Adams and M. Orgel, "Through the Mental Health Maze" (Health Research Group, 2000 P Street, N.W., Washington, D.C. 20036, 1975).

4. Strupp, Hadley, and Gomes-Schwartz, *Psychotherapy*, p. 137.

5. A. Leighton, "Discussion," in *Transcultural Psychiatry*, ed. A. V. S. De Rueck and R. Porter (Boston: Little, Brown, 1965).

Bibliography

Abel, T. "Cultural Patterns as They Affect Psychotherapeutic Procedures." *American Journal of Psychotherapy* 10 (1956), 728–40.

Ackerknecht, E. H. "Natural Diseases and Rational Treatment in Primitive Medicine." *Bulletin of the History of Medicine* 19 (1946), 467–97.

———. "Problems of Primitive Medicine." *Bulletin of the History of Medicine* 11 (1942), 503–21.

———. "Psychopathology, Primitive Medicine, and Primitive Culture." *Bulletin of the History of Medicine* 14 (1943), 30–67.

Adams, S., and M. Orgel. *Through the Mental Health Maze.* Washington, D.C.: Health Research Group, 1975.

Ader, R., ed. *Psychoneuroimmunology.* New York: Academic Press, 1981.

"African Sees Gain for Mentally Ill." *New York Times*, March 24, 1968.

Akstein, D. "Terpsichore Trance Therapy: A Form of Group Psychotherapy Based on Ritual Possession." *Transcultural Psychiatric Research* 5 (April 1968), 74–5.

Albee, G. W. "Myths, Models and Manpower." *Mental Hygiene* 52, no. 2 (1968), 168–80.

274

Alegria, D., E. Guerra, C. Martinez, G. G. Meyer. "El Hospital Invisible: A Study of Curanderismo." *Archives of General Psychiatry* 34 (1977), 1354–7.

Alexander, C. A., and M. K. Shivaswamy. "Traditional Healers in a Region of Mysore." *Social Science and Medicine* 5 (1971), 595–601.

Allport, G. W., and T. F. Pettigrew. "Cultural Influences on the Perception of Movement: The Trapezoidal Illusion Among the Zulus." *Journal of Abnormal Psychology* 55, no. 1 (1957), 104–13.

Altschule, M. D. *Origins of Concepts in Human Behavior.* New York: John Wiley, 1977.

Aspy, D. N. "A Study of Three Facilitative Conditions and Their Relationships to the Achievement of Third Grade Students." Ph.D. diss., University of Kentucky, 1965. Summarized in Truax, C. B., and R. R. Carkhuff. *Toward Effective Counseling and Psychotherapy: Training and Practice.* Chicago: Aldine Publishing Company, 1967.

Aveline, M. "What Price Psychiatry Without Psychotherapy?" *Lancet* 2 (1984), 856–8.

Baasher, T. A. "Traditional Psychotherapeutic Practices in the Sudan," *Transcultural Psychiatric Review* 4 (October 1967), 158–60.

Becker, E. "The Relevance to Psychiatry of Recent Research in Anthropology," *American Journal of Psychotherapy* 16, no. 4 (1962), 600–17.

Beitman, B. D. "The Demographics of American Psychotherapists: A Pilot Study." *American Journal of Psychotherapy* 37 (1983), 37–48.

Belo, J. *Trance in Bali.* New York: Columbia University Press, 1960.

Benoist, A., et al. "Depression Among French Canadians in Montreal." *Transcultural Psychiatric Research* 2 (April 1965), 52–4.

Berenson, B. G., and R. R. Caukhuff, eds. *Sources of Gain in Counseling and Psychotherapy.* New York: Holt, Rinehart and Winston, 1967.

Bergin, A. E. "The Effects of Psychotherapy: Negative Results Revisited." *Journal of Counseling Psychology* 10 (1963), 244–55.

———. "Psychotherapy Can Be Dangerous." *Psychology Today,* November 1975, 96–104.

———. "Some Implications of Psychotherapy Research for Therapeutic Practice," *Journal of Abnormal Psychology* 71, no. 1 (1966), 235–46.

Bergman, A. B., S. W. Dassel, and R. J. Wedgewood. "Time-Motion

Study of Practicing Pediatricians." *Pediatrics* 38, no. 2 (1966), 254–63.

———, J. L. Probstfield, and R. J. Wedgwood. "Task Identification in Pediatric Practice." *American Journal of the Diseases of Children* 118 (1969), 459–68.

Bergman, R. L. "Navaho Medicine and Psychoanalysis." *Human Behavior* 8–15, July 1973.

———. "Paraprofessionals in Indian Mental Health Programs." *Psychiatric Annals* 4 (1974), 76–84.

———. "A School for Medicine Men." *American Journal of Psychiatry* 130 (1973), 663–6.

Berlin, I. N. "Resistance to Change in Mental Health Professionals." *American Journal of Orthopsychiatry* 39, no. 1 (January 1969), 109–15.

Bermann, G. "China." In *Psychiatry in the Communist World,* edited by A. Kiev. New York: Science House, 1968.

Berndt, C. H. "The Role of Native Doctors in Aboriginal Australia." In *Magic, Faith and Healing,* edited by A. Kiev. New York: The Free Press, 1964.

Berne, E. "The Cultural Problem: Psychopathology in Tahiti." *American Journal of Psychiatry* 116 (1960), 1076–81.

Bishop, M. M., and G. Winokur. "Cross-Cultural Psychotherapy." *Journal of Nervous and Mental Disease* 123 (1956), 369–75.

Blachly, P. H., H. J. Osterud, and R. Josslin. "Suicide in Professional Groups." *New England Journal of Medicine* 268, no. 23 (1963), 1278–82.

Bloch, S., G. Bond, B. Qualls, I. Yalom, E. Zimmerman. "Patients' Expectations of Therapeutic Improvement and Their Outcomes." *American Journal of Psychiatry* 133 (1976), 1457–60.

Bloom, L. "The Izinyanga of Durban, South Africa." *Transcultural Psychiatric Research* 14 (April 1963), 43–5.

Bluestone, H., R. Bisi, and A. J. Katz. "The Establishment of a Mental Health Service in a Predominantly Spanish-Speaking Neighborhood of New York City." *Behavioral Neuropsychiatry* 1, no. 5 (1969), 12–16.

Boas, F. "On Grammatical Categories." In *Language in Culture and Society,* edited by D. Hymes. New York: Harper & Row, 1964.

Boghen, D., and M. Boghen. "Medical Attitudes, Beliefs and Practices in Martinique." *Transcultural Psychiatric Research* 3 (April 1966), 47–9.

Bogoras, W. *The Chukchee.* New York: American Museum of Natural History, 1907.

Bolman, W. "Cross-Cultural Psychotherapy." *American Journal of Psychiatry* 124, no. 9 (1968), 1237–44.

Borus, J. F., M. Anastasi, R. Casoni, et al. "Psychotherapy in a Goldfish Bowl." *Archives of General Psychiatry* 36 (1979), 187–90.

Bourguignon, E. "The Theory of Spirit Possession." In *Context and Meaning in Cultural Anthropology,* edited by M. Spiro. New York: The Free Press, 1965.

Boyer, L. B. "Folk Psychiatry of the Apaches of the Mescalero Indian Reservation." In *Magic, Faith and Healing,* edited by A. Kiev. New York: The Free Press, 1964.

———. "Further Remarks Concerning Shamans and Shamanism." *The Israel Annals of Psychiatry and Related Disciplines* 2, no. 2 (1964), 235–57.

———. "Notes on the Personality Structure of a North American Indian Shaman." *Journal of Hillside Hospital* 10 (January 1961), 14–33.

———. "Remarks on the Personality of Shamans." *Psychoanalytic Study of Society* 2 (1961), 233–54.

———, et al. "Comparison of the Shamans and Pseudoshamans of the Apaches of the Mescalero Indian Reservation: A Rorschach Study." *Journal of Projective Techniques and Personality Assessment* 28, no. 2 (1964), 173–80.

Braceland, F. J., ed. *Faith, Reason and Modern Psychiatry.* New York: P. J. Kennedy and Sons, 1955.

Bram, J. "Spirits, Mediums and Believers in Contemporary Puerto Rico." *Transactions of the New York Academy of Sciences,* 1957, 340–47.

Brewer, M. "We're Gonna Tear You Down and Put You Back Together." *Psychology Today,* August 1975, 35–89.

Bromberg, W. *The Mind of Man: A History of Psychotherapy and Psychoanalysis.* New York: Harper and Brothers, 1959.

Brown, B. M. "Cognitive Aspects of Wolpe's Behavior Therapy." *American Journal of Psychiatry* 124 (December 1967), 6.

Brown, D. *Bury My Heart at Wounded Knee.* New York: Bantam, 1972.

Brown, R. W., and E. Lenneberg. "A Study in Language and Cognition." *Journal of Abnormal and Social Psychology* 49 (1954), 454–62.

Burton-Bradley, B. G., and C. Julius. "Folk Psychiatry of Certain Villages in the Central District of Papua." *Transcultural Psychiatric Research* 3 (April 1966), 22–4.

Bustamente, J. A. "Importance of Cultural Patterns in Psychotherapy." *American Journal of Psychotherapy* 11 (1957), 803–12.

Calestro, K. M. "Psychotherapy, Faith Healing and Suggestion." *International Journal of Psychiatry* 10 (1972), 83–113.

Cannon, W. B. "Voodoo Death." *American Anthropologist* 46 (1942), 169–81.

Caplan, G., and H. Grunebaum. "Perspectives on Primary Prevention." *Archives of General Psychiatry* 17, no. 3 (1967), 331–46.

Carkhuff, R. R., and C. B. Truax. "Lay Mental Health Counseling: The Effects of Lay Group Counseling." *Journal of Consulting Psychology* 29 (1965), 426.

———, and C. B. Truax. "Training in Counseling and Psychotherapy: An Evaluation of an Integrated Didactic and Experimental Approach." *Journal of Consulting Psychology* 29 (1965), 333–6.

Carstairs, G. M. "Medicine and Faith in Rural Rajasthan." In *Health, Culture and Community,* edited by B. D. Paul. New York: Russell Sage Foundation, 1955.

———. "Psychiatric Problems in Developing Countries." *British Journal of Psychiatry* 123 (1973), 271–7.

———, and R. L. Kapur. *The Great Universe of Kota.* Berkeley: University of California Press, 1976.

Casper, E. G., and M. J. Philippus. "Fifteen Cases of Embrujada (bewitched)." *Hospital and Community Psychiatry* 26 (1975), 273–4.

Castaneda, C. *The Teachings of Don Juan: A Yaqui Way of Knowledge.* New York: Ballantine Books, 1969.

Caudill, W. "Around the Clock Patient Care in Japanese Psychiatric Hospitals: The Role of the Tsukisoi." *American Sociological Review* 26, no. 2 (April 1961), 204–14.

———. "Observations on the Cultural Context of Japanese Psychiatry." In *Culture and Mental Health,* edited by M. Opler. New York: The Macmillan Company, 1959.

———, and C. Schooler. "Symptom Patterns and Background Characteristics of Japanese Psychiatric Patients." *Transcultural Psychiatric Research* 5 (October 1968), 133–7.

Cawte, J. *Medicine Is the Law.* Honolulu: University of Hawaii Press, 1974.

Cawte, J. E. "Australian Ethnopsychiatry in the Field: A Sampling in North Kimberley." *Medical Journal of Australia* 1 (1964), 467–72.

———, and M. A. Kidson. "Australian Ethnopsychiatry: The Walbiri Doctor." *Medical Journal of Australia* 2 (1964), 977–83.

Cerletti, U. "Old and New Information About Electroshock." *American Journal of Psychiatry* 107 (1950), 87–94.

Cernay, J. "Psychiatry in China." *Ceskoslovenska Psychiatrie* 59, no. 4 (1963), 273–82. Reported in *Transcultural Psychiatric Research* 1 (April 1964), 34–6.

Charatan, F. B., and I. Rosenblatt. "Psychotherapy: The Views of Psychiatrists from Scotland and Nassau County, New York." *American Journal of Psychiatry* 125, no. 8 (1969), 1120–2.

Clark, M. *Health in the Mexican-American Culture: A Community Study.* Berkeley: University of California Press, 1959.

Colby, K. M. "Computer Simulation of Change in Personal Belief Systems." *Behavioral Science* 12, no. 3 (1967), 248–53.

———. "Computer Simulation of Neurotic Processes." In *Computers in Biomedical Research,* edited by R. W. Stacey and B. Waxman. New York: Academic Press, 1965.

———, J. B. Watt, and J. P. Gilbert. "A Computer Method of Psychotherapy: Preliminary Communication." *Journal of Nervous and Mental Disease* 142, no. 2 (1966), 148–52.

Conklin, H. "Hanunoo Color Categories." *Southwest Journal of Anthropology* 9 (Winter 1955), 339–44.

Corin, E., and G. Bibeau. "Psychiatric Perspectives in Africa." *Transcultural Psychiatric Research Review* 17 (1980), 205–33.

Cowen, E. L., E. A. Gardner, and M. Zax. *Emergent Approaches to Mental Health Problems.* New York: Appleton-Century-Crofts, 1967.

Currier, R. L. "The Hot-Cold Syndrome and Symbolic Balance in Mexican and Spanish-American Folk Medicine." *Ethnology* 5, no. 3 (1966), 251–63.

D'Andrade, R. G. "Anthropological Studies of Dreams." In F. L. K. Hsu. *Psychological Anthropology.* Homewood, Ill.: Dorsey Press, 1961.

Dauth, J. "Malaysia's Bomohs." *World Health*, November 1977, 4–7.

Davis, K. "Mental Hygiene and the Class Structure." *Psychiatry* 1 (1938), 55–65.

Dawson, J. "Urbanization and Mental Health in a West African Community." In *Magic, Faith and Healing*, edited by A. Kiev. New York: The Free Press, 1964.

Dean, S. R., and D. Thong. "Shamanism Versus Psychiatry in Bali, 'Isle of the Gods': Some Modern Implications." *American Journal of Psychiatry* 129 (1972) 59–62.

Deane, W. N. "The Culture of the Patient: An Underestimated Dimension in Psychotherapy." *International Journal of Social Psychiatry* 7 (1961), 181–6.

Del Pozo, E. C. "Empiricism and Magic in Aztec Pharmacology." In *Ethnopharmacologic Search for Psychoactive Drugs*, edited by D. H. Efron, B. Holmstedt, and N. Kline. Public Health Service Publication no. 1645. Washington, D.C.: U.S. Government Printing Office, 1967.

Denko, J. D. "How Preliterate Peoples Explain Disturbed Behavior." *Archives of General Psychiatry* 15 (1966), 398–409.

DeReuck, A. V. S., and R. Porter, eds. *Transcultural Psychiatry.* Boston: Little, Brown and Company, 1965.

Devereux, G. "Dream Learning and Individual Ritual Differences in Mohave Shamanism." *American Anthropologist* 59 (1957), 1036–45.

———. *Mohave Ethnopsychiatry and Suicide: The Psychiatric Knowledge and the Psychic Disturbances of an Indian Tribe.* Bureau of American Ethnology Bulletin no. 175. Washington, D.C.: Smithsonian Institution, 1961.

——. *Reality and Dream: Psychotherapy of a Plains Indian*. New York: International Universities Press, 1950.

——. "Shamans as Neurotics." *American Anthropologist* 63 (1961), 1088–90.

——. "Three Technical Problems in Psychotherapy of Plains Indian Patients." *American Journal of Psychotherapy* 5 (1951), 411–23.

Diaz-Guerrero, R. "Neurosis and the Mexican Family Structure." *American Journal of Psychiatry* 112 (1955), 411–17.

Dobkin, M. "Folk Curing with a Psychedelic Cactus in the North Coast of Peru." *International Journal of Social Psychiatry* 15 (1968), 23–32.

——. "Fortune's Malice." *Journal of American Folklore* 82 (1969), 132–41.

Douyon, E. "Trance in Haitian Voodoo." *Transcultural Psychiatric Research* 2 (October 1965), 155–9.

Dubos, R. *Man Adapting*. New Haven: Yale University Press, 1965.

Dumont, M. P. "Tavern Culture: The Sustenance of Homeless Men." *American Journal of Orthopsychiatry* 37, no. 5 (October 1967), 938–45.

Durlak, J. A. "Comparative Effectiveness of Paraprofessional and Professional Helpers." *Psychological Bulletin* 86 (1979), 80–92.

Edgerton, R. B., M. Karno, and I. Fernandez. "Curanderismo in the Metropolis: The Diminished Role of Folk Psychiatry Among Los Angeles Mexican-Americans." *American Journal of Psychotherapy* 24 (1970), 124–34.

Edsman, C. M., ed. *Studies in Shamanism*. Stockholm: Almquist and Weksell, 1967.

Efron, D. H., B. Holmstedt, and N. Kline, eds. *Ethnopharmacologic Search for Psychoactive Drugs*. Public Health Service Publication no. 1645. Washington, D.C.: U.S. Government Printing Office, 1967.

Egbert, C. D., G. E. Battit, C. E. Welch, and M. K. Bartlett. "Reduction of Postoperative Pain by Encouragement and Instruction of Patients." *New England Journal of Medicine* 170, no. 16 (1964), 825–7.

Eliade, M. *Shamanism: Archaic Techniques of Ecstasy*. Translated by W. R. Trask. New York: Pantheon, 1964.

El-Islam, M. F. "Arabic Cultural Psychiatry." *Transcultural Psychiatric Research Review* 19 (1982), 5–24.

Ellsworth, R. B. *Nonprofessionals in Psychiatric Rehabilitation.* New York: Appleton-Century-Crofts, 1968.

Erasmus, C. J. "Changing Folk Beliefs and the Relativity of Empirical Knowledge." *Southwest Journal of Anthropology* 8 (1952), 411–28.

Erikson, E. H. *Observations on the Yoruk: Childhood and World Image.* University of California Publications in American Archaeology and Ethnology. Berkeley: University of California Press, 1943. Quoted in S. H. Posinsky, "Yoruk Shamanism," *Psychiatric Quarterly* 39 (1965), 227–43.

Eysenck, H. J. "The Effectiveness of Psychotherapy: The Specter at the Feast." *Behavioral and Brain Sciences* 6 (1983), 290.

———. "The Effects of Psychotherapy: An Evaluation." *Journal of Consulting Psychology* 16 (1952), 319–24.

Ezriel, H. "Experimentation Within the Psychoanalytic Session," *British Journal of Philosophy and Science* 7 (1956), 25. Quoted in W. M. Mendel, "The Non-Specifics of Psychotherapy," *International Journal of Psychiatry* 5, no. 5 (1968), 400–2.

Favazza, A. R., and A. D. Faheem, eds. *Themes in Cultural Psychiatry: An Annotated Bibliography, 1975–1980.* Columbia: University of Missouri Press, 1982.

Fejos, P. "Magic, Witchcraft and Medical Theory in Primitive Cultures." In *Man's Image in Medicine and Anthropology*, edited by I. Galdston. New York: International Universities Press, 1963.

Fiedler, F. E. "A Comparison of Therapeutic Relationships in Psychoanalytic, Non-Directive and Adlerian Therapy." *Journal of Consulting Psychology* 14 (1950), 436–45.

Field, M. J. *Search for Security: An Ethnopsychiatric Study of Rural Ghana.* Evanston, Ill.: Northwestern University Press, 1960.

———. "Witchcraft as a Primitive Interpretation of Mental Disorder." *Journal of Mental Science* 101 (1955), 826–33.

Fisch, S. "Botanicas and Spiritualism in a Metropolis." *Milbank Memorial Fund Quarterly* 46 (1968), 377–88.

Fisher, S., and R. P. Greenberg. *The Scientific Credibility of Freud's Theories and Therapy.* New York: Basic Books, 1977.

Ford, C. S., and F. A. Beach. *Patterns of Sexual Behavior.* New York: Harper and Brothers, 1951.

Foster, G. M. "Nagualism in Mexico and Guatemala." *Acta Americana* 2 (1944), 85–105.

———. "Relationships Between Spanish and Spanish-American Folk Medicine." *Journal of American Folklore* 66 (1953), 201–17.

Fox, J. R. "Pueblo Baseball: A New Use for Old Witchcraft." *Journal of American Folklore* 74 (1961), 291.

———. "Witchcraft and Clanship in Cochiti Therapy." In *Magic, Faith and Healing,* edited by A. Kiev. New York: The Free Press, 1964.

Frake, C. O. "The Diagnosis of Disease Among the Subanun of Mindanao." *American Anthropologist* 63 (1961), 113–32.

Frank, J. D. *Persuasion and Healing.* Baltimore: Johns Hopkins Press, 1961.

———. "Psychotherapy: The Restoration of Morale." *American Journal of Psychiatry* 131 (1974), 271–4.

———. "The Role of Hope in Psychotherapy." *International Journal of Psychiatry* 5, no. 5 (May 1968), 383–412.

———, E. H. Nash, A. R. Stone, and S. D. Imber. "Immediate and Long-Term Symptomatic Course of Psychiatric Outpatients." *American Journal of Psychiatry* 120 (1963), 429–39.

———, R. Hoehn-Saric, S. D. Imber, B. L. Liberman, and A. R. Stone. *Effective Ingredients of Successful Psychotherapy.* New York: Brunner Mazel, 1978.

Freeman, D. "Shaman and Incubus." *Psychoanalytic Study of Society* 4 (1967), 315–43.

Freeman, W. "Psychiatrists Who Kill Themselves: A Study in Suicide." *American Journal of Psychiatry* 124, no. 6 (1967), 846–7.

Freud, S. *Collected Papers.* Vol. 1, 2d ed. London: Hogarth Press, 1940, 249–63.

Friedman, H. J. "Patient-Expectancy and Symptom Reduction." *Archives of General Psychiatry* 8 (1963), 61–7.

Fuchs, S. "Magic Healing Techniques Among the Balahis in Central India." In *Magic, Faith and Healing,* edited by A. Kiev. New York: The Free Press, 1964.

Galdston, I., ed. *Man's Image in Medicine and Anthropology*. New York: International Universities Press, 1963.

Gardner, G. G. "The Psychotherapeutic Relationship." *Psychological Bulletin* 61 (1964), 426–37.

Garrison, V. "Doctor, Espiritista or Psychiatrist?: Health-Seeking Behavior in a Puerto Rican Neighborhood in New York City." *Medical Anthropology* 1 (1977), 65–180.

Gavin, J., and A. Ludwig. "A Case of Witchcraft." *Journal of Nervous and Mental Disease* 133 (1961), 161–8.

Gelfand, M. "Psychiatric Disorder as Recognized by the Shona." In *Magic, Faith and Healing*, edited by A. Kiev. New York: The Free Press, 1964.

Gibbs, J. L. "The Kpelle Moot: A Therapeutic Model for the Informal Settlement of Disputes." *Journal of Africa* 33, no. 1 (1963), 1–11.

Giel, R., Y. Gezahegn, and J. N. van Luijk. "Faith Healing and Spirit Possession in Ghion, Ethiopia." *Transcultural Psychiatric Research* 5 (April 1968), 64–7.

Gill, M., and M. Brenman. *Hypnosis and Related States: Psychoanalytic Studies of Regression*. New York: International Universities Press, 1961.

Gillin, J. "Magical Fright." *Psychiatry* 11 (November 1948), 387–400.

Gliedman, L. H., E. H. Nash, S. D. Imber, A. R. Stone, and J. D. Frank. "Reduction of Symptoms by Pharmacologically Inert Substances and by Short-Term Psychotherapy." *American Medical Association Archives of Neurology and Psychiatry* 79 (1958), 345–51.

Goldstein, A. P., "Domains and Dilemmas," *International Journal of Psychiatry* 7, no. 3 (1969), 128–34.

———. *Therapist-Patient Expectancies in Psychotherapy*. New York: Pergamon Press, 1962.

Goleman, D. "Social Workers Vault into a Leading Role in Psychotherapy: Psychiatrists and Psychologists Defend Territory as Competition Increases." *Washington Post*, April 30, 1985.

Goodman, G. "An Experiment with Companionship Therapy: College Students and Troubled Boys—Assumptions, Selection, and Design."

American Journal of Public Health 62, no. 10 (October 1967), 1772–7.

Greden, J. F., and J. I. Casariego. "Controversies in Psychiatric Education: A Survey of Residents' Attitudes." *American Journal of Psychiatry* 132 (1975), 270–3.

Greenberg, D. S. "Washington Report." *New England Journal of Medicine* 303 (1980), 539–40.

Greenblatt, M., and D. Kantor. "Student Volunteer Movement and the Manpower Shortage." *American Journal of Psychiatry* 118 (1962), 809–14.

Greenspoon, J. "The Reinforcing Effect of Two Spoken Sounds on the Frequency of Two Responses." *American Journal of Psychology* 68 (1955), 409–16.

Gross, M. L. *The Psychological Society.* New York: Random House, 1978.

Gursslin, O. R., R. G. Hunt, and J. L. Roach. "Social Class and the Mental Health Movement." In F. Riessman, J. Cohen, and A. Pearl, *Mental Health of the Poor.* New York: The Free Press, 1964.

Hadley, S. W., and H. H. Strupp. "Contemporary Views of Negative Effects in Psychotherapy." *Archives of General Psychiatry* 33 (1976), 1291–1302.

Haley, J. *Strategies of Psychotherapy.* New York: Grune and Stratton, 1963.

Hallaji, J. "Hypnotherapeutic Techniques in a Central Asian Community." *International Journal of Clinical and Experimental Hypnosis.* Reported in *Transcultural Psychiatric Research* 1 (October 1964), 110–11.

Hallowell, A. I. "Ojibwa Ontology, Behavior and World View." In *Culture in History,* edited by S. Diamond. New York: Columbia University Press, 1960.

———. "Some Empirical Aspects of Northern Salteaux Religion." *American Anthropologist* 36 (1934), 389–405.

Handelman, D. "The Development of a Washo Shaman," *Ethnology* 6, no. 4 (1967), 444–64.

Hansell, N., M. Wodarczyk, and H. M. Visotsky. "The Mental Health Expediter: A Review After Two Years of the Project and One Year of the Expediter in Action." *Archives of General Psychiatry* 18 (April 1968), 392–99.

Harding, T. "Psychosis in a Rural West African Community." *Social Psychiatry* 8 (1973), 198–203.

Harlow, H. F. "The Nature of Love." *American Psychologist* 13 (1958), 673–85.

———. "Primary Affectional Patterns in Primates." *American Journal of Orthopsychiatry* 30 (1960), 676–84.

Harner, M. *The Way of the Shaman: A Guide to Power and Healing.* New York: Harper and Brothers, 1950.

Harrison, T. J. "Training for Village Health Aides in the Kotzebue Area of Alaska." *Public Health Reports* 80, no. 7 (1965), 565–72.

Harwood, A. "The Hot-Cold Theory of Disease: Implications for Treatment of Puerto Rican Patients." *Journal of the American Medical Association* 216 (1971), 1153–8.

———. *Rx: Spiritist as Needed: A Study of a Puerto Rican Community Mental Health Resource.* New York: John Wiley and Sons, 1977.

"Healer Offers Unique Brand of Psychotherapy." *Medical World News,* September 29, 1967.

Heine, R., ed. *The Student Physician as Psychotherapist.* Chicago: University of Chicago Press, 1962.

Henry, J. "The Inner Experience of Culture." *Psychiatry* 14 (1951), 87–103.

Herbert, W. "Taking Therapists to Court." *Washington Post Book World,* August 18, 1985.

Herink, R., ed. *The Psychotherapy Handbook: The A to Z Guide to More Than 250 Different Therapies in Use Today.* New York: New American Library, 1980.

Hertz, D. "Problems of Urbanization in Liberia as Reflected in the Mental Health Services." *Transcultural Psychiatric Research* 1 (April 1964), 58–60.

Hes, J. P. "The Changing Social Role of the Yemenite Mori." In *Magic, Faith and Healing,* edited by A. Kiev. New York: The Free Press, 1964.

Hessin, A. L. "Treatment of the Mentally Ill by San Blas Indian Healers (Panama)." *Transcultural Psychiatric Research* 15 (October 1963), 70.

Hilgard, J. R., D. C. Staight, and U. S. Moore. "Better-Adjusted Peers as Resources in Group Therapy with Adolescents." *Journal of Psychology* 73 (1969), 75–100.

————, and U. S. Moore. "Affiliative Therapy with Young Adolescents." *Journal of the American Academy of Child Psychiatry* 8, no. 4 (1969), 577–605.

Hill, D. *Magic and Superstition*. New York: Hamlyn Publishing, 1968.

Hilts, P. "Psychotherapy Put on Couch by Government." *Washington Post*, September 14, 1980.

Hoehn-Saric, R., B. Liberman, S. D. Imber, A. R. Stone, S. K. Pande, J. D. Frank. "Arousal and Attitude Change in Neurotic Patients." *Archives of General Psychiatry* 26 (1972), 51–6.

Holland, W. R. "Mexican-American Medical Beliefs: Science or Magic?" *Arizona Medicine* 20 (May 1963), 89–102.

————, and R. G. Tharp. "Highland Maya Psychotherapy." *American Anthropologist* 66 (February 1964), 41–52.

Hollingshead, A. B., and F. C. Redlich. *Social Class and Mental Illness*. New York: John Wiley and Sons, 1958.

Holt, R. R., and L. Luborsky. *Personality Patterns of Psychiatrists*. New York: Basic Books, 1958.

Holtved, E. "Eskimo Shamanism." In *Studies in Shamanism*, edited by C. M. Edsman. Stockholm: Almquist and Weksell, 1967.

Howell, W., and D. J. S. Bailey. *A Sea Dyak Dictionary*. Singapore: American Mission Press, 1900.

Hudson, W. M., ed. *The Healer of Los Olmos*. Texas Folklore Society Publication no. 24. Dallas: Southern Methodist University Press, 1951.

Hunt, R. G. "Social Class and Mental Illness: Some Implications for Clinical Theory and Practice." *American Journal of Psychiatry* 116 (June 1960), 1065–9.

Huxley, A. *The Devils of Loudon*. London: Chatto and Windus, 1961.

Indian Health Highlights. Washington, D.C.: Department of Health, Education and Welfare, 1966.

Inkeles, A., and D. J. Levinson. "National Character: The Study of Modal Personality and Socio-Cultural Systems." In *Handbook of Social Psychology,* edited by G. Lindzey. Cambridge, Mass.: Addison-Wesley, 1954.

"Innovations in Mental Health Training: Summaries of Experimental and Special Training Projects." Washington, D.C.: National Institute of Mental Health Division of Manpower and Training, 1969. Mimeographed.

Jaco, E. G. "Mental Health of the Spanish-American in Texas." In *Culture and Mental Health,* edited by M. K. Opler. New York: The Macmillan Company, 1959.

Jahoda, G. "Traditional Healers and Other Institutions Concerned with Mental Illness in Ghana." *International Journal of Social Psychiatry* 7, no. 4 (1961), 245–68.

James, D. W. "Chinese Medicine." *The Lancet* 1 (1958), 1068–9.

Janis, I. L. *Psychological Stress.* New York: John Wiley and Sons, 1958.

Janov, A., and E. M. Holden. *Primal Man: The New Consciousness.* New York: Thomas Y. Crowell, 1975.

Jarvis, D. C. *Folk Medicine: A Vermont Doctor's Guide to Good Health.* New York: Henry Holt and Company, 1958.

Jilek, W. G. "Altered States of Consciousness in North American Indian Ceremonials." *Ethos* 10 (1982), 326–43.

——. "The Image of the African Medicine-Man." In N. Petrilowitsch, "Contributions to Comparative Psychiatry," *Bibliotheca Psychiatrica et Neurologica* 133, no. 6 (1967), 165–78.

——. "Native Renaissance: The Survival and Revival of Indigenous Therapeutic Ceremonials Among North American Indians." *Transcultural Psychiatric Research Review* 15 (1978), 117–47.

——, and N. Todd. "Witchdoctors Succeed Where Doctors Fail." *Canadian Psychiatric Association Journal* 19 (1974), 351–6.

Johnson, D. L., and C. A. Johnson. "Totally Discouraged: A Depressive Syndrome of the Dakota Sioux." *Transcultural Psychiatric Research* 2 (October 1965), 141–3.

"Joint Venture in Mental Health, 1968." Report of the Ad Hoc Comprehensive Mental Health Planning Committee for Santa Clara County. San Jose, California, 1968.

Jones, R. "Ethnic Family Patterns: The Mexican Family in the United States." *American Journal of Sociology* 53 (1948), 450–2.

Kahn, M. W., and J. Delk. "Developing a Community Mental Health Clinic on the Papago Indian Reservation." *International Journal of Social Psychiatry* 19 (1973), 299–306.

———, J. Henry, and J. Cawte. "Mental Health Services by and for Australian Aborigines." *Australian and New Zealand Journal of Psychiatry* 10 (1976), 221–8.

———, C. Williams, E. Glavez, L. Lejoro, R. Conrad, and G. Goldstein. "The Papago Psychology Service: A Community Mental Health Program on an American Indian Reservation." *American Journal of Community Psychology* 3 (1975), 81–97.

Kaplan, B., ed. *Studying Personality Cross-Culturally.* New York: Row, Peterson and Company, 1961.

———, and D. Johnson. "The Social Meaning of Navaho Psychopathology and Psychotherapy." In *Magic, Faith and Healing,* edited by A. Kiev. New York: The Free Press, 1964.

Karno, M. "The Enigma of Ethnicity in a Psychiatric Clinic." *Archives of General Psychiatry* 14, no. 5 (1966), 516–20.

———, and R. B. Edgerton. "Perception of Mental Illness in a Mexican-American Community." *Archives of General Psychiatry* 20 (1969), 233–8.

———, R. N. Ross, and R. A. Caper. "Mental Health Roles of Physicians in a Mexican-American Community." *Community Mental Health Journal* 5, no. 1 (1969), 62–9.

Katz, R. *Boiling Energy: Community Healing Among the Kalahari Kung.* Cambridge: Harvard University Press, 1982.

———. "Empowerment and Synergy: Expanding the Community's Healing Resources." *Prevention in Human Services* 3 (1983/84), 201–26.

Kellaway, P. "The Part Played by Electric Fish in the Early History of Bioelectricity and Electrotherapy." *Bulletin of the History of Medicine* 20 (1946), 112–37.

Kelley, H. H. "The Effects of Expectations upon First Impressions of Persons." *American Psychologist* 4 (1949), 252.

Kelly, Isabel. *Folk Practices in North Mexico.* Austin: University of Texas Press, 1965.

Kelly, J. G. "The Mental Health Agent in the Urban Community." In *Urban America and the Planning of Mental Health Services.* Symposium no. 10. New York: Group for the Advancement of Psychiatry, 1964.

Kennedy, J. G. "Nubian Zar Ceremonies as Psychotherapy." *Human Organization* 26 (1967), 185–94.

Khajavi, F., and H. Hekmat. "A Comparative Study of Empathy: The Effects of Psychiatric Training." *Archives of General Psychiatry* 25 (1971), 490–3.

Kiev, A. *Curanderismo: Mexican-American Folk Psychiatry.* New York: The Free Press, 1968.

———. "Prescientific Psychiatry." in *American Handbook of Psychiatry,* edited by S. Arieti. Vol. 3. New York: Basic Books, 1966.

———. "Primitive Holistic Medicine." *International Journal of Social Psychiatry,* 8, no. 1 (1962), 58–61.

———. "Primitive Therapy: A Cross-Cultural Study of the Relationship Between Child Training and Therapeutic Practices Related to Illness." In *Psychoanalytic Study of Society,* edited by W. Muensterberger and S. Axelrod. Vol. 1. New York: International Universities Press, 1961.

———. "The Psychotherapeutic Aspects of Primitive Medicine." *Human Organization* 21 (1962), 25–9.

———. "Psychotherapy in Haitian Voodoo." *American Journal of Psychotherapy* 16 (July 1962), 469–76.

———. "Spirit Possession in Haiti." *American Journal of Psychiatry* 118 (1961), 133–8.

———, ed. *Magic, Faith and Healing.* New York: The Free Press, 1964.

Kim, H. "Folk Psychiatry in Korea." *Transcultural Psychiatric Research Review* 11 (1974), 40–2.

———. Review of "Shamanist Healing Ceremonies in Korea" by K. I. Kim. *Transcultural Psychiatric Research Review* 10 (1973), 124–5.

Kim, H. A. Review of "Analytic Psychological Study Regarding the Treatment of the Spirits of the Dead in Korean Shamanistic Cults," by B. Y. Rhi. *Transcultural Psychiatric Research Review* 9 (1972), 117–20.

Kimball, C. P. "Psychologic Responses to Open Heart Surgery." *American Journal of Psychiatry* 126 (1969), 348–59.

Kline, L. Y. "Some Factors in Psychiatric Treatment of Spanish-Americans." *American Journal of Psychiatry* 125, no. 12 (June 1969), 1674–81.

Kluckhohn, C., and D. Leighton. *The Navaho.* Garden City, N.Y.: Anchor Books, 1962.

Knupfer, G., D. D. Jackson, and G. Krieger. "Personality Differences Between More and Less Competent Psychotherapists as a Function of Criteria of Competence." *Journal of Nervous and Mental Disease* 129 (1959), 375–84.

Kolata, G. B. "Clinical Trial of Psychotherapists Is Under Way." *Science* 212 (1981), 432–3.

Kolman, P. B. R. "A Study of Psychiatric Patients of the University of Malaya Medical Centre Who Also Consult Indigenous Healers." *Social Psychiatry* 11 (1976), 127–34.

Kora, T. "Morita Therapy." *Transcultural Psychiatric Research* 2 (October 1965), 101–3.

Koss, J. D. "Ritual Healing and the Reduction of Psychic Stress." Paper presented at Fifth World Congress of International College of Psychosomatic Medicine, Jerusalem, 1979.

Kramer, B. H. "Psychotherapeutic Implication of a Traditional Healing Ceremony: The Malaysian Main Puteri." *Transcultural Psychiatric Research Review* 7 (1970), 149–51.

Krasner, L. "Studies of the Conditioning of Verbal Behavior," *Psychological Bulletin* 55 (1958), 148–70.

Krauthammer, C. "The Twilight of Psychotherapy." *Washington Post* December 27, 1985.

Kroeber, A. L. "Psychosis or Social Sanction." In *The Nature of Culture.* Chicago: University of Chicago Press, 1952.

Kubie, L. S. "The Need for a New Subdiscipline in the Medical Profession." *Archives of Neurology and Psychiatry* 78 (September 1957), 283–93.

LaBarre, W. "Confession as Cathartic Therapy in American Indian Tribes." In *Magic, Faith and Healing,* edited by A. Kiev. New York: The Free Press, 1964.

———. "Primitive Psychotherapy in Native American Cultures: Peyotism and Confession." *Journal of Abnormal and Social Psychology* 42 (1947), 294–309.

Lambo, T. A. "Patterns of Psychiatric Care in Developing African Countries." In *Magic, Faith and Healing,* edited by A. Kiev. New York: The Free Press, 1964.

———. "Psychotherapy in Africa." *Psychotherapy and Psychosomatics* 24 (1974), 311–26.

———. "Psychotherapy in Africa." *Human Nature* 1 (1978) 32–40.

———, ed. *First Pan-African Psychiatric Conference.* Ibadan, Nigeria: Government Printer, 1962.

Lamson, H. D. *Social Pathology in China.* Shanghai: Commercial Press, 1928.

Langner, T. S. "Psychophysiological Symptoms and the Status of Women in Two Mexican Communities." In *Approaches to Cross-Cultural Psychiatry,* edited by J. M. Murphy and A. H. Leighton. Ithaca, N.Y.: Cornell University Press, 1965.

Lateef, N. V. "Diverse Capacities of the Marabout." *Transcultural Psychiatric Research Review* 11 (1974), 181–5.

Leavitt, E. E. "The Results of Psychotherapy with Children." *Journal of Consulting Psychology* 21 (1957), 189–96.

Lebra, W. P. "The Okinawan Shaman." In *Ryukyuan Culture and Society,* edited by A. H. Smith. Honolulu: University of Hawaii Press, 1964.

———. "Shaman and Client in Okinawa." in *Mental Health Research in Asia and the Pacific,* edited by W. Caudill and T. Lin. Honolulu: East-West Center Press, 1969.

Lefebvre, P. Review of "Process in Instant Cure," by E. Hoch. *Transcultural Psychiatric Research Review* 13 (1981), 130–1.

Leighton, A., and D. Leighton. "Elements of Psychotherapy in Navaho Religion." *Psychiatry* 4 (1941), 515–23.

Leighton, A. H. "Therapeutic Process in Cross-Cultural Perspective." *American Journal of Psychiatry* 124 (1968), 1176–8.

Levenson, A. I., et al. "Manpower and Training in Federally-Funded Community Mental Health Centers." *Hospital and Community Psychiatry*, March 1969.

Levinson, P., and J. Schiller. "Role Analysis of the Indigenous Nonprofessional." *Social Work* 11, no. 3 (1966), 95–101.

Lévi-Strauss, C. *Structural Anthropology.* New York: Basic Books, 1963.

Levy, R. I. "Tahitian Folk Psychotherapy." *International Public Health Research Newsletter* 9, no. 4 (1967), 12–15. Abstracted in *Transcultural Psychiatric Research* 6 (April 1969), 51–5.

Lewin, L. *Phantastica: Narcotic and Stimulating Drugs.* New York: E. P. Dutton and Company, 1964. (First published in 1924.)

Lewis, L. S. "Rational Behavior and the Treatment of Illness." *Journal of Health and Human Behavior* 4, no. 4 (Winter 1963), 235–9.

Lewis, O. "The Culture of Poverty," *Scientific American* 215, no. 1 (1966), 19–25.

———. *Life in a Mexican Village: Tepoztlán Restudied.* Urbana: University of Illinois Press, 1951.

Lindemann, E. "The Health Needs of Communities." In *Hospitals, Doctors and the Public Interest,* edited by J. H. Knowles. Cambridge, Mass.: Harvard University Press, 1965.

Linton, R. *Culture and Mental Disorders.* Springfield, Ill.: Charles C. Thomas, 1956.

Loeb, E. "Shaman and Seer." *American Anthropologist* 31 (1929), 61–84.

Lubchansky, I., G. Egri, and J. Stokes. "Puerto Rican Spiritualists View Mental Illness: The Faith Healer as a Paraprofessional." *American Journal of Psychiatry* 127 (1970), 312–21.

Luborsky, L., B. Singer, and L. Luborsky. "Comparative Studies of Psychotherapies. Is It True That 'Everyone Has Won and All Must Have Prizes'?" *Archives of General Psychiatry* 32 (1975), 995–1008.

———, A. T. McLellan, G. E. Woody, C. P. O'Brien, and A. Auerbach. "Therapist Success and Its Determinants." *Archives of General Psychiatry* 42 (1985), 602–11.

Luce, G. "The Importance of Psychic Medicine: Training Navaho Medicine Men." In *Mental Health Program Reports,* edited by J. Segal. Vol. 5. Washington, D.C.: National Institute of Mental Health, 1971.

Maddox, J. L. *The Medicine Man: A Sociological Study of the Character and Evolution of Shamanism.* New York: The Macmillan Company, 1923.

Madsen, W. *The Mexican-Americans of South Texas.* New York: Holt, Rinehart and Winston, 1964.

————. *Society and Health in the Lower Rio Grande Valley.* Austin: Hogg Foundation for Mental Health, University of Texas, 1961.

————. "Value Conflicts and Folk Psychotherapy in South Texas." In *Magic, Faith and Healing,* edited by A. Kiev. New York: The Free Press, 1964.

Maretzki, T. W. "Culture and Psychopathology in Indonesia." *Transcultural Psychiatric Research Review* 18 (1981), 237–56.

Margetts, E. L. "The Future of Psychiatry in East Africa." *East African Medical Journal* 37 (1960), 448–56.

————. "Traditional Yoruba Healers in Nigeria." *Man* 102 (1965), 115–8.

Margolin, S. G. "On Some Principles of Therapy." *American Journal of Psychiatry* 114 (1958), 1087–94.

Martinez, C., and H. W. Martin. "Folk Diseases Among Urban Mexican-Americans." *Journal of the American Medical Association* 196 (1966), 161–4.

Masserman, J. H. "The Timeless Therapeutic Trinity." In *Current Psychiatric Therapies,* edited by J. H. Masserman. Vol. 7. New York: Grune and Stratton, 1967.

McCartney, J. L. "Neuropsychiatry in China: A Preliminary Observation." *China Medical Journal* 40 (1926), 617–26.

Meadow, A., and D. Stoker. "Symptomatic Behavior of Hospitalized Patients: A Study of Mexican-American and Anglo-American Patients." *Archives of General Psychiatry* 12 (March 1965), 267–77.

Mendel, W. M. "The Non-Specifics of Psychotherapy." *International Journal of Psychiatry* 5, no. 5 (1968), 400–2.

"Mental Health Activities in the Indian Health Program." Washington, D.C.: Department of Health, Education and Welfare, 1967.

Messing, S. D. "Group Therapy and Social Status in the Zar Cult in Ethiopia." In *Culture and Mental Health*, edited by M. K. Opler. New York: The Macmillan Company, 1959.

Metzger, D., and G. Williams. "Tenejapa Medicine I: The Curer." *Southwestern Journal of Anthropology* 19 (1963), 216–34.

Meyer, G. G. "Curanderos and Psychiatrists as Professional Healers." Paper presented at Fifth World Congress of Psychiatry, Mexico City, 1971.

Michaelson, M. "Can a 'Root Doctor' Actually Put a Hex On or Is It All a Great Put-On?" *Today's Health*, March 1972, 39–60.

Miller, N. E. "Learning of Visceral and Glandular Responses." *Science* 163, no. 3866 (January 31, 1969), 434–5.

Miner, H. "Body Ritual of the Nacirema." *American Anthropologist* 58 (1956), 503–7.

Mischel, W., and F. Mischel. "Psychological Aspects of Spirit Possession." *American Anthropologist* 60 (1958), 249–60.

Mitchell, W. E. "The Group and Primitive Therapy: New Guinea." Paper presented at Northeastern Association for Group Psychotherapy, Boston, March 31, 1973.

Mumford, E., H. J. Schlesinger, G. V. Glass, C. Patrick, and T. Cuerdon. "A New Look at Evidence About Reduced Cost of Medical Utilization Following Mental Health Treatment." *American Journal of Psychiatry* 141 (1984), 1145–58.

Murase, T., and F. Johnson. "Naikan, Morita and Western Psychotherapy." *Archives of General Psychiatry* 31 (1974), 121–8.

Murdock, G. P. "Tenino Shamanism," *Ethnology* 4 (1965), 165–71.

Murphy, J. M. "Psychotherapeutic Aspects of Shamanism on St. Lawrence Island, Alaska." In *Magic, Faith and Healing*, edited by A. Kiev. New York: The Free Press, 1964.

———, and A. H. Leighton. "Native Conceptions of Psychiatric Disorders." In *Approaches to Cross Cultural Psychiatry*, edited by J. M. Murphy and A. H. Leighton. Ithaca, N.Y.: Cornell University Press, 1965.

Nall, F. C., and J. Speilberg. "Social and Cultural Factors in the Responses of Mexican-Americans to Medical Treatment." *Journal of Health and Social Behavior* 8, no. 4 (December 1967), 299–308.

Navarro, V. "Health, Health Services and Health Planning in Cuba." *International Journal of Health Services* 2 (1972), 397–431.

Neher, A. "A Physiological Explanation of Unusual Behavior in Ceremonies Involving Drums." *Human Biology* 34 (1962), 151–60.

Neki, J. S. "Psychiatry in South-East Asia." *British Journal of Psychiatry* 123 (1973), 257–69.

———. "A Reappraisal of the Guru-Chela Relationship as a Therapeutic Paradigm." *International Mental Health Research Newsletter* 16 (1974), 2–7.

———. "*Sahaja:* An Indian Ideal of Mental Health." *Psychiatry* 38 (1975), 1–10.

Nelson, S. H., and E. F. Torrey. "The Religious Functions of Psychiatry." *American Journal of Orthopsychiatry* 43 (1973), 362–7.

Ness, R. C., and R. M. Wintrob. "Folk Healing: A Description and Synthesis." *American Journal of Psychiatry* 138 (1981), 1477–81.

Nishimaru, S. "Mental Climate and Eastern Psychotherapy." *Transcultural Psychiatric Research* 2 (April 1965), 24.

Nisson, M. P., and K. E. Schmidt. "Land-Dayak Concepts of Mental Illness." *Medical Journal of Malaya* 21, no. 4 (June 1967), 352–7.

———, and K. E. Schmidt. "Land-Dayak Concepts of Mental Illness." *Transcultural Psychiatric Research* 3 (April 1966), 21–2.

Opler, M. E. "Some Points of Comparison and Contrast Between the Treatment of Functional Disorders by Apache Shamans and Modern Psychiatric Practice." *American Journal of Psychiatry* 92 (1936), 1371–87.

Opler, M. K. *Culture, Psychiatry and Human Values.* Springfield, Ill.: Charles C. Thomas, 1956.

———. "Dream Analysis in Ute Indian Therapy." In *Culture and Mental Health,* edited by M. K. Opler. New York: The Macmillan Company, 1959.

Orne, M. T. "On the Nature of Effective Hope." *International Journal of Psychiatry* 5, no. 5 (1968), 403–10.

Otsyula, W. "Native and Western Healing: The Dilemma of East African Psychiatry." *Journal of Nervous and Mental Disease* 156 (1973), 297–9.

Oyebola, D. D. O. "The Method of Training Traditional Healers and Midwives Among the Yoruba of Nigeria." *Social Science and Medicine* 14A (1980), 31–7.

———. "Traditional Medicine and Its Practitioners Among the Yoruba of Nigeria: A Classification." *Social Science and Medicine* 14A: (1980), 23–9.

Ozturk, O. M. "Folk Treatment of Mental Illness in Turkey." In *Magic, Faith and Healing,* edited by A. Kiev. New York: The Free Press, 1965.

Pande, S. K. "The Mystique of 'Western' Psychotherapy: An Eastern Interpretation." *Journal of Nervous and Mental Disease* 146, no. 6 (1968), 425–32.

Parks, W. Z. "Paviotso Shamanism." *American Anthropologist* 36 (1934), 98–113.

———. *Shamanism in Western North America.* Chicago: Northwestern University Press, 1938.

Parloff, M. B. "Can Psychotherapy Research Guide the Policymaker?" *American Psychologist* 34 (1979), 296–306.

———. "How Werner Got It." *Psychology Today,* November 1978, 136–47.

———. "Psychotherapy Research Evidence and Reimbursement Decisions: Bambi Meets Godzilla." *American Journal of Psychiatry* 139 (1982), 718–27.

———. "Shopping for the Right Therapy." *Saturday Review,* February 21, 1976.

———, I. E. Waskow, and B. E. Wolfe. "Research on Therapist Variables in Relation to Process and Outcome." In *Handbook of Psychotherapy and Behavior Change,* edited by S. L. Garfield and A. E. Bergin. New York: John Wiley, 1978.

Paulbaum, P. J. "Apprenticeship Revisited." *Archives of General Psychiatry* 13 (1965), 304–9.

Peck, H. B., T. Levin, and M. Roman. "The Health Careers Institute: A

Mental Health Strategy for an Urban Community." *American Journal of Psychiatry* 129, no. 9 (March 1969), 1180–6.

Pelto, P. J. "Psychological Anthropology." In *Biennial Review of Anthropology*, edited by B. J. Siegel and A. R. Beals. Stanford, Cal.: Stanford University Press, 1967.

Perham, J. "Manangism in Borneo." *Journal of the Straits Branch of the Royal Asiatic Society* (Singapore, 1887), 87–103.

Peterson, I. "State Finds Quacks in Mental Therapy." *New York Times*, December 7, 1972.

Pfeiffer, W. M. "Meditation and Trance States in Indonesian Tribes." *Transcultural Psychiatric Research* 2 (October 1965), 106–10.

Pfister, O. "Instinctive Psychoanalysis Among the Navahos." *Journal of Nervous and Mental Disease* 76 (1932), 234–54.

Pigache, P. "The Witch Doctor as Psychotherapist—Science or Suggestion?" *World Medicine*, May 16, 1973, 45–7.

Pollack, I. W., F. M. Ochberg, and E. Meyer. "Social Class and the Subjective Sense of Time." *Archives of General Psychiatry* 21 (July 1969), 1–14.

Poser, E. G. "The Effect of Therapists' Training on Group Therapeutic Outcome." *Journal of Consulting Psychology* 30, no. 4 (1966), 283–9.

Posinsky, S. H. "Yoruk Shamanism." *Psychiatric Quarterly* 39 (1965), 227–43.

Prince, R. "Indigenous Yoruba Psychiatry." In *Magic, Faith and Healing*, edited by A. Kiev. New York: The Free Press, 1964.

———. "Psychotherapy and the Chronically Poor: What Can We Learn from Primitive Psychotherapy?" In *Social Change, Poverty, and Mental Health*, edited by J. Finney. Lexington: University of Kentucky Press, 1968.

———. "Psychotherapy as the Manipulation of Indigenous Healing Mechanisms: A Transcultural Survey." *Transcultural Psychiatric Research Review* 13 (1976), 115–33.

———. "Some Notes on Yoruba Native Doctors and Their Management of Mental Illness." In *First Pan-African Psychiatric Conference*, edited by T. A. Lambo. Ibadan, Nigeria: Government Printer, 1962.

———. "The Use of Rauwolfia for the Treatment of Psychoses by Nigerian Native Doctors." *American Journal of Psychiatry* 118 (1960), 147–9.

———, ed. *Trance and Possession States.* Montreal: R. M. Bucke Memorial Society, 1968.

———, A. Leighton, and R. May. "The Therapeutic Process in Cross-Cultural Perspective: A Symposium." *American Journal of Psychiatry* 124, no. 9 (March 1968), 1171–6.

———, and E. D. Wittkower. "The Care of the Mentally Ill in a Changing Culture (Nigeria)." *American Journal of Psychotherapy* 18, no. 4 (1964), 644–8.

Proleau, L., M. Murdock, N. Brody. "An Analysis of Psychotherapy Versus Placebo." *Behavioral and Brain Sciences* 6 (1983), 275–85.

Radin, P. *Primitive Religion: Its Nature and Origin.* New York: Dover Publications, 1937.

Ramirez, S., and R. Parres. "Some Dynamic Patterns in the Organization of the Mexican Family." *International Journal of Social Psychiatry* 3 (1957), 18–21.

Rappaport, H. "The Tenacity of Folk Psychiatry: A Functional Interpretation." *Social Psychiatry* 12 (1977), 127–32.

Ravenscroft, K. "Voodoo Possession and Hypnosis." *International Journal of Clinical and Experimental Hypnosis* 13, no. 3 (1965), 157–82.

Redlich, F. C., and D. X. Freedman. *The Theory and Practice of Psychiatry.* New York: Basic Books, 1966.

Rieff, R., and F. Riessman. "The Indigenous Non-Professional." New York: National Institute of Labor Education, 1964.

Riessman, F. "The 'Helper' Therapy Principle." *Social Work* 10 (April 1965), 27–32.

———, E. F. Lynton, M. Ginsberg, S. Barr, and M. Battle. "The New Nonprofessional." *American Child* 49, no. 1 (Winter 1967), 1–32.

———, J. Cohen, and A. Pearl, eds. *Mental Health of the Poor.* New York: The Free Press, 1964.

Rin, H. "A Study of the Aetiology of Koro in Respect to the Chinese Concept of Illness." *International Journal of Social Psychiatry* 11, no. 1 (1965), 7–13.

Rioch, M. J. "Changing Concepts in the Training of Therapists." *Journal of Consulting Psychology* 30, no. 4 (1966), 290–2.

———. "Pilot Projects in Training Mental Health Counselors." In *Emergent Approaches to Mental Health Problems*, edited by E. L. Cowen, E. A. Gardner, and M. Zax. New York: Appleton-Century-Crofts, 1967.

Rioch, M. J., C. Elkes, A. A. Flint, B. S. Usdansky, R. G. Newman, and E. Silber. "National Institute of Mental Health Pilot Study in Training Mental Health Counselors." *American Journal of Orthopsychiatry* 33 (1963), 678–89.

Robinson, H. A., F. C. Redlich, and J. K. Myers. "Social Structure and Psychiatric Treatment." *American Journal of Orthopsychiatry* 24, no. 2 (1954), 307–16.

Rock, J. F. "Contributions to the Shamanism of the Tibetan-Chinese Borderland." *Anthropos* 54 (1959), 796–818.

Rogers, C. R. "The Necessary and Sufficient Conditions of Therapeutic Personality Change." *Journal of Consulting Psychology* 21 (1957), 95–103.

———, and R. F. Dymond, eds. *Psychotherapy and Personality Change.* Chicago: University of Chicago Press, 1954.

Rogler, L. H., and A. B. Hollingshead. "The Puerto Rican Spiritualist as Psychiatrist." *American Journal of Sociology* 67 (1961), 17–21.

Romney, A. K., and R. G. D'Andrade, eds. "Transcultural Studies in Cognition." *American Anthropologist* 66, no. 3 (Special Edition, 1964).

Rosenbaum, M. "Some Comments on the Use of Untrained Therapists." *Journal of Consulting Psychology* 30, no. 4 (1966), 292–4.

Rosenthal, R. "Changes in Some Moral Values Following Psychotherapy." *Journal of Consulting Psychology* 19 (1955), 431–6.

Rothenberg, A. "Puerto Rico and Aggression." *American Journal of Psychiatry* 120 (1964), 962–70.

Rubel, A. J. *Across the Tracks: Mexican Americans in a Texas City.* Austin: University of Texas Press, 1966.

———. "Concepts of Disease in Mexican-American Culture." *American Anthropologist* 62 (1960), 793–814.

———. "The Epidemiology of a Folk Illness: Susto in Hispanic America." *Ethnology* 3 (1964), 268–83.

Ruiz, P. "Folk Healers as Associate Therapists." In *Current Psychiatric Therapies*, edited by J. H. Masserman. New York: Grune and Stratton, 1976.

———. "Santeros, Botanicas and Mental Health: An Urban View." *Transcultural Psychiatric Research Review* 9 (1972), 176–7.

———. "Spiritism, Mental Health and the Puerto Rican: An Overview." *Transcultural Psychiatric Research Review* 16 (1979), 28–43.

———, and J. Langrod. "Psychiatry and Folk Healing: A Dichotomy?" *American Journal of Psychiatry* 133 (1976), 95–7.

———, and J. Langrod. "The Role of Folk Healers in Community Mental Health Services." *Community Mental Health Journal* 12 (1976), 392–8.

Sachs, W. *Black Hamlet*. Boston: Little, Brown and Company, 1947.

Sandner, D. F. "Navaho Medicine Men—The Psychological Cure." Paper presented at annual meeting of American Psychiatric Association, San Francisco, 1970.

Sangmuah, E. "The Healing (Spiritual) Therapy in Ghana." Paper presented at the second Pan-African Conference on Psychiatry, Dakar, 1968.

Sargant, W. *The Mind Possessed: A Physiology of Possession, Mysticism and Faith Healing*. Philadelphia: J. B. Lippincott, 1974.

———. "Witch Doctoring, Zar and Voodoo: Their Relation to Modern Psychiatric Treatments." *Transcultural Psychiatric Research* 5 (October 1968), 130–2.

Sasaki, Y. "Psychiatric Study of the Shaman in Japan." In *Mental Health Research in Asia and the Pacific*, edited by W. Caudill and T. Lin. Honolulu: East-West Center Press, 1969.

Sauna, V. D. "Socio-Cultural Aspects of Psychotherapy and Treatment: A Review of the Literature." In *Progress in Clinical Psychology*, edited by L. E. Abt and B. F. Riess. New York: Grune and Stratton, 1966.

———. "Psychological Intervention in the Arab World." *Transcultural Psychiatric Research Review* 14 (1979), 205–8.

Saunders, L. *Cultural Differences and Medical Care: The Case of the*

Spanish-Speaking People of the Southwest. New York: Russell Sage Foundation, 1954.

―――. "Healing Ways in the Spanish Southwest." In *Patients, Physicians, and Illnesses,* edited by E. G. Jaco. New York: The Free Press, 1958.

―――, and J. Samora. "A Medical Care Program in a Colorado County." In *Health, Culture and Community,* edited by B. Paul. New York: Russell Sage Foundation, 1955.

Scheibe, K. E. "College Students Spend Eight Weeks in a Mental Hospital." *Psychotherapy* 2 (1965), 117–20.

Schimmel, E. M. "The Hazards of Hospitalization." *Annals of Internal Medicine* 60, no. 1 (January 1964), 100–10.

―――. "The Physician as Pathogen." *Journal of Chronic Disease* 16 (1963), 1–4.

Schmidt, K. E. "Folk Psychiatry in Sarawak: A Tentative System of Psychiatry of the Iban." In *Magic, Faith and Healing,* edited by A. Kiev. New York: The Free Press, 1964.

Schofield, W. *Psychotherapy: The Purchase of Friendship.* Englewood Cliffs, N.J.: Prentice-Hall, 1964.

Schulman, S., and A. M. Smith. "The Concept of 'Health' Among Spanish-Speaking Villages in New Mexico and Colorado." *Journal of Health and Human Behavior* 4, no. 4 (Winter 1963), 226–34.

Scott, C. S. "Health and Healing Practices Among Five Ethnic Groups in Miami, Florida." *Public Health Reports* 89 (1974), 524–32.

Segall M. H., D. T. Campbell, and M. J. Herskovits. *The Influence of Culture on Visual Perception.* Indianapolis: The Bobbs-Merrill Company, 1966.

Seguin, C. A. "Language and Psychotherapy." *Journal of Nervous and Mental Disease* 121 (1955), 564–7.

Senter, D. "Witches and Psychiatrists." *Psychiatry* 10 (1947), 49–56.

Sereno, R. "Obeah, Magic and Social Structure in the Lesser Antilles." *Psychiatry* 11 (1948), 15–31.

Seward, G. *Psychotherapy and Culture Conflict.* New York: The Ronald Press, 1956.

Shapiro, A. K. "The Placebo Effect in the History of Medical Treatment:

Implications for Psychiatry." *American Journal of Psychiatry* 116 (1959), 298–304.

Shapiro, E. T., and H. Pinsker. "Shared Ethnic Scotoma." *American Journal of Psychiatry* 130 (1973), 1338–41.

Shapiro, J. "Dominant Leaders Among Slum Hotel Residents." *American Journal of Orthopsychiatry* 39, no. 4 (July 1969), 644–50.

Shepherd, M. "Comparative Psychiatric Treatment in Different Countries." In *Aspects of Psychiatric Research*, edited by D. Richter, J. M. Tanner, L. Taylor, and O. L. Zangwill. London: Oxford University Press, 1962.

――――. "The Statutory Registration of Psychotherapists?" *Bulletin of the Royal College of Psychiatrists*, November 1980, 166–9.

Sigerist, H. *History of Medicine*. Vol. 1. New York: Oxford University Press, 1951, 175.

Silver, H. K., L. C. Ford, and L. R. Day. "The Pediatric Nurse-Practitioner Program." *Journal of the American Medical Association* 204, no. 4 (1968), 298–302.

Silverman, J. "Shamans and Acute Schizophrenia." *American Anthropologist* 69, no. 1 (1967), 21–31.

Simmons, O. G. "The Mutual Images and Expectations of Anglo-Americans and Mexican-Americans." *Daedalus* 90 (Spring 1961), 286–99.

Singer, P., E. Araneta, and L. Aarons. "Integration of Indigenous Healing Practices of the Kali Cult with Western Psychiatric Modalities in British Guiana," *Transcultural Psychiatric Research* 4 (April 1967), 65–7.

――――, E. Araneta, and J. Naidoo. "Learning of Psychodynamic, History, Diagnosis, Management, Therapy by a Kali Cult Indigenous Healer in Guyana." Paper presented at International Congress of Anthropological and Ethnological Sciences, Chicago, August 28, 1973.

Sloane, R. B., F. R. Staples, A. H. Cristol, N. J. Yorkston, and K. Whipple. "Short-Term Analytically Oriented Psychotherapy Versus Behavior Therapy." *American Journal of Psychiatry* 132 (1975), 373–7.

Smith, M. L., G. V. Glass, T. I. Miller. *The Benefit of Psychotherapy*. Baltimore: Johns Hopkins University Press, 1980.

Soddy, K., ed. *Identity: Mental Health and Value Systems.* London: Tavistock Publications, 1961.

Stead, E. A. "Training and Use of Paramedical Personnel." *New England Journal of Medicine* 277, no. 15 (1967), 800–1.

Stewart, K. *Pygmies and Dream Giants.* London: Victor Gollancz, 1955.

Strupp, H. H. "Needed: A Reformulation of the Psychotherapeutic Influence." *International Journal of Psychiatry* 10 (1972), 114–20.

———. "On the Technology of Psychotherapy." *Archives of General Psychiatry* 26 (1972), 270–8.

———. "The Vanderbilt Psychotherapy Research Project: Past, Present, and Future." In *Psychotherapy Research,* edited by J. B. W. Williams and R. L. Spitzer. New York: Guilford Press, 1984.

———, and A. E. Bergin. "Some Empirical and Conceptual Bases for Coordinated Research in Psychotherapy." *International Journal of Psychiatry* 7, no. 2 (1969), 18–90.

———, and S. W. Hadley. "Specific Versus Nonspecific Factors in Psychotherapy." *Archives of General Psychiatry* 36 (1979), 1125–36.

———, S. W. Hadley, and B. Gomes-Schwartz. *Psychotherapy for Better or Worse.* New York: Jason Aronson, 1977.

Stunkard, A. "Some Interpersonal Aspects of an Oriental Religion." *Psychiatry* 14 (1951), 419–31.

Suicide and Homicides Among Indians. Washington: Department of Health, Education and Welfare, 1969.

Szasz, T. S. *The Ethics of Psychoanalysis.* New York: Basic Books, 1965.

Taube, C. A., B. J. Burns, and L. Kessler. "Patients of Psychiatrists and Psychologists in Office-Based Practice: 1980." *American Psychologist* 39 (1984), 1435–47.

Taylor, R. L. *Mind or Body: Distinguishing Psychological from Organic Disorders.* New York: McGraw-Hill, 1982.

Toffelmier, G., and K. Luomala. "Dreams and Dream Interpretation of the Diegueño Indians of Southern California." *Psychoanalytic Quarterly* 2 (1936), 195–225.

Torrey, E. F. "The Case for the Indigenous Therapist." *Archives of General Psychiatry* 20 (1969), 365–73.

———. "A Medical Survey of the Saysay People in the Blue Nile Gorge." *Ethiopian Medical Journal* 4 (July 1966), 4–11.

———. "Mental Health Services for American Indians and Eskimos." *Community Mental Health Journal* 6, no. 6 (1970), 455–63.

———. "The Primal Therapy Trip: Medicine or Religion?" *Psychology Today*, December 1976, 62–8.

———. *Surviving Schizophrenia: A Family Manual.* New York: Harper & Row, 1983.

———. "The Zar Cult in Ethiopia." *International Journal of Social Psychiatry*, 13, no. 3 (1967), 216–23.

———, ed. *An Introduction to Health and Health Education in Ethiopia.* Addis Ababa: Berhanena Selam Press, 1966.

———, F. J. Van Rheenan, and H. A. Katchadourian. "Problems of Foreign Students: An Overview." *Journal of the American College Health Association* 19, no. 2 (1970), 83–6.

"Traditional Medical Practitioners: Pros and Cons." *Lancet* 1 (1980), 963–4.

Truax, C. B., and R. R. Carkhuff. *Toward Effective Counseling and Psychotherapy: Training and Practice.* Chicago: Aldine Publishing Company, 1967.

———, and D. Wargo. "Human Encounters that Change Behavior for Better or Worse." *American Journal of Psychotherapy* 20 (1966), 499–520.

———, D. Wargo, J. Frank, S. Imber, C. Battle, R. Hoehn-Saric, E. Nash, and A. Stone. "Therapeutic Empathy, Genuineness, and Warmth and Patient Therapeutic Outcome." *Journal of Consulting Psychology* 30 (1966), 395–401.

Trumbull, R. "Eskimo Mental Ills Tied to New Life." *New York Times*, July 15, 1974.

Tseng, W. S. "Psychiatric Study of Shamanism in Taiwan." *Archives of General Psychiatry* 26 (1972), 561–5.

———, and J. F. McDermott. "Psychotherapy: Historical Roots, Universal Elements, and Cultural Variations." *American Journal of Psychiatry* 132 (1975), 378–84.

Turner, V. W. "An Ndembu Doctor in Practice." In *Magic, Faith and Healing*, edited by A. Kiev. New York: The Free Press, 1964.

Tyhurst, L. "Displacement and Migration." *American Journal of Psychiatry* 108 (1951), 561–8.

Uhlenhuth, E. H., and D. B. Duncan. "Subjective Change with Medical Student Therapists: Course of Relief in Psychoneurotic Outpatients." *Archives of General Psychiatry* 18 (April 1968), 428–38.

————, and D. B. Duncan. "Subjective Change with Medical Student Therapists: Some Determinants of Change in Psychoneurotic Outpatients." *Archives of General Psychiatry* 18 (May 1968), 532–40.

Umbarger, C. C., J. S. Dalsimer, A. P. Morrison, and P. R. Breggin. *College Students in a Mental Hospital.* New York: Grune and Stratton, 1962.

Vahia, N. S., S. L. Vinekar, and D. R. Doongaji. "Some Ancient Indian Concepts in the Treatment of Psychiatric Disorders." *British Journal of Psychiatry* 112, no. 489 (1966), 1089–96.

Vandenbos, G. R., J. Stapp, and R. R. Kilburg. "Health Services Providers in Psychology." *American Psychologist* 36 (1981), 1395–1418.

Vidaver, R. M. "The Mental Health Technician: Maryland's Design for a New Health Career." *American Journal of Psychiatry* 125, no. 8 (February 1969), 1013–23.

Wakefield, D. *Island in the City.* Boston: Houghton Mifflin Company, 1959.

Wallace, A. F. C. "Cultural Determinants of Response to Hallucinatory Experience." *Archives of General Psychiatry* 1, no. 1 (July 1959), 58–69.

————. *Culture and Personality.* New York: Random House, 1961.

————. "Dreams and the Wishes of the Soul: A Type of Psychoanalytic Theory Among Seventeenth Century Iroquois." *American Anthropologist* 60 (1958), 234–48.

————. "The Institutionalization of Cathartic and Control Strategies in Iroquois Religious Psychotherapy." In *Culture and Mental Health*, edited by M. K. Opler. New York: The Macmillan Company, 1959.

Wallace, M. E. "Private Practice: A Nationwide Study." *Social Work* 27 (1982), 262–7.

Weed, V., and W. H. Denham. "Toward More Effective Use of the Nonprofessional Worker." *Social Work* 6 (October 1963), 29.

Weil, A. *Health and Healing: Understanding Conventional and Alternative Medicine.* Boston: Houghton Mifflin, 1983.

Weinberg, S. K. "Mental Healing and Social Change in West Africa." *Social Problems* 2, no. 3 (1964), 257–69.

Weinstein, E. A. *Cultural Aspects of Delusion: A Psychiatric Study of the Virgin Islands.* New York: The Free Press, 1962.

Whisson, M. G. "Some Aspects of Functional Disorders Among the Kenya Luo." In *Magic, Faith and Healing,* edited by A. Kiev. New York: The Free Press, 1964.

Whiting, J. W., and I. L. Child. *Child Training and Personality: A Cross-Cultural Study.* New Haven: Yale University Press, 1953.

Whorf, B. L. "Science and Linguistics." In *Language, Thought and Reality,* edited by J. B. Carroll. Cambridge, Mass.: The Technology Press of Massachusetts Institute of Technology, 1957.

Wilkins, W. "Expectancy of Therapeutic Gain: An Empirical and Conceptual Critique." *Journal of Consulting and Clinical Psychology* 40 (1973), 69–77.

Williams, J. B. W., and R. L. Spitzer. *Psychotherapy Research: Where Are We and Where Should We Go?* New York: Guilford Press, 1984.

Wilmer, H. A. "Transference to a Medical Center." *California Medicine* 96, no. 3 (1962), 173–80.

Winkelman, N. W., and S. D. Saul. "The Riddle of Suggestion." *American Journal of Psychiatry* 129 (1972), 477–81.

Wintrob, R., and E. D. Wittkower. "Magic and Witchcraft in Liberia: Their Psychiatric Implications." *Transcultural Psychiatric Research* 3 (October 1966), 149–52.

Wise, H. B., E. F. Torrey, A. McDade, and H. Bograd. "The Family Health Worker." *American Journal of Public Health* 58, no. 10 (1968), 1828–38.

Wittkower, E. D., H. B. Murphy, J. Fried, and H. Ellenberger. "Cross-Cultural Inquiry into the Symptomatology of Schizophrenia." *Annals of the New York Academy of Sciences* 84 (1960), 854–63.

———, and H. Warnes. "Cultural Aspects of Psychotherapy." *American Journal of Psychotherapy* 28 (1974), 566–73.

Workineh, H. M. "Teaching of the Ethiopian Orthodox Church on Matters Related to Health and Disease." In *An Introduction to Health and Health Education in Ethiopia,* edited by E. F. Torrey. Addis Ababa: Berhanena Selam Press, 1966.

World Health Organization, "The Promotion and Development of Traditional Medicine." WHO Technical Report Series no. 622. Geneva: WHO, 1978.

Yamamoto, J., Q. C. James, and N. Palley. "Cultural Problems in Psychiatric Therapy." *Archives of General Psychiatry* 19 (1968), 45–9.

Yap, P. M. "Mental Diseases Peculiar to Certain Cultures: A Survey of Comparative Psychiatry." *Journal of Mental Science* 97 (1951), 313–27.

Zempleni, A. "Traditional Interpretation and Therapy of Mental Disorder Among the Wolof and the Lebou of Senegal." *Transcultural Psychiatric Research* 6 (1969), 69–74.

Index